Black Men Teaching in Urban Schools

This volume follows 11 Black male teachers from an urban, predominantly Black school district to reveal a complex set of identity politics and power dynamics that complicate these teachers' relationships with students and fellow educators. It provides new and important insights into what it means to be a Black male teacher and suggests strategies for school districts, teacher preparation programs, researchers and other stakeholders to rethink why and how we recruit and train Black male teachers for urban K–12 classrooms.

Edward Brockenbrough is Associate Professor in Teaching, Learning, and Leadership at the University of Pennsylvania Graduate School of Education, Philadelphia, PA, USA.

Routledge Critical Studies in Gender and Sexuality in Education

Series Editors Wayne Martino, Emma Renold, Goli Rezai-Rashti, Jessica Ringrose and Nelson Rodriguez

Black Men Teaching in Urban Schools

Reassessing Black Masculinity

Edward Brockenbrough

Routledge
Taylor & Francis Group

NEW YORK AND LONDON

First published 2018
by Routledge
711 Third Avenue, New York, NY 10017

and by Routledge
2 Park Square, Milton Park, Abingdon, Oxon, OX14 4RN

Routledge is an imprint of the Taylor & Francis Group, an informa business

© 2018 Taylor & Francis

Library of Congress Cataloguing-in-Publication Data
A catalog record for this book has been requested

ISBN: 978-1-138-90329-6 (hbk)
ISBN: 978-1-315-69699-7 (ebk)

Typeset in Sabon
by Apex CoVantage, LLC

Contents

Acknowledgments

This book draws upon questions, conundrums, insights, inspirations, and experiences spanning my 20+ year career as an educator and my nearly decade-long journey as an educational scholar. As I wrestled with the ideas that would eventually crystallize in the form of this book, I crossed paths with numerous individuals who sustained, encouraged, and celebrated me along the way. I never could have made it this far without the support of my extended village, and I will be forever grateful to all of its members. You are too numerous to name in entirety here, but I hope you know how indebted I am to all of you.

Several individuals provided supports that were particular to this book project, and I do want to take this opportunity to specifically name and thank them. First, I am extremely grateful to Wayne Martino, whose mentorship sustained me as I negotiated the unforeseen challenges of culling my thoughts into my first book-length manuscript. Not only do I draw upon Wayne's scholarship in this book, but I also try to model my own work after his incisive analyses of masculinity in educational contexts. I cannot underscore enough how thankful I am for Wayne's guidance.

I also want to thank several individuals who supported me during the early stages of my scholarly inquiries on Black male teachers' experiences. Chief among them are Kathy Schultz, Lisa Bouillion-Diaz, James Earl Davis, and Howard Stevenson, my all-star dissertation committee members. These four scholars modeled rigorous and loving academic mentorship for me, and I will always be grateful for their collective commitment to my success. I am thankful as well for George Wimberly, who helped me to capitalize on the unique platform for my work provided by a 2007 dissertation fellowship from the American Educational Research Association and the Institute of Educational Sciences (AERA-IES Grant R305U000003), which funded the research that is presented in this book. Additionally, I want to thank Amy Bach, Jas Dhillon, Jeannine Dingus-Eason, Adrienne Dixson, Liz ErkenBrack, Logan Hazen, Jayne Lammers, Joanne Larson, Kevin Meuwissen, and Julia White for their feedback on earlier drafts of the work that appears in this book.

My scholarship on the experiences of Black male teachers has been influenced by and in dialogue with works by other scholars who have studied Black men's participation in the American teaching profession. These scholars include Thurman Bridges, Travis Bristol, Anthony Brown, Cleveland Hayes, Tyrone Howard, Tambra Jackson, Chance Lewis, Marvin Lynn, Rich Milner, Amber Pabon, Ivory Toldson, and Ashley Woodson. I consider it an honor to be in their scholarly company, and I thank them for inspiring, responding to, and deepening my contributions to our shared field of study. Additionally, the analyses presented in this book were informed by my engagements with a larger community of scholars who have brought critical perspectives to bear on examinations of race, gender, and social justice in American education. These individuals include (but are not limited to!) Judy Alston, Tomás Boatwright, Roland Sintos Coloma, Cindy Cruz, T. Elon Dancy, Cynthia Dillard, Ezekiel Dixon-Román, Michael Dumas, Jillian Carter Ford, Marcelle Haddix, Shaun Harper, Kevin Lawrence Henry, Marc Lamont Hill, Nikola Hobbel, Lionel Howard, Darrell Hucks, Jason Irizarry, Korina Jocson, Hilton Kelly, Valerie Kinloch, Kevin Kumashiro, Bettina Love, Rigoberto Marquez, Lynnette Mawhinney, Lance McCready, Steve Mobley, Joseph Nelson, Steven Thurston Oliver, Leigh Patel, Emery Petchauer, Rosalie Rolón-Dow, Sonia Rosen, Camika Royal, Yolanda Sealey-Ruiz, Sam Stiegler, and Chezare Warren. I thank these scholars for their intellectual fellowship.

As I worked on various iterations of this project, I often found myself thinking about the influence in my life of four very special Black male teachers: Wade Hanley, Brooks Morris, Elmo Terry-Morgan, and Dwight Vidale. These four men embodied a commitment to academic excellence and radical love that distinguished them as educators, and I am deeply grateful for the many lessons that I learned from them. I also want to thank my former teaching colleague and co-conspirator, Imani Matthews, whose patience with me as a proto-feminist educator enabled the critical feminist consciousness that pervades this book, and that takes center stage in Chapter 5. And of course, I am forever indebted to my 11 study participants who graciously, honestly, and courageously told their stories to me. Listening to their narratives taught me more about being a Black male teacher than any other experience in my life. My hope is that others will benefit as I did from my participants' willingness to share their journeys.

Finally, this book is dedicated to my father, Edward Brockenbrough: my first—and best—Black male teacher.

1 Introduction

"Acting Tougher"

It did not take long for Quincy Stinson[1] to come face-to-face with the unique challenges of being a Black male teacher in an urban school. In fact, as Quincy recalled one afternoon, some of those challenges greeted him on his first day in the classroom:

> The first day last year, a kid was kind of like, "You know, you kinda sweet, Mr. Stinson, you kinda soft. You not gonna be able to teach us. You're gonna be gone soon." Just like that, the very first day I came in, that was what one of the kids, who was pretty decent all along, but that's what he said to me. I'm like, if they've already pegged me for somebody who's gonna quit the first day, I gotta start acting tougher.

"Acting tougher" is exactly what he did. During his entire first year as a humanities teacher at a predominantly Black, under-resourced urban public school, Quincy was required to demonstrate his ability to keep his students in check. Battles for authority in the classroom ensued on a regular basis, especially between Quincy and the Black male students in his classes. When admonished by Quincy for not following his instructions, some Black male students would dismiss him by declaring, "You can't talk to me that way, you're not my father." Others would engage Quincy in heated verbal exchanges that escalated to threats of physical retaliation against him. Surrounded by a schoolwide culture of violence, Quincy knew of a few Black male colleagues in his building who would occasionally take disruptive male students into the hallway and either slam them into lockers or lightly punch them. Quincy never went to such extremes, but he did engage in daily struggles for power with his Black male students. All the while, it was clear to Quincy that his ability to perform a particular brand of Black masculinity was being tested. Through baptism by fire, Quincy was introduced during his first year as a full-time teacher to an unwritten yet undeniable job requirement: the ability to prove an invincible Black manhood.

The fraught participation in the urban teaching profession of Quincy and the ten other Black male teachers whose narratives are featured in this book should not be terribly surprising. As evidenced by critical scholarship on Black masculinity, a conflicted mix of fascinations and fears toward Black male bodies has always haunted Black men's navigations of American social and institutional contexts (Carbado, 1999b; Gates, 1997; Majors, 1992; Neal, 2013; Richardson, 2007), and public schools are no exception in this regard (Ferguson, 2000; McCready, 2010; Noguera, 2008). Yet strikingly, prevailing cultural discourses on Black men in urban teaching routinely underestimate, and sometimes completely overlook, how the experiences of Black male teachers may be complicated by culture-wide and school-specific anxieties toward Black men. For nearly two decades, a large chorus of educational scholars, urban school reformers, public intellectuals, community advocates, and other stakeholders has called for efforts to increase the pool of Black male teachers, which estimates place at slightly less than 2% of the nation's teaching force (Toldson, 2011). Appeals for more Black male teachers have repeatedly envisioned these men as role models and surrogate father figures for Black youth, especially Black boys, who may lack supportive male adults in their homes and communities (Basinger, 1999; Hawkins, 2015; Miller, 2016; Nazaryan, 2015; Richard, 2005; Taylor, 2016). Relying at times on patriarchal logics, recurrent discourses on Black male teachers as role models and father figures leave little room for these men to express uncertainty, vulnerability, or defeat. Moments like the ones recalled by Quincy—of authority lost, of Black masculine legitimacy impugned—fall beyond the boundaries of Black macho-pedagogical fantasies. Against a backdrop of systemic inequities that have contributed to current trends of Black educational underachievement, Black male teachers are imagined as a patriarchal panacea to the plight of Black children in America's urban schools and communities. With stakes this high, these men must remain indomitable.

To be sure, patriarchal discourses on male teachers are not a new phenomenon. As I discuss later in this chapter, contemporary calls for more Black male teachers build upon a century-long angst over the dearth of men in the teaching profession. This angst has coincided with periodic cultural panics over the state of American masculinities, sparking rallying cries for more male teachers to save American boys by modeling a rugged and reliable manhood in schools. Like male educators collectively, Black male teachers are expected to serve their students by operating as benevolent yet exacting patriarchs who can restore a normative gender order in the lives of American youth, especially Black boys. But when the logics of patriarchy and their intersections with race are called into question, the recent push for more Black male teachers raises several sets of concerns that warrant deeper investigation. For instance:

1) Given the surveillance and distrust of Black male bodies within American urban schools and across American cultural landscapes, why is the Black male teacher triumphed by such a diverse array of stakeholders as a legitimate agent of patriarchal power? What political, pedagogical, and ideological projects are being served by positioning Black male teachers, particularly in predominantly Black urban classrooms, as surrogate fathers and role models?

2) In a society where Black masculinity is both lauded and loathed, what perceptions of adult Black men do teachers, administrators, parents, and students bring to their encounters with Black male teachers, and how do those perceptions affect Black male teachers' experiences? How do Black male teachers negotiate their relationships with these stakeholder groups?

3) How do Black male teachers' lived experiences as Black men in America inform their sense of self, their career aspirations, their pedagogical work, and their strategies for participating in the urban teaching profession?

4) What exactly does it mean for Black male teachers to serve as father figures and role models for Black children? How do these men make sense of and respond to these highly touted, yet often unpacked, expectations?

5) Are there, in fact, unique cultural and pedagogical insights that Black male teachers bring to bear on their work with Black students in urban schools? If so, how, if at all, can those insights be shared with and taken up by other urban educators?

As these questions indicate, a host of weighty concerns about the nature, trajectory, and impact of Black men's participation in the urban teaching profession resides below surface-level valorizations of Black male teachers. Common-sense rhetoric on the need for more Black men in teaching belies the political and pedagogical complexities associated with choosing certain types of adults to engage certain types of strategies to teach, mentor, and socialize certain types of children. Thus, it is crucial that calls to recruit and retain more Black male teachers be informed by critical considerations of who these men are and what they are being asked to do.

Advancing critical analyses of the lives and work of Black men in the nation's urban teaching ranks is the goal of this book. In the chapters that follow, I set the stage for and then share findings from a study that I conducted on the experiences of 11 Black male teachers who worked in a predominantly Black urban school district on the east coast of the

United States. Mirroring the questions I posed earlier, my project was driven by dual desires to develop a nuanced portrait of how my 11 study participants made sense of their experiences as Black male teachers and to consider how their insights might bring more complexity to popular and scholarly discourses on Black men in urban teaching. Grounded in life history methodology and informed by Black masculinity studies, my project enabled study participants to explain how dominant cultural and institutional constructions of Black manhood were used by a variety of stakeholders to promote, prescribe, and police their participation as Black male teachers in their schools, thus forcing them into complex negotiations of identity, pedagogy, and power. This book focuses closely and critically on those complex negotiations.

Although the 11 men in my study cited joyful and successful moments from their teaching experiences that echoed public perceptions of them as role models, father figures, and effective instructors for Black children, their detailed accounts of the contentious identity politics and power dynamics that unfolded in classrooms and hallways illuminated personal, professional, and pedagogical dilemmas that have often gone unaccounted for in portrayals of Black male teachers. Bringing these dilemmas to the forefront creates important opportunities to critically unpack certain silences within popular discourses on Black male teachers—namely, the silences around Black patriarchy unfulfilled, as illustrated earlier in Quincy's narrative excerpt. The vulnerabilities, doubts, and failures articulated by the men in my study force us to question what ideological projects would depend on the erasure of such moments from popular discourses on Black male teachers. More than simply allowing us to hear these men's stories, the narratives presented in this book help us to think more deeply about how the stories of Black male teachers may be used to reproduce—and, under different circumstances, transform—racial, gender, cultural, and educational hierarchies that both include and extend beyond the experiences of Black men in the urban teaching profession.

That said, Black male teachers' stories, on their own terms and for their own sake, also matter. A more nuanced appreciation of what these men see, hear, feel, and confront along their journeys toward and through the urban teaching profession is one of this book's most significant contributions. A major assertion throughout this text is that the identities and pedagogies of my 11 study participants did not always fit into the presumed and prescribed roles awaiting them as Black men in urban teaching contexts. The resulting dissonance between who these Black male teachers were and who they were expected to be was something that these men, in the absence of intentional supports, were frequently left to negotiate on their own. If teacher education programs, urban school districts, and other stakeholders are truly invested in recruiting and retaining more Black men in the urban teaching profession, then they must delve below essentialist and cursory valorizations of Black male teachers as father figures and role models to attend to dilemmas around race, masculinity, and pedagogy that can undermine retention efforts. By paying close attention to moments of disconnect between dominant discourses on Black male teachers and the individual lives of Black men in the profession, this book spotlights the thorny negotiations of identity and power that must inform attempts to understand and support Black male teachers.

Black Teachers, Male Teachers

Throughout this book, I devote considerable attention to a range of discourses that shapes our understandings of and investments in Black male teachers. When discussing discourses, I draw upon Foucault's notion of discourses as "ways of constituting knowledge, together with the social practices, forms of subjectivity and power relations which inhere in such knowledges and the relations between them" (Weedon, 1987, p. 108). Discourses are complex constellations of meaning-making that encompass what we know, how we articulate what we know, and how we influence—or even enforce—particular ways of being that fortify particular truths about ourselves and our worlds. For my analyses of Black men's experiences in urban teaching, two discursive strands emerge as particularly important: popular discourses on adult Black men in general, and on Black male teachers more specifically, that circulate in mass media and are consumed by wide potential audiences; and scholarly discourses on Black masculinity and Black male teachers that critically interrogate the production of knowledge about Black maleness. These discourses repeatedly come to the fore of my analysis and are defined more thoroughly as this book unfolds.

But before delving into deeper considerations of the meaning-making specifically around Black male teachers, it is crucial that I first highlight some broader discourses on teaching that have influenced prevailing perceptions of Black men's presence within the field. Black male teachers are situated at the intersection of (at least) two significant political and intellectual projects that target the American teaching profession: the validation of Black educators' culturally and politically mediated pedagogical work with Black students; and the push for male teachers to perform conventional modes of American masculinity within K–12 classrooms. Separate overviews of the discourses on Black teachers and male teachers are offered here as backdrops to this book's analyses of the lives and work of Black male teachers.

Black Teachers

Over the past three decades, a rich corpus of scholarship has considered the significance of Black participation in the American teaching profession. Many of the claims throughout this scholarly literature shine an intentional light on the affordances of Black teachers' culturally responsive pedagogies.[2] In contrast to one-size-fits-all approaches to curriculum and instruction, culturally responsive pedagogies recognize cultural background as one factor that can shape how students learn and engage differently within educational spaces, and they seek curricular content, instructional techniques, and community-building strategies that capitalize on students' cultures to enhance their learning experiences (Gay, 2010; Irvine, 2002; Ladson-Billings, 1995; Villegas & Lucas, 2002). Scholarship on culturally responsive pedagogies has outlined several characteristics that distinguish these pedagogical approaches as responsive to students' cultural identities and backgrounds. These include a respect for students' cultures that intentionally counters deficit-oriented perspectives on racial and ethnic minority students (Gay, 2010; Ladson-Billings, 2009; Milner, 2011; Villegas & Lucas, 2002), engagements with students' culturally specific modes of knowing and being when determining curriculum content and designing learning experiences (Gay, 2010; Ladson-Billings, 2009; Milner, 2011; Villegas & Lucas, 2002), and modes of care that are culturally recognizable to traditionally marginalized students (Dixson, 2003; Gay, 2010; Lynn, 2006b; Milner, 2011; C. R. Monroe, 2009). These and other factors distinguish culturally responsive pedagogies as valuable frameworks for classroom learning.

Across numerous scholarly accounts, Black teachers are credited for developing culturally responsive pedagogies that allow them to effectively engage Black students. Rooted in their own daily participation in Black cultural contexts, Black teachers' communicative expressions, interactional styles, racial bonds to other Blacks, and emic understandings of Black culture are all cited as powerful tools for connecting with, gaining trust from, and improving the achievement of Black students (Cook & Dixson, 2013; Foster, 1994, 1997; Howard, 2001; Irvine, 1990, 2002; W. Johnson, Nyamekye, Chazan, & Rosenthal, 2013; Milner, 2006). Black teachers' pedagogical effectiveness with Black students is also attributed to stern, no-nonsense approaches to discipline and classroom management that mirror the disciplinary styles frequently encountered by Black children in their familial contexts, and that stem from culturally specific modes of care for Black children (Delpit, 1995; Ford & Sassi, 2014; Foster, 1994; Howard, 2001; Irvine, 2002; Milner, 2012; C. Monroe & Obidah, 2004; C. R. Monroe, 2009). These modes of care are characterized in a number of scholarly works as a family-like concern for Black students' success that ultimately positions Black educators as surrogate parental figures—or other mothers (Beauboeuf-Lafontant, 2002; Case, 1997; Dixson, 2003; Dixson & Dingus, 2008; Foster, 1993; Irvine, 2002) and other fathers (Bridges, 2011; Lynn, 2006b)—for Black youth. While some works have emphasized the possibilities for non-Black teachers to engage in culturally responsive pedagogical interactions with Black students (Ford & Sassi, 2014; Ladson-Billings, 2009; Milner, 2011), Black teachers have remained by and large at the center of this literature, thus affirming the special pedagogical resonance of their culturally mediated ties to Black youth.

Along with describing their pedagogical expertise in educating Black students, the scholarship on Black teachers has also cast these educators as agents of Black racial uplift. Dating back to the late 19th century, racial uplift campaigns, often led by members of the Black professional classes, have focused on educational attainment, moral respectability, and racial solidarity as tools for resisting White supremacy and achieving Black social, political, and economic progress (Carlton-LaNey & Burwell, 1996; Glaude, 2000; Whitaker, 2005; D. G.White, 1993). Across numerous scholarly works, particularly those that focus on segregated Black schools in the Jim Crow-era American South, Black teachers' commitment to Black students' achievement and self-worth is ascribed anti-racist and pro-uplift pedagogical aims. For instance, in her classic account of an all-Black high school in segregated North Carolina, Walker (1996) explores how Black teachers articulated a "countermessage" of Black humanity and self-worth that defied the logics of Jim Crow antiblackness, asserted the possibilities of Black student success, and stressed the need for Black youth to work harder than their White counterparts to ensure Black racial progress. Similarly, Beauboeuf-Lafontant (1999) argues that 19th-century racial uplift narratives informed an "oppositional consciousness," or a deliberate stance against White supremacy, among Black educators that shaped their efforts to subvert White supremacist messages of Black inferiority through their teaching. Echoing Walker and Beauboeuf-Lafontant, other scholars offer accounts of Black teachers in segregated Black schools who instilled racial pride in Black students to counter the effects of White supremacy (Celeski, 1994; Dempsey & Noblit, 1993; Fairclough, 2007; Franklin, 1990; Kelly, 2010; Savage, 2001; Tillman, 2004), and some scholars draw connections between Black teachers' anti-racist work and the civil rights activism that transpired throughout the segregated American South (Baker, 2011; Walker, 2013). Across these and other texts, the pre-integration Black teacher emerges as a race worker whose classroom functioned as a site for resisting racial oppression.

Moving from pre- to post-integration, many scholarly accounts have portrayed Black teachers' continued efforts following de jure segregation to uplift Black youth and prepare them to succeed in the White-dominated spheres of schooling and work (Cook & Dixson, 2013; Delpit, 1995; Dixson, 2003; Dixson & Dingus, 2008; Irvine, 2002; W. Johnson et al., 2013; Milner, 2006, 2012). However, the palpable reverence for Black teachers' efforts during segregation speaks to a larger racial project behind the scholarship on Blacks in teaching.

Because desegregation efforts in the 1960s and 1970s reproduced deficit lenses on the quality of segregated Black schools, many Black teachers lost their jobs as newly integrated schools refused to place the education of White students in the hands of purportedly under-qualified Black educators (Delpit, 1997; Fairclough, 2007; Tillman, 2004; Walker, 2001). As some stakeholders contend, the loss of Black teachers and the demise of care-centered, all-Black schools have left the fate of Black children's education in the hands of White teachers who lack culturally responsive pedagogical insights and anti-racist political commitments (BeauboeufLafontant, 1999; Dempsey & Noblit, 1993; Foster, 1990). In stark contrast to these White teachers, Black educators, with their ability to connect with Black students, collectively represent the promise of racial solidarity and progress through education. As stated by one Black teacher who was quoted in several of Foster's publications on Blacks in teaching, Black teachers and Black students are "part of that Black umbilical cord," and if Black teachers do not realize how they and their Black students "are of the same umbilical cord and do not strive to make us more connected to that cord, with a common destiny, then we're lost" (1991, p. 274, 1993, pp. 379–380, 1994, p. 230). Foster's reference to this comment in multiple publications underscores how the Black umbilical cord metaphor speaks powerfully to the perceived significance of Black teachers, especially in the post-Jim Crow milieu. Amidst the cultural and political dislocation pervading post-civil rights Black life, Black teachers represent an intergenerational lifeline that can reestablish Black education as a collective, anti-racist project. The "common destiny" symbolized by the umbilical cord attests to a belief in the shared plight of Blacks in America and the power of education—under the guidance of Black teachers—to collectively uplift the race.

The correlation between racial solidarity and the effectiveness of Black teachers has gained a renewed urgency amidst ongoing struggles to recruit and retain Blacks in the American teaching profession. Following Black teachers' loss of jobs during desegregation initiatives in the 1960s and 1970s, the numbers of Blacks in the nation's teaching force have steadily declined. While commonly cited reasons for teacher job dissatisfaction, like low salaries and poor work conditions, have contributed to this (Farinde, Allen, & Lewis, 2016; Ingersoll & May, 2011), so, too, have persistent structural barriers that appear to disproportionately affect Black participation in teaching. These barriers include entrance examinations that prevent access to the profession for some potential Black teaching candidates (Mawhinney, 2014; Petchauer, 2016) and neoliberal educational reforms like state takeovers and school turnaround plans, the undermining of unions, and the reliance on alternative-route teacher certification programs, all of which have had the collective impact of diminishing the presence of Black teachers in predominantly Black classrooms (Cook & Dixson, 2013; Dixson, Buras, & Jeffers, 2015; T. White, 2016). Set against the backdrop of Black students' academic plights in

American K–12 schools, the scholarly literature on Black teachers suggests that these educators can, and should, play a central role in improving the educational and social futures of Black children.

While the scholarship on Black teachers has made significant contributions to historical, political, and pedagogical perspectives on teaching, much of it has relied on two increasingly tenuous premises: first, that Black teachers and Black students continue to possess a common cultural identity and background; and, second, that Black teachers can continue to wield that shared identity and background to connect with, gain insights into, and motivate Black students. In their compelling critique of Black educational scholarship, O'Connor, Lewis, and Muller (2007) explore how blackness as an analytic category frequently ignores historical timeframe, regional location, class status, ethnicity, and national origin as salient mediating factors in Black cultural and educational experiences. Applying this critique to scholarship on Black teachers, I have noted the potential challenges posed by intraracial differences between Black male teachers and Black students in earlier iterations of my work (Brockenbrough, 2012a, 2013). Other scholars have pointed to class tensions between Black middle-class educators and the Black students and communities they served (Dingus, 2006; Fairclough, 2007) and to other cultural disconnects between teachers of color and students of color (Achinstein & Aquirre, 2008). None of these works necessarily precludes the possibilities of cultural connectedness between Black teachers and Black students, but they do raise important questions. Namely, as various forms of intraracial difference become more visible and potentially disruptive in Black communities (Dyson, 2005; Kunkle, 2015; Pew Research Center, 2007), how does the increasing heterogeneity within and across these communities shape the work of Black teachers? In what ways do evolving constructions of blackness in the United States not only enable, but possibly confound, a cultural connectedness between Black teachers and Black students? And, what are the implications for how we understand the larger racial project—symbolized by the image of the Black umbilical cord—undergirding the valorization of Black teachers' work with Black youth? To be clear, I do not raise these questions with the intention of dismissing the value of Black teachers, or Black male teachers specifically, as culturally responsive pedagogues or agents of racial uplift. Rather, what I am attempting to underscore here is the rationale for questioning the extent to which Black male teachers may continue to serve in these capacities, and may do so without contention. Amidst shifting conditions for the construction of racial identities and experiences in Black communities, American society, and American urban schools, the affordances and constraints of Black male teachers' culturally responsive pedagogies and race work warrant close attention. This book takes up that charge.

Male Teachers

Along with the research literature on the histories and pedagogies of Blacks in teaching, scholarship on men's participation in the teaching profession also serves as an important backdrop for this book's focus on Black male teachers. A significant corpus of historical and sociological work has chronicled the feminization of American teaching (Apple, 1986; Hoffman, 1981; Perlmann & Margo, 2001; Prentice & Theobald, 1991; Strober & Tyack, 1980; Tyack & Strober, 1981; Weiler, 1989), whereby shifting economic and cultural landscapes facilitated the influx of women into the ranks of the profession. This influx transformed teaching from a male bastion at the beginning of the 19th century to "women's work" by century's end. While teaching remains a predominantly female field, calls for more male teachers have resurfaced throughout the past century as educators, psychologists, policy-makers, and others have sought remedies for the purported demise of American manhood. In fact, current calls for more male teachers continue to reproduce the rhetoric of masculinity in crisis, and any analysis of Black men in the classroom must consider how the experiences of these teachers have been shaped by broader cultural discourses on masculinity in teaching. Mirroring the focus on race in the preceding review of scholarship on Black teachers, the goal of this current section is to frame how cultural constructions of gender have shaped men's participation in the American teaching profession.

At the heart of recurring discourses on men in teaching is the quest to reproduce selective notions of what it means to be a man. Scholarship from the interdisciplinary field of masculinity studies underscores the significance of calling such constructions of manhood into question (Adams & Savran, 2002; Pascoe & Bridges, 2016; Reeser, 2010). Central to this body of scholarship is what Connell (1995) definitively characterized as hegemonic masculinity, or the brand of masculine identity and expression heralded at a given historical moment as evidence of true manhood. In modern Western societies, hegemonic masculinity typically has been associated with men who exhibit "physical strength, adventurousness, emotional neutrality, certainty, control, assertiveness, self-reliance, individuality, competitiveness, instrumental skills, public knowledge, discipline, reason, objectivity and rationality" (Skelton, 2001, p. 50). Where power is contingent on a decisive and domineering manhood, the men who come closest to possessing these traits are desired, emulated, and called to lead. It is thus the approximation of a culturally esteemed masculinity, and not simply the biological inheritance of maleness, that places certain men at the helm of modern-day male domination. By denaturalizing maleness, and by attributing specific modes of maleness to control over specific historical arrangements of power, scholarly works from masculinity studies delimit hegemonic masculinity as a cultural, political, economic, and ideological phenomenon with intentional boundaries and far-reaching consequences.[3]

Calls to recruit more men into the teaching force are examples of hegemonic masculinity at work in the American imaginary. Throughout the 20th century, alarmist accounts of the "woman peril" in education—or the preponderance of women teachers who allegedly produced effeminized boys incapable of fulfilling their manly duties later in life (S. Johnson, 2008; Kimmel, 1987; Pleck, 1987; Weiler, 1989)—led to appeals for virile, red-blooded men to save boys by modeling an authentic masculinity at the head of the classroom. Artifacts like Phi Delta Kappa's *Teaching as a Man's Job* (1938) and Sexton's *The Feminized Male* (1969) underscored the need for real men to become teachers in order to counter boys' overexposure to the feminized culture of American schools. By the late 1990s and early 2000s, as academic indicators like testing scores and college enrollment rates generated new concerns about the underachievement of boys in American schools (Sax, 2007; Sommers, 2000; Tyre, 2006), and as data from the National Education Association revealed new historic lows in the numbers of male teachers nationwide (National Education Association, 2004), a new panic over the "boy crisis" in American K–12 schools sparked yet another round of calls to recruit men into teaching. In popular media coverage, this latest clamor for more male teachers has routinely imagined these men as adult male role models, effective disciplinarians, and father figures, especially for boys and for children from single-mother homes (Bolch, 2006; Gormley, 2012; James, 2013; Lobron, 2005; MacPherson, 2003; McWeeney, 2014; Milloy, 2003; National Education Association, 2004; Rowden-Racette, 2005; Snyder, 2008). It has also bemoaned persistent barriers to recruiting male teachers, including the profession's image as women's work, the difficulty of providing for families on low teacher salaries, and the threat of accusations of sexual impropriety during physical interactions with students (Abdul-Alim, 2004; Bolch, 2006; James, 2013; Lobron, 2005; Milloy, 2003; National Education Association, 2004; Rowden-Racette, 2005; Simpson, 2011; Snyder, 2008). Like past appeals to increase men's presence in the classroom, recent popular discourses on the need for male teachers cite crisis rhetoric on the plight of boys to demand a more male-centered culture of teaching. In doing so, these latest calls for more male teachers assure prospective recruits and the general public that the right men can save American boys by bringing hegemonic masculinity and patriarchal oversight into the teaching profession.

The taken-for-granted rationales behind calls to recruit more male teachers speak to the necessity of critical scholarship on masculinity politics in teaching. Outside of the United States, a substantive body of scholarly work emerging from Australia, Canada, and the United Kingdom has addressed this need. Informed by conceptualizations of gender and power from feminism and masculinity studies, this corpus of literature advances four general claims regarding contemporary discourses on men in teaching. First, the panics over boys' "laddish" behaviors and academic underperformance relative to girls, and the subsequent calls for more male teachers, reproduce patriarchal commitments to the preservation of male power while further marginalizing feminist concerns over the classroom experiences of girls and the status of women teachers under patriarchal educational bureaucracies (Lingard & Douglas, 1999; W. Martino & Frank, 2006; Mills, 2004; Mills, Martino, & Lingard, 2004; Thornton & Bricheno, 2006). Second, calls for more male teachers, along with publicly and privately funded recruitment initiatives, rely on minimal and/or inconclusive evidence of the efficacy of male teachers as role models for boys (Carrington et al., 2007; Carrington, Tymms, & Merrell, 2008; Francis et al., 2008; Marsh, Martin, & Cheng, 2008; Martin & Marsh, 2005; Sokal & Katz, 2008; Watson, 2017) and miss opportunities for structural analyses of the forces that impact boys' academic performance (Tarrant et al., 2015; Watson, 2017). Third, in the absence of critical examinations of masculinity politics in schools, male teachers may respond to the policing of their identities with misogynist and homophobic performances of hegemonic masculinity (Francis & Skelton, 2001; W. Martino & Frank, 2006; Roulston & Mills, 2000). And, fourth, schools need more male teachers to disrupt rather than reproduce hegemonic masculinity and model gender equity (Lingard & Douglas, 1999; Roulston & Mills, 2000; Skelton, 2009; Thornton & Bricheno, 2006). Collectively, this body of work has made important contributions to our knowledge of how masculinity can mediate identity, pedagogy, and power in the teaching profession.

In contrast to the literature focused on national contexts beyond the United States, a relatively small body of scholarship has provided critical analyses of masculinity politics in the lives of American male teachers. This includes works by Allan (1994) and Sargent (2001), who explore how male elementary teachers negotiated contradictory pressures to perform hegemonic masculinities while engaging in the nurturing, caring, and traditionally feminized cultures of elementary classrooms, and Weaver-Hightower's (2011) description of how male pre-service teachers responded to gender-based discouragements from peers and family members about their pursuit of feminized work. Additionally, Weaver-Hightower, as well as King (1998, 2004), Crisp and King (2016), and Sargent (2001), consider how male teachers, especially in early childhood and elementary settings, must manage suspicions of their sexualities as queer and/or pedophilic. Looking at broader cultural discourses, Martino (2008) traces the historical emergence of discourses on male teachers as role models, and he closely examines their resurgence in recent popular media in the United States and Canada. His extensive analysis reveals how role modeling discourses serve an anti-feminist project to re-masculinize schools by imagining strictly heteronormative male teachers. Similarly, Sternod (2011) explores how contemporary American media coverage of men in teaching attempts to resituate a proper masculinity and male authority in the classroom while unintentionally creating opportunities to disrupt hegemonic masculinity politics, and S. Johnson (2008) considers how tensions between American rural life and urbanization may have informed popular discourses on male teachers in the first half of the 20th century. Overall, there are certainly fewer analyses of masculinity politics and male teachers that focus specifically on American cultural and educational contexts. Nevertheless, the works that do exist underscore the need to understand how masculinity politics shape male teachers' daily experiences, and how calls for more male teachers may advance anti-feminist agendas to recuperate hegemonic masculinity in American schools.

A larger corpus of scholarship on masculinity politics in the lives of American male teachers would afford deeper reckonings with hegemonic masculinity and its consequences in schools. Additionally, expanding this body of literature would create more opportunities to examine the intersections of race and masculinity.[4] In the extant literature, Sternod (2011) briefly considers how race alters the boy crisis discourse to position Black male teachers more as disciplinarians of, rather than role models for, Black boys, and S. Johnson (2008) briefly notes that the slower feminization of teaching in segregated Black schools produced a slower disappearance of Black male teachers from those classrooms. Sargent (2001) acknowledges the barriers that men of color face when trying to access the spoils of hegemonic masculinity, but he does not interrogate the significance of race for either the men of color or the White men in his study. Weaver-Hightower (2011) identifies his study participants as White but does not address race in his analysis, and Allan (1994) and King (1998, 2004) also leave race untouched. While the minimal or absent attention to race in these works in no way invalidates their contributions, it does point to the need for more scholarship that explores the intersections of race and masculinity politics in the lives of American male teachers.

In the case of Black male teachers in American schools, exploring the intersections of race and masculinity politics requires a special attention to the interplay between privilege and marginality. A dubious history of surveillance and punishment has targeted Black male bodies throughout American society (Carbado, 1999b; Gates, 1997; Neal, 2013; Richardson, 2007) and within American schools (Ferguson, 2000; McCready, 2010; Noguera, 2008), consequently challenging Black men's access to the trappings of (White) patriarchal power. By contrast, the male teacher, as discussed, has been repeatedly imagined as a commanding patriarch who can re-masculinize American classrooms and American boys. Given their overlapping subjectivities as Black men and as male teachers, how do Black male teachers experience the convergence of these contradictory legacies? In other words, how can Black male teachers embody the privileged, masculine authority of the prototypical male teacher when their Black male bodies represent a threat that must be contained? How do these seemingly contrary embodiments shape how Black male teachers see themselves and define their mission? Additionally, does the inattention to racial difference in much of the scholarly literature cited suggest that the hegemonic masculinity ascribed to male teachers is an extension of whiteness? If so, are the popular media coverage and growing body of scholarship specifically on Black male teachers, both of which are examined in Chapter 2 of this book, merely attempts to recast male domination in the classroom in blackface? To be clear, I raise these questions here—just as I raised questions in response to my earlier review of the scholarship on Black teachers—not to dismiss the need for male teachers, or Black male teachers in particular. Instead, my intention is to question, and possibly reimagine, the logics upon which that need is often articulated. If hegemonic masculinity is not presumed as a pedagogical good, what becomes possible for Black men's participation in the teaching profession? This question is crucial for ongoing scholarly inquiries into the lives and work of Black male teachers, and it is considered closely in this text.

Origins of the Project

It happened one morning during my second year as a middle and high school history teacher at an independent school in New York City. While conducting a routine homework check in my first period class, I admonished a Black male student who was engaged at the time in some form of tomfoolery. As I continued checking assignments, I heard this student mumble something under his breath: "batty man." For a few moments, all I could do was stare at the Coke can and half-eaten bagel on my desk. "Batty man," a Jamaican epithet for homosexual men, was infamously popularized for American audiences in Buju Banton's, 1992 reggae song, "Boom Bye Bye," in which the unapologetically homophobic rasta chanted "boom bye bye inna batty bwoy head" (Myrie, 1992). (Rough translation: Shoot a gay man.) This student, who happened to be of Caribbean descent, belonged to a cadre of Black and Latino boys who had subtlety yet routinely taunted me for my heretofore unannounced queerness. About three or four seconds passed until I caught my breath, turned to the student, and asked him in an unavoidably menacing tone, "What did you call me?" He did not reply, but I kicked him out of my class nonetheless. Two days later, I officially came out to the school, becoming the only openly queer teacher on the faculty. And, from that point on, I never fully regained the favor of some of those Black and Latino male students.

A radically different story unfolded three years later when I served as a faculty chaperone for a trip to a student diversity conference in San Francisco. On the final evening of the trip, my faculty colleagues and I treated our cohort of New York City student delegates to a touristy feast near the city's famed Chinatown district. One of the students on the trip was a Black male upperclassman who had taken two of my classes and had participated in practically every extracurricular activity for which I was a faculty advisor. Upon some nagging on my part to hurry him up, this student replied, "Gosh, Mr. Brock, you're like my dad!" To this day, I have yet to fully determine why this moment stirred so much angst within me. I had always known that our relationship was special; I had always known that I could influence this particular student in ways that his other teachers, none of whom were Black men, seemingly could not. But I guess being likened to his dad announced a level of responsibility and a degree of emotional attachment that, at best, had only been hinted at before that moment. Somehow I had never prepared myself for the possibility that I might be seen as a father figure by this Black male student—a young man who, in his own father's absence, had impressively assumed a paternal role for his younger siblings. A few seconds elapsed before I managed an awkward smirk and retorted, "I don't have no kids." I then ushered all of the students onto a trolley heading to Chinatown and waited for the blurred boundaries between pedagogue and father to come back to order.

The significance of my presence as an adult Black man was marked in countless ways during my five years as a middle and high school history teacher, but the two preceding anecdotes have always stood out in my mind. Throughout those inaugural years of my career, I was constantly assured by administrators, faculty members, students, parents, friends, media, and any other source that cared to comment that it was important to have more Black male teachers like me in the classroom, particularly to serve as role models for Black boys. Yet outside of a handful of conversations with other Black male teachers, which were few and far between, the muddy terrains below those surface-level celebrations of Black men in the teaching ranks were never acknowledged. There were certainly no considerations of how the bonds between Black male teachers and Black male students, as in my experience, might be confounded by ethnic divides and homophobia; Black male identity was never imagined in such heterogeneous and conflicted terms. Even the presumably positive possibility of being a role model for Black boys, or better yet a father figure, was presented without recognitions of the emotional and psychic onus of such a connection. As an early 20-something still learning to care for myself, how was I supposed to assume the responsibilities of surrogate fatherhood? Even though my work as a Black male teacher entailed so much more than my encounters with Black boys, those specific encounters were repeatedly invested with such symbolic weight that they continue to dominate my early memories of my teaching career. While myriad sources pronounced the importance of being a Black male teacher, few if any seemed to recognize its complexities. Often, I found myself trying to sift through those complexities on my own.

My isolation during those years helps to explain the search for answers that led to this project. For nearly 15 years now, I have worked with preservice and in-service teachers who have enrolled in my teacher education courses, attended my professional development workshops, or participated in research studies that I have led or supported. When engaging other Black male teachers during those encounters, not only have I recognized the familiar quandaries of negotiating one's place, pedagogy, and mission as a Black man in teaching, but I have also discovered the unique affordances of my multiple identities as a Black male university researcher, teacher education instructor, and former K–12 classroom teacher to create spaces in which other Black male teachers can engage in critical reflections on their experiences. Frequently, my conversations with these teachers have provided outlets that were unavailable in their teacher education programs or workplaces. To be sure, my identities, experiences, and perspectives as a Black male educator sometimes varied from those of my newfound colleagues; we did not seamlessly fit into some essentialist and overdetermined category of "The Black Male Teacher," nor did we necessarily reach consensus on the various issues that we contemplated. However, our collective familiarity with dominant discourses on Black male teachers created a common meeting ground for critical dialogues across our individual differences.

These dialogues with other Black male teachers have led me to three pivotal realizations: (1) dominant discourses on Black men in teaching can provide a rich backdrop for Black male educators' collective interrogations of their experiences; (2) my firsthand encounters with those dominant discourses lends me a vital degree of credibility with other Black male teachers, both as a discussant on the state of Black men in teaching and as a source of support for Black male teachers in K–12 classrooms; and (3) my status as a university researcher and instructor who enjoys a degree of in-group access to Black male teachers' perspectives uniquely positions me as a potential advocate for Black male teachers' interests. These three realizations speak to my intellectual, professional, political, and personal investments in the project described in this book. As an educational researcher, I understand how the teaching profession can function as a repository for social and cultural anxieties around identity, power, and schooling, and I want to produce scholarship that troubles the reproduction of dubious racial and gender projects through the bodies of Black male teachers. As a former K–12 educator, I still empathize with well-intentioned Black male educators who heed the call to enter the classroom, yet find little guidance and few supports for the unique challenges and opportunities that greet them upon their arrival. And as a Black male teacher educator, I want to produce work that can be used by Black male teachers and their allies to think more critically about the presence and needs of Black men in the American teaching profession. Since prior publications of my research on Black male teachers have appeared primarily in academic journals with limited distribution (Brockenbrough, 2012b, 2012c, 2012a, 2014), and since those publications and one other text (Brockenbrough, 2013) have not covered all of my study findings, this book marks my attempt to share the full picture provided by my research with a wider audience. My hope is that this book will allow multiple stakeholder groups to collectively participate in more critical and nuanced considerations of why Black male teachers matter in American K–12 schools.

The Study

Study Methods

This book presents findings from *Black Men Teaching: The Identities and Pedagogies of Black Male Teachers*, my doctoral dissertation study that was supported by funding from the American Educational Research Association and the United States Department of Education's Institute of Educational Sciences (Grant R305U000003). Since the aim was to develop a deeper understanding of what it means to be a Black man in the teaching profession, this study drew methodologically on life history narrative inquiry. Like other forms of narrative inquiry, life history narratives draw on Bruner's assertion that people lead "storied lives" (cited in Alsup, 2006) and that the process of narrating our life stories reveals how we construct and understand our sense of self. What gets included in one's narrative, how narrative elements are ordered, and the perspectives that shape the meaning of the narrative as a whole all serve as windows into the self (Souto-Manning & Ray, 2007). By providing subjects with multiple opportunities to recount and construct their life stories, life history narrative research enables examinations of how social and historical forces have acted on and shaped individuals; how individuals have exercised agency in the midst of larger social and historical forces to construct their own identities; and how life experiences across temporal and spatial contexts have combined to inform individuals' emergent sense of self (Denzin, 1989; Goodson & Sikes, 2001; Munro, 1998). In this study, the use of life history narratives afforded rich and in-depth analyses of each participant's understanding of his life experiences as a Black man in the United States and his professional experiences as a Black male teacher in an urban school.

With life history narrative inquiry as a methodological anchor, data collection procedures for this study were designed to provide participants with multiple opportunities to construct and reflect on their lived experiences as Black men and as Black male teachers. The sequence of data collection procedures was guided by Seidman's (1998) regimen for in-depth interviewing, which calls for three separate interviews with each study participant: (1) an initial life history interview, which helps to situate the participant's experiences with a particular social phenomenon within the context of his or her life circumstances; (2) a second interview focusing on specific details of the participant's lived experiences with the social phenomenon in question; and (3) a concluding interview in which the participant clarifies details from the previous interviews and reflects on the overall meaning of the experiences he or she has recounted. This three-interview sequence provides the researcher with each study participant's account of his or her experience with the phenomenon under investigation, while also supplying additional biographical information that is crucial for contextualizing each participant's account.

Protocols for all data collection sessions appear in the Appendix. Following Seidman's (1998) regimen, data collection began with an in-depth life history interview with each participant. After responding to several "warm-up" questions regarding background information, entry into the teaching profession, and current teaching assignments, the bulk of the first interview explored participants' racial and gendered identity formation experiences across their life spans. Asking participants to define their racial and gender identities allowed me as the researcher to honor their definitions of self and to tailor interview questions accordingly. Using identity terminology provided by participants, I asked the men in this study during the first interview to explain the relationship between their racial and gender identities and to describe how their racial and gender identities had shaped childhood, adolescent, and adulthood experiences across multiple social contexts. The first interview concluded with prompts for participants to describe identities other than race and gender that had played significant roles in informing their sense of self, thus allowing them to provide additional layers of specificity and complexity to their identity narratives.

After generating rich biographical overviews of participants' life experiences as Black men during the first interview, a narrower focus on their teaching experiences defined the second of the three study interviews. I asked participants to consider the potential influence of several factors on their professional experiences as Black male teachers, including their pedagogical stances, instructional practices, classroom management styles, and relationships with students, fellow teachers, administrators, and parents. As participants reflected on these factors, I asked them to describe the particular role, if any, of Black maleness in shaping various aspects of their experiences in the teaching profession. The emphasis throughout the second interview on the challenges and opportunities characterizing participants' professional experiences offered an ideal backdrop for questions about available or potential supports for Black men in teaching, which were posed at the end of this interview.

The third and final one-on-one interview provided participants with the chance to speak about their involvement in this study. After participants reflected on any major issues that had emerged in their teaching experiences since previous study-related contacts, I asked them to recall their reasons for agreeing to take part in this study, describe what, if anything, they had gained from or enjoyed about their participation in the study, and suggest which aspects of the study design might be modified in future iterations of this project. I also asked participants to describe their hopes for how the study findings would ultimately be used. This third interview thus enabled the men in this study to offer their unique feedback on this research project as the individuals who had experienced it, and the interview also allowed me as the researcher to take stock of the wishes of those who had made invaluable contributions to this scholarly investigation.

In addition to the one-on-one interviews, focus group sessions were conducted to enable study participants to collectively explore and negotiate the significance of their experiences as Black male teachers. There were two one-time sessions, Focus Group A and Focus Group B, with four and five participants, respectively. The composition of each focus group was determined by the participants' availability, with no participant attending both focus groups. During both sessions, I asked participants to revisit three major themes that had emerged across one-on-one interviews: the presumed status of Black male teachers as role models and father figures; the relationships between Black male teachers and Black male students; and potential strategies for recruiting, retaining, and supporting Black men in the teaching profession. These topics were intentionally revisited during both focus groups to generate more opportunities for triangulation across data sources and to enable participants to discuss their perspectives on these key issues with other Black male teachers. Several related topics also emerged during both focus groups, and time was deliberately reserved toward the end of the sessions for participants to raise concerns that had not been addressed.

Protocols for the one-on-one interviews and focus group sessions were informed by an earlier pilot study (Brockenbrough, 2006) during which I conducted in-depth interviews with six Black male teachers to develop an initial sense of key themes to target. Although the pilot study identified several themes that seemed worthy of further exploration, I conducted all data collection sessions for the dissertation study as semi-structured interviews to allow for unanticipated topics and insights to surface while still ensuring some continuity of themes across data sources. I also employed several strategies for in-depth interviewing described by Lichtman (2006) to make sure that key issues were addressed while enabling enough flexibility for participants to narrate their life experiences on their own terms. These strategies included introductory questions that framed key themes broadly enough to allow participants a number of possible angles from which to respond, and probing questions that asked participants to clarify their statements and provide illustrative anecdotes when possible. Another interviewing strategy, the repetition of participant responses in the interviewer's own words, allowed me as the researcher to check my understanding of participants' statements with their intended meanings. In several cases, this strategy prompted participants to iden- tify and correct my misinterpretations or critique my assumptions about the relevance of emergent study themes to their particular life narratives. Together, the use of semi-structured interviews and in-depth interview- ing techniques helped me to wed pre-study conceptual frameworks with iterative adaptations of those frameworks that more accurately captured participants' insights and perspectives.

In all, data collection extended from January to October 2007 for nine study participants, and from October 2007 to February 2008 for two participants who were enrolled later in the study and consequently were not included in focus group sessions. Each of the first two in-depth inter- views lasted an average of 90 minutes, and the third an average of 30 minutes. Each focus group lasted just under two hours. In total, approxi- mately 44 hours of one-on-one and focus group interviews were recorded for this study, producing lengthy and detailed accounts that allowed for rich descriptions of participants' perspectives. All data collection ses- sions were recorded with a digital audio recorder and then transcribed verbatim to ensure accurate reproductions of participants' narratives. Table 1.1 lists all of the data collections sessions in which each teacher in this study participated.

Whereas data analysis was iterative and ongoing throughout the study, formal analytic procedures lasted from September 2007 to April 2008. Two principal concerns—participants' constructions and negotiations of their identities as Black men, and participants' perspectives on their peda- gogies and professional experiences as Black male teachers—drove the

Table 1.1 Data Collected for Each Subject

Participant	1st interview	2nd interview	3rd interview	Focus Group A[a]	Focus Group B[b]
Bill	X	X	X	X	
Damon	X	X	X	X	
Felix	X	X	X	X	
Greg	X	X	X		X
Ira	X	X	X		
Karl	X	X	X		X
Mitch	X	X	X		
Oliver	X	X	X		X
Quincy	X	X	X		X
Solomon	X	X	X	X	
Victor	X	X	X		X

a Focus Group A: Bill, Damon, Felix, & Solomon.
b Focus Group B: Greg, Karl, Oliver, Quincy, & Victor.

generation and arrangement of coding schemes. Overall, data analysis consisted of three phases. In the first phase of analysis, I reviewed one-on-one interview and focus group transcripts to develop an initial sense of the range of themes across data sources. Based on this review, I generated a tentative list of coding schemes. In the second phase of analysis, I revisited data on each participant and triangulated those data across lengthy narrative passages to construct an individual participant profile. Although certain codes began to emerge as recurrent across several participant profiles, the primary focus during the second phase of data analysis remained on identifying the significant themes in and specific nuances of each participant's life narrative. Constructing individual participant profiles before triangulating data across multiple participant narratives helped me as the researcher to avoid misinterpretations of the former in service of the latter; in other words, individual participant profiles forced a reckoning with each participant's narrative on its own terms, regardless of whether those terms seemed to indicate a significant study finding. In the third phase of data analysis, I analyzed participant profiles together to finish honing codes and arranging them into overarching categories, and to apply codes to the triangulation of data across multiple participant narratives. Most of the emergent themes that came into relief during this third phase of data analysis recurred in multiple passages across four or more participant narratives. Overall, the three phases of data analysis afforded in-depth examinations of each participant's negotiations of the challenges and triumphs he had experienced over his life as a Black man and as a Black male teacher, as well as broader considerations of the commonalities that spanned multiple participants' life narratives.

The data collection and analysis procedures described were crucial for allowing me to achieve my research aims. The goal of this study was not to test a particular hypothesis about Black male teachers, but rather to explore the ways in which the experiences of being Black men in the teaching profession were meaningful for study participants. Thus, it was crucial for me to obtain and identify multiple indications of what being a Black male teacher meant for the men in this study. The three in-depth interviews with each participant, along with the two focus groups, provided these indications in a rich and nuanced fashion. As noted, the semi-structured interview format and the intentional use of various in-depth interviewing techniques allowed for some continuity of themes across data sources while also enabling participants to correct any misinterpretations on my part and raise questions or concerns that I may have overlooked, thus helping me to produce accurate representations of participants' perspectives. Revisiting emergent themes from previous data collection sessions during the third one-on-one interviews and during the focus groups was another strategy that allowed me to check my understanding of participants' perspectives. Feedback from members of my peer writing group also helped me to refine the analysis of data from this study.

Research Context and Participants

Pseudonyms for the research context and study participants are used throughout this article to protect participants' anonymity. All the participants in this study were employed at the time of data collection in the public school system in Brewerton, aka the Brew, a large urban center on the east coast with sizeable Black and White populations, and smaller but growing Latino and Asian communities. Black youth constituted the majority of the Brewerton School District's student body (roughly two-thirds), followed in descending order by smaller numbers of Latino, White, and Asian students. Most Brewerton schools offered free or reduced-price meal programs for all their students, suggesting a prevalence of working-class and poor families being served by Brewerton public schools. Like many urban districts, the Brewerton School District struggled with scarce financial and material resources, student underperformance on high-stakes testing, high student dropout rates, and high teacher and administrative turnover. These challenges were exacerbated by the shifting social and economic landscape of Brewerton, with its growing disparities between rich and poor residents, the disappearance of manufacturing jobs for blue-collar workers, and the concentration of drugs, violence, poor housing, and poor access to health care in impoverished, predominantly minority neighborhoods. Together, school district and citywide indices depict an inner-city educational system that struggled to apply limited resources in an equitable fashion to the schooling of Brewerton children. This is not to suggest that educators and residents in Brewerton were completely without agency and hope. Rather, this overview is intended to generate an appreciation of the structural barriers in Brewerton schools and communities that made educational and social change a Herculean yet urgent project.

All of the participants in this study were Black male teachers who were employed in Brewerton public schools during the time of this study. Ten of the eleven participants were teaching 6th–12th grade; one participant, Greg, was teaching on the K–5 level but had previously spent half of his career in middle schools. Participation was limited to educators with middle and high school teaching experience to enable this study to draw upon and speak to the issues facing Black male teachers in those grade levels, who existed in larger numbers than their elementary peers. Efforts were also made to recruit teachers from schools with sizeable percentages of Black students in order to investigate scholarly and popular claims of a special connectedness between Black male teachers and Black youth. Of the 11 participants in the study, nine were teaching in schools with predominantly Black student bodies. The two remaining participants, Greg and Karl, were teaching in schools that were predominantly minority but had pluralities of Latino and Asian students, respectively. Both of these teachers still reported significant contacts with the Black students in their schools, and Greg also made a number of references to his prior teaching experience at a predominantly Black school in the Brewerton School District.

Prospective participants were identified and recruited through personal contacts and professional networks in Brewerton educational circles to which I had access, and purposeful sampling was used to bring some diversity of background experiences and teaching subjects. Recruits received a one-page description of the study via email, followed by an in-person overview of study objectives and design, and they were given opportunities to ask questions and express any concerns prior to enrolling in the study. Participation in this study was on a voluntary basis only, and each participant signed a consent form prior to entering the study to confirm that his participation was voluntary and informed.

Recruitment of participants began in January of 2007. By March of 2007, ten men were enrolled in the study. One of those men became unavailable following his first one-on-one interview, and he was subsequently withdrawn from the study. Of the nine that remained, the majority was under the age of 30 and had been teaching for less than five years. To bring more diversity to the study sample, efforts were made in September of 2007 to find three more participants over the age of 30 with at least ten years of teaching experience. Those efforts secured two new participants, one (Ira) who was over 30 and had five to nine years of teaching experience, and the other (Mitch) who neither was over 30 nor had more than ten years of teaching experience but still made invaluable contributions to the project.

Table 1.2 provides a demographic summary of the study participants. In addition to assigning pseudonyms to the participants, the descriptions of age, grade level, subject area, and years of teaching experience

Table 1.2 Demographic Summary of Study Participants

Participant	Age	Grade Level	Subject Area	Years of Teaching
Bill Drexler	<30	High School	Humanities	< 5
Damon Hubert	<30	Middle School	Humanities	< 5
Felix Jones	<30	High School	Math/Science	< 5
Greg Poland	30–39	Middle School*	Humanities	> 10
Ira Walker	30–39	High School	Humanities	5–9
Karl Reardon	<30	Middle School	Humanities	< 5
Mitch Abrams	<30	Middle School	Math/Science	< 5
Oliver Currington	>40	High School	Humanities	> 10
Quincy Stinson	<30	Middle School	Humanities	< 5
Solomon Yardley	<30	High School	Math/Science	< 5
Victor Rollins	>40	Middle School	Humanities	5–9

* Grade level prior to study, comprising half of overall teaching experience are presented in broad categories that help to situate the participants while also protecting their anonymity. Additional details about participants' backgrounds and lives are provided in the report of study findings as they become relevant, and pseudonyms or generic descriptors (for instance, "university" in place of the actual names of the universities they attended) are used when referring to places of origin, college alma maters, current workplaces, names of students or colleagues, and the like. Although these measures are taken to protect the participants' anonymity, all of the teachers in this study were informed at the beginning of each interview that they could pass on questions with which they felt uncomfortable or request that the digital audio recorder be stopped. Nevertheless, given the sensitive nature of some of the themes that surfaced, and out of respect for participants' willingness to share their stories so honestly and thoughtfully, this book attempts to protect their anonymity while preserving as much as possible the integrity and original intent of their voices.

A Few Challenges

Any attempt to investigate some aspect of the human condition, regardless of how thoroughly and carefully conducted, inevitably tells only parts of the story at hand. This study is no exception. As discussed earlier in this chapter, my status as a Black male researcher, teacher educator, and former K–12 instructor has afforded a unique rapport with other Black male educators and instinctual insights into their professional and personal experiences. Yet despite my insider status, my lens on the issues facing Black male teachers invariably privileged certain intellectual, political, and pedagogical concerns. For instance, I often found myself drawn to gender, sexuality, and class dynamics as a queer, middle-class researcher. While my attention to these issues generated invaluable insights from study participants, it also meant that other concerns may not have surfaced as clearly as they would have for a researcher driven by different sets of interests.

An even bigger challenge for me at times was the negotiation of my role as a researcher. Since my research aim was to uncover the meaning that study participants ascribed to their experiences as Black male teachers, I tried to refrain from challenging them on remarks that were at odds with my own stances, opting instead to pose follow-up questions that elicited elaboration without exposing my own opinions or casting judgments. While this seemed to contribute to a safe space in which participants could speak openly, it may have resulted in some missed opportunities to push dialogues even further when I felt that doing so could have made participants uncomfortable. Additionally, since participants shared their stories with me in relatively safe spaces, I struggled with the degree to which I should relay those stories in potentially unsafe spaces beyond the participatory contexts of this study. As noted earlier in this chapter and reiterated in later chapters, portions of the copious details collected during interviews have been withheld at times in this book in order to further protect participants' anonymity. While this strategy felt like the most responsible way to handle certain data, it admittedly constrained some segments of analysis for this book.

Since the portrait presented in this project is of Black male teachers specifically in Brewerton, working in public schools and teaching at the middle and high school levels, the findings of this study cannot be generalized as reflective of all Black male teachers. What these findings can do, however, is spark important questions and concerns for teacher education programs, school districts, and educational researchers who want to build a substantial body of critical knowledge on the experiences of Black men in the teaching profession. Despite being confined to a particular locale and certain grade levels, this study uncovered themes that countered supposedly universal claims about Black male teachers. Presenting these contradictions in this book will hopefully guide further interrogations of current (mis)understandings of Black men in the classroom.

Organization of the Book

The goals of this opening chapter were to introduce the overarching aims of the book and provide some initial context for understanding why those aims are worth pursuing. Building on this chapter's discussions of the discourses on Black teachers and male teachers in American education, Chapter 2 focuses more directly on how the intersections of Blackness and maleness make the recruitment of Black male teachers a complex and consequential cultural project. Drawing upon critical perspectives from Black masculinity studies, I examine what I refer to as "saviorist" discourses that depict Black male teachers as savior-like figures who, as both culturally responsive pedagogues and models of hegemonic masculinity, can save Black children, especially Black boys. As I assert, these discourses appear on the surface to celebrate Black men, but they do so through bounded constructions of Black manhood that are not necessarily attainable by all potential Black male teachers, and that may not always serve the best interests of Black youth. I then follow this analysis of saviorist discourses at large with an examination in Chapter 3 of how the men in my study took up these discourses to explain their motivations for entering and participating in urban teaching. This chapter confirms the relevance of saviorist discourses as a backdrop for understanding my participants' narratives while also capturing some of their hopes and goals as Black men in the teaching profession.

From there, I venture into the tensions surrounding saviorist discourses in study participants' narratives. In Chapter 4, I explore how patriarchal constructions of Black male teachers as disciplinarians and father figures presented several dilemmas for the men in my study. Contrary to scholarly and popular discourses that cast Black male teachers as ideal role models and father figures for Black students, the findings shared in this chapter reveal how patriarchal constructions of Black male teachers can produce pedagogical quandaries for Black men in urban classrooms. In Chapter 5, I examine the dilemmas that study participants encountered as they negotiated their relationships with women colleagues in the predominantly female workplace of schools. Here, the focus is on patriarchal gender ideologies that fueled participants' contentious encounters with women in positions of authority, as well their desire for more male-defined spaces in their professional lives as teachers. Together, Chapters 4 and 5 trace complicated gender politics that often elude saviorist discourses on Black male teachers, and that definitely warrant closer attention.

Continuing with the dilemmas associated with saviorist discourses, Chapter 6 analyzes the challenges experienced by the queer men who participated in my study. While none of these men were openly queer at work, some still found themselves targeted by students' homophobic surveillance and speech acts, making their closeted status the subject of contentious teacher-student power struggles in their classrooms. By spotlighting the narratives of the Black queer men in my study, this chapter exposes and challenges the heteronormativity of saviorist discourses on Black male teachers while also considering what agency may look like for these men. This analysis is followed by an exploration in Chapter 7 of the affordances of study participants' culturally responsive pedagogies. By highlighting participants' pedagogical successes with Black students, this chapter provides an important balance to the emphasis elsewhere on the tensions and dilemmas in participants' narratives. Finally, in Chapter 8, I conclude by considering how this book provides the basis for reimagining the work and lives of Black male teachers beyond the confines of saviorist discourses on Black masculinity, and I offer several broader strategies for how teacher education programs, school districts, and policy-makers can grapple with the dilemmas chronicled in this text as they recruit, train, and support Black male teachers.

A quick note on the presentation of study findings: Since I draw upon multiple and lengthy life narratives from each of the 11 study participants when sharing study findings in this book, I had to strike a balance between reproducing some narrative excerpts verbatim while just summarizing key themes from others. This strategy was necessary to make the presentation of study findings manageable within this book's word limitation. The verbatim excerpts that do appear were chosen for their evocative nature, which hopefully will compensate for the narrative passages that are summarized instead of reproduced in this text.

Notes

1. Pseudonyms are used for all of the men who participated in my study.
2. Other terms have been used to describe the culturally mediated nature of pedagogical interactions, most notably culturally relevant pedagogy, while still evoking similar sets of concerns. See Gay (2010), Ladson-Billings (2009), and Milner (2011, 2016) for examples.
3. For more examples of works from masculinity studies that explore these issues, see Connell (2000), Kimmel (2012), and Pascoe (2007).
4. As discussed in Chapter 2, some of the scholarship on Black male teachers analyzes the intersections of race and masculinity in these teachers' experiences. Here, however, I am focusing on scholarly examinations of male teachers' experiences that do not focus specifically on Black men in teaching. A more rigorous engagement with race is an area for growth in this body of work.

2 Saving Black Boys

Black Male Teachers and Saviorist Black Masculinity

In Chapter 1, I offered separate reviews of the scholarly literatures on Black teachers and male teachers, underscoring how the politics of blackness and maleness, respectively, have influenced participation in the American teaching profession. For Black teachers, culturally responsive pedagogies and racial solidarities mark longstanding commitments to preparing Black youth to succeed in the face of White supremacist oppression. For male teachers, the performance of hegemonic masculinity in the classroom reflects cultural anxieties around the "boy crisis" in K–12 schools and the fate of American manhood at large. As Black and male members of the nation's teaching force, Black male teachers are situated at the intersection of the profession's relationships to blackness and maleness. How that intersection produces specific expectations for Black men's participation in teaching, and how Black male teachers negotiate those expectations, warrant close and critical consideration.

In this chapter, I turn to the intersection of blackness and maleness to explore how Black masculinity politics position Black men in the nation's teaching ranks. Specifically, I argue that popular discourses on Black male teachers have relied on a saviorist Black manhood to define expectations for and justify the recruitment and retention of Black men in teaching. I use the term "saviorist" to mark the construction of Black male teachers as savior-like figures who, as both culturally responsive pedagogues and models of hegemonic masculinity, are able to manage, inspire, and ultimately save Black children, especially Black boys.[1] As I discuss in this chapter, saviorist discourses appear on the surface to celebrate Black men, but they do so by reproducing a racialized patriarchy and hegemonic masculinity that may not be in the best interests of Black male teachers or the Black youth they serve.

To contextualize this argument, I first draw upon Black masculinity studies to explain two premises that ground my conceptualization of Black masculinity. I then build upon those premises to analyze popular discourses on Black men as savior-like figures in the lives of Black male youth, and I follow that analysis with an even closer look at saviorist popular discourses on Black male teachers. I conclude the chapter by reviewing scholarly literature on Black male teachers, with a particular attention to how critical scholarship—including the analyses offered in this book—can complicate our understanding of Black men's participation in the American teaching profession.

Analyzing Black Masculinity: Two Premises

By now, a widely circulated litany of statistics on incarceration, homicide, unemployment, homelessness, educational underachievement, mental and physical health disparities, and other chronic blights has documented the bleak realities facing many Black males in America (M. Alexander, 2012; Anderson, 2008; Centers for Disease Control and Prevention, 2016; Feierman, 2014; G. Graham & Gracia, 2012; Noguera, 2008; Schott Foundation for Public Education, 2012). These oft-cited indices of Black male disenfranchisement illustrate the cumulative impact of structural forces that have systematically eroded Black men's life chances and, thus, loom ominously over any attempts to transform the exigencies of Black men's lives. Understanding how the plights and possibilities of the Black male condition are produced, encountered, embodied, conceptualized, and negotiated is at the crux of a rich corpus of scholarship known collectively as Black masculinity studies. The works that comprise this cross-disciplinary field engage a range of academic lenses to trace a multifaceted yet related set of concerns around the nature and consequences of Black masculinity (Drake, 2016; Jenkins & Hine, 2001; Richardson, 2007; M. O. Wallace, 2002; Young, 2007). University courses (Adejumo, 2015; Neal, n.d.), academic conferences (Williams, 2005), academic journals (Strayhorn & Jeffries, 2012), and scholarly anthologies (R. P. Byrd & Guy-Sheftall, 2001; Carbado, 1999a; R. L. Jackson & Hopson, 2011; Mutua, 2006b; Slatton & Spates, 2014) all attest to the presence and impact of this field. Given its intellectual diversity, Black masculinity studies, like any such field, consists of multiple and divergent strands, from Afrocentric thought (Akbar, 1991; Kunjufu, 2005; Madhubuti, 1990, 2002) to queer perspectives (B. K. Alexander, 2006; E. P. Johnson, 2008; McCune, 2014) and beyond. This intellectual diversity speaks to the range of thinkers and audiences with a stake in the field, marking the critical analysis of Black masculinity as a significant scholarly endeavor.

Across Black masculinity studies, the complexities of Black male subjectivity emerge as a clear priority. Indeed, a defining concern of this field of study is the contested and contradictory processes through which knowledge about Black male subjects is produced, and within, against, and around which Black males define their identities and participation across sociohistorical, cultural, and institutional contexts. Examples include works that examine the politics of Black male hypermasculinity and hypersexuality (R. L. Jackson, 2006; Lemelle, 2010; Neal, 2013; Poulson-Bryant, 2005; Slatton & Spates, 2014); Black males' fraught performances of boyhood (Dumas & Nelson, 2016; Ferguson, 2000) and fatherhood (Green, 2009; Neal, 2006); the intersections of Black masculinity and class politics (P. B. Harper, 1996; Neal, 2005; T. L. Taylor & Johnson, 2011; Young, 2007); Black male navigations of schooling (B. K. Alexander, 2006; Dancy, 2012; J. E. Davis, 2001; McCready, 2010); and the experiences of Black queer males (E. P. Johnson, 2008; McCune, 2014; Mumford, 2016; Reid-Pharr, 2001). In these and numerous other examples from Black masculinity studies, what it means to be a certain type of Black male—a macho Black male, a queer Black male, a Black father—is not a given. Despite material and ideological conditions that have systematically reproduced the marginalized social positionalities of Black males as a whole, factors such as social and cultural contexts and intersecting multiple identities inevitably nuance how Black male subjectivity is understood and enacted by various social actors across particular times and spaces. The field of Black masculinity studies has made an important contribution by coupling grand narratives of the Black male experience with careful accounts of when and how those narratives splinter.

The complex and contradictory processes through which we produce and respond to knowledge about Black male subjects informs the first premise of my analysis of Black masculinity: A full grasp of Black masculinity's significance and effects demands a critical investigation of how individual Black men agentically negotiate prevailing constructions of Black male subjectivity. Throughout this book, I trace the circulation of discourses that reflect deep investments—across American culture at large, within Black America, and within educational contexts—in particular modes of Black male subjectivity, and I consider how the participants in my study and other Black male teachers like them may align with, oppose, and/or rework the truths about Black men that emerge from those investments. Doing so enables me to recognize the expectations facing Black male teachers as a collective while also exploring how individual Black male teachers exercise their agency to position themselves in a variety of ways within schools. Admittedly, this approach to making sense of the impact of broader cultural discourses on teachers' lived experiences is not new.[2] However, as I discuss later in this chapter, popular discourses on Black men in teaching have often relied on common-sense claims about the need for Black male teachers. Consequently, there has been relatively little exploration of how individual Black male teachers, especially those who diverge from saviorist constructions of Black manhood, variably negotiate what it means to be a Black man in the teaching profession. As calls to increase the numbers of Black men in teaching spawn more and more attempts to create, replicate, and scale-up recruitment and retention initiatives (Chapman & Colangelo, 2015; Fenwick, 2010; Hawkins, 2015; Irvin, 2015; Reckdahl, 2015), it is crucial to consider how the diverse identities and experiences of Black male teachers should inform efforts to engage these men. Failure to do so may destine recruitment and retention efforts to reproduce limited constructions of the desirable Black male teacher.

Along with its nuanced considerations of how Black male subjectivity is produced and negotiated, Black masculinity studies informs my analysis through another offering: its critique of patriarchal constructions of Black manhood. This critique derives from the influence of Black feminist scholarship since the late 1970s that has modeled critical interventions against patriarchal regimes within Black communities (Hill Collins, 2000, 2005; hooks, 1981; Smith, 1983; M. Wallace, 1979). While some Black masculinity scholars have actually promoted patriarchal models of Black manhood (djvlad, 2016; Hare & Hare, 1984, 1985; Kunjufu, 1985b; Madhubuti, 1990, 2002; VIPMediaBlogs, 2017), others have followed Black feminism's lead by decrying the equation of Black liberation to the restoration of Black male patriarchy (Awkward, 1999; R. P. Byrd, 2001; Carbado, 1999b; Guy-Sheftall, 2006; Lemons, 2001; Mutua, 2006a; Neal, 2005; White, 2008). With the recent introduction of "toxic masculinity" into the American cultural lexicon (Hamblin, 2016; Holloway, 2015), Black feminist-informed sensibilities on Black manhood have also driven efforts to contend with the lure of toxic masculinity for Black men (Armah, 2016; Asadulla, 2016; T. W. Harris, 2017). Additionally, queer critiques have converged with Black feminist-informed works in Black masculinity studies to trouble Black patriarchy's anti-queer impulses (Drake, 2016; P. B. Harper, 1996; Neal, 2005, 2013; Riggs, 2006; Ron Simmons, 1991). Collectively, these ruminations explore the possibilities of Black male ontologies that eschew patriarchal domination and heteronormative regulation as the foundations of Black manhood (R. P. Byrd, 2001; Drake, 2016; Mutua, 2006c; Neal, 2005, 2013; White, 2008). As a disruptive intervention, the critical stances toward patriarchal discourses within Black masculinity studies have generated significant explorations of Black male subjectivities that resist and seek alternatives to hegemonic modes of masculinity.

Black feminist and queer-inspired work from Black masculinity studies informs the second analytical premise of my project: Disrupting patriarchal and heteronormative constructions of Black maleness is essential for enabling counterhegemonic Black masculinities. This premise grounds my critical disposition toward certain logics that get reproduced in calls for more Black male teachers. As I discuss further in this chapter, contemporary discourses on Black male teachers have frequently beckoned these men to fill a perceived void in the lives of Black youth by serving as patriarchs in the classroom. Those who appear to perform the hegemonic masculinity envisioned for Black patriarchs are cast as role models and father figures who can save Black children and, in some cases, the Black community as a whole. Echoing concerns from Black feminist and queer-inspired scholarship on Black masculinity, my analyses throughout this book explore the consequences of linking Black male teachers to forms of power that historically have organized male dominance, cisgenderism, and heteronormative repression in Black social and political contexts. These consequences are frequently overshadowed by the allure of having more positive Black male role models in the classroom, which is why this book works tirelessly to bring them into the spotlight. My analyses also question the pedagogical and emotional consequences of patriarchy for Black male teachers, who may or may not desire to align themselves with this construction of Black manhood, and they consider alternative modes of participation for these men within the teaching profession. Combining both of my analytical premises on Black masculinity, this book pays particular attention to how Black male teachers negotiate dominant discourses on Black manhood, and it strives to envision counterhegemonic possibilities for their gender work in American K–12 schools.

Saviorist Black Masculinity

Building upon my engagement with Black masculinity studies, a core concern of this project is the saviorist Black masculinity permeating popular discourses on Black male teachers. As a widely circulated and highly regarded mode of Black masculine being, saviorist Black masculinity situates Black male teachers within a larger political project—one that seeks to validate hegemonic masculinity and confirm patriarchy within Black educational and cultural contexts. To frame my analysis of saviorist Black masculinity, I offer an overview of the deep-seated anxieties surrounding the legitimacy and respectability of Black men's masculinities. With these anxieties as a backdrop, I then cite examples from a variety of sources to illustrate how Black male adults are imagined as savior-like figures in the lives of Black youth, especially Black boys, and I raise several concerns that should inform analyses of saviorist Black masculinity.

In his in-depth and illuminating review of social science and educational literatures on Black males in the United States from the 1930s to the beginning of the 21st century, Brown (2012) traces longstanding anxieties around the masculine legitimacy of Black men. As Brown notes, scholarship from the 1930s through the 1950s often described Black men as absent from their families and adrift in society at large, unable to live up to the responsibilities of a proper patriarchal manhood. This literature was followed by works in the 1960s that tended to cast Black men as emasculated by matriarchal Black family structures and prone to violence and hypersexuality as means to reassert their masculinity. After a focal turn in the 1970s to the soulful and adaptive subcultures of Black men, alarm over Black male homicide and incarceration rates fueled depictions of Black males in the 1980s and 1990s as an "endangered species" living in a perpetual state of crisis. As Brown argues, despite slight shifts in emphasis and tone from decade to decade, the underlying message of these discourses remained consistent: "The Black male is hypermasculine and oppositional to the norms and expectations of schools and society" (p. 2068). More specifically, these prevailing discourses on the Black male subject repeatedly depicted adult Black men's failures at participating in the economy at large and the Black family in particular—failures that led to their reactionary, hypermasculine coping strategies—and they attributed the maladaptive behaviors of Black boys to the absence in their lives of responsible Black men. In Brown's poignant words, these discourses established "an essentialized story that has closed off the kinds of questions that one can ask to account for and address the social needs of African American males" (p. 2049).

Covering almost a century's worth of knowledge production on Black males in America, Brown's analysis provides an illuminating backdrop for understanding contemporary discourses on Black men and Black boys. As Black boys in the United States continue to experience high drop-out rates from K–12 schools, high unemployment rates, overrepresentation in the school-to-prison pipeline, a range of health disparities, and related dilemmas (Anderson, 2008; Feierman, 2014; G. Graham & Gracia, 2012; Howard, 2014; Schott Foundation for Public Education, 2012; Tavis Smiley Reports, 2011), numerous stakeholders continue to ascribe the plight of Black boys to the paucity of adult Black men in their lives. Absentee fathers especially are blamed for Black boys' raw psychological scars and sense of abandonment (Anderson, 2008; Green, 2009), their strained and sometimes oppositional relationships with their mothers (Cuffee, 2008; Hare & Hare, 1985), and their attraction to gangs and male-centered street culture (Anderson, 2008; Boyd-Franklin & Franklin, 2000; Cuffee, 2008; T. Harris & Taylor, 2012). Although a growing number of scholars has troubled the reliance on Black male role models as remedies to the deep and enduring structural inequities that produce Black youth marginality (T. O. Jackson, Boutte, & Wilson, 2013; James, 2012; W. Martino & Rezai-Rashti, 2012), the absent Black father repeatedly emerges in cultural discourses as a major cause of Black boys' miseries.

If absentee Black fathers are understood as the root cause of the perceived waywardness of Black boys, then a sensible remedy would be to reengage those fathers and/or find suitable surrogates. This rationale has fueled pervasive calls over the past three decades for Black men to take responsibility for raising their children and to serve as role models and mentors for fatherless Black boys. Evidence of such rhetoric can be found in everything from articles and opinion pieces on the need for active Black fathers in Black boys' lives (Campbell, 2011; Glaude & Glaude, 2016; Gregory, 2016) to high-profile speeches on Black paternal accountability by Barack Obama that underscored his own status as a symbol of responsible Black fatherhood (Bryant, 2013; Dyson, 2008). Viral internet clips have generated praise for Black fathers who spend quality time with

Black boys (Brett, 2015; Ramirez, 2017; Sonny, 2015; "Videos of father and son goes [sic] viral for their incredible dancing," 2017) and for Black fathers and other Black male adults who provide Black boys with discipline and guidance (Healey, 2012; Judge, 2017; Worley, 2011). A slew of popular films and television shows has underscored the significance of Black father figures' relationships with Black male youth (Barris, Patel, Brown, Patel, & Asher, 2014; Romanski, Gardner, Kleiner, & Jenkins, 2016; Lee, 1996; Singleton, 1991, 2001), and Black male public figures have used their platforms to promote Black fatherly support and mentorship of Black boys (Cosby & Poussaint, 2007; H. Harper, 2006; Lattimore, 2014). One public figure, educator and media commentator Steve Perry, even hosted a television series titled *Save Our Sons* (R. Brown & Armstead, 2012) in which he and other respectable Black men intervened in the lives of wayward Black boys, many of whom were being raised by overwhelmed single mothers. These are but a few examples of the widespread public discourses that promote responsible Black father figures and role models as antidotes to the plight of Black boys in America.

In addition to the examples cited, a corpus of literature on how to raise and support Black boys also underscores the urgency of Black male role models. Mixing insights from psychological and educational scholarship with Afrocentric edicts and self-help mantras, this body of work routinely centers cultural anxieties regarding the prevalence of Black boys being raised by single mothers (Boyd-Franklin & Franklin, 2000; Brewster & Stephenson, 2013; Cuffee, 2008; Kunjufu, 1985a; F. D. D. Lewis, 2010; Moore & Moore, 2013). It also frequently asserts the importance of finding adult Black men—especially those who are college-going or college educated, employed, and morally respectable—to serve as role models for Black boys (Boyd-Franklin & Franklin, 2000; Cuffee, 2008; T. Harris & Taylor, 2012; Kunjufu, 1985b, 2005; F. D. D. Lewis, 2010). The positive influence of responsible and upstanding Black male adults becomes the foil to the deleterious impact exerted by gangs and street culture in lowincome neighborhoods, particularly on Black boys from single-mother households (Boyd-Franklin & Franklin, 2000; T. Harris & Taylor, 2012; F. D. D. Lewis, 2010). This literature goes on to laud the transformative power of rites of passage ceremonies and mentoring programs led by Black men specifically for Black boys (Cuffee, 2008; Hare & Hare, 1985; Kunjufu, 2005; F. D. D. Lewis, 2010). In all, the Black male role model and father figure, whether biological kin or community surrogate, emerges throughout this literature as a critical solution to the plight of Black boys.

All of the examples cited speak to an important backdrop for scholarship on Black male teachers: the savior narrative that repeatedly gets invoked to envision and justify Black men's roles in the lives of Black boys. The savior is a popular archetype in western culture, used to depict and describe everything from messianic religious figures (Holderness,

2015; Humphries-Brooks, 2006) and charismatic political leaders (Bobic, 2016; Gerson, 2016; Weisenthal, 2013) to heroic filmic and literary protagonists (Adney, 2005; Hughey, 2014; Klein, 2012; Punt, 2004; Sirota, 2013) and inspirational educators (A. Brown, 2013; Horan, 2015). Although savior-like figures are not completely identical across contexts, their narratives frequently include three common factors. First, the savior is routinely the central agent of change. In contrast to the helplessness generally exhibited by those in peril, the savior possesses the knowledge, skills, motivation, and spirit to uplift the imperiled from their downtroddenness. Second, the savior is admirable. The ingenuity, courage, benevolence, and moral authority demonstrated by the savior distinguish him or her as a paragon of virtue. These two factors often overshadow any missteps or character flaws, as heroism ultimately emerges as the savior's defining trait. And, for this heroism, the beneficiaries of the savior's good deeds are typically depicted as grateful.[3]

Building on the narrative template of saviorism, some striking similarities emerge throughout the previously reviewed discourses on the role of Black men in the lives of Black boys. First, like other saviors' encounters with the victimized and powerless, the Black male adult is summoned by a crisis: the plight of Black boys. Across numerous examples cited earlier (Anderson, 2008; Boyd-Franklin & Franklin, 2000; Campbell, 2011; Cuffee, 2008; Green, 2009; Gregory, 2016; T. Harris & Taylor, 2012; Lee, 1996; Singleton, 1991, 2001), Black boys in peril are a central justification behind calls for Black male role models and father figures. Second, upon their arrival in the lives of Black boys, Black male adults, not unlike other savior-like figures, are central agents of change. As previously cited, from films and TV shows on saving Black male youth to male-centered mentoring programs (Brewster & Stephenson, 2013; R. Brown & Armstead, 2012; Campbell, 2011; Gregory, 2016; Hare & Hare, 1985; Kunjufu, 2005; Lattimore, 2014; Lee, 1996; Lewis, 2010), Black male adults are essential players in the uplift of Black boys, reproducing an adult/child binary that privileges adult agency and authority. That Black men are frequently called upon to do what single mothers and other women apparently cannot—save Black boys—underscores the distinctiveness and necessity of their agency. Finally, for his good deeds, the Black male adult, as typical of a savior, is to be admired. A strong reverence is consistently expressed toward Black men who answer the call to take responsibility for Black boys' futures (Campbell, 2011; Judge, 2017; Lattimore, 2014; Ramirez, 2017; Sonny, 2015). Responsible and respectable, Black male role models and father figures are cast as virtuous, and as such, deserving of appreciation.

To be clear, this comparison of Black male role models and father figures to the trope of saviorism is not intended to dismiss the importance of Black men in Black boys' lives. As discussed further in the chapters to come, I am eager to think critically about the supportive role of Black male teachers in the lives of their Black male students. By referencing saviorism here, my intention is to trouble *the manner* in which Black men are often imagined in the lives of Black boys. The marginalization of Black male youth in American society is a systemic injustice that requires coordinated efforts by multiple stakeholder groups working across policy-making, educational, economic, familial, communal, and other contexts. Yet the recurrent focus on savior-like Black men as the fundamental antidote to the misery of Black boys singles out these men as agents of change, often with little-to-no attention paid to the burdens experienced by these men or the structural remedies needed to resolve the plight of Black boys. The inattention to these factors is problematic and warrants pushback. Additionally, the focus on Black male role models and father figures described above consistently relies on an allegiance to Black patriarchy. Appeals for responsible fathers, dedicated role models, and male-centered mentoring programs center adult Black men who can save Black boys by modeling and enacting a patriarchal manhood. Despite Black women's invaluable labor in raising and supporting Black boys, the sidelining of single mothers and other women makes sense when calls for more savior-like Black men are understood as part of a larger cultural project to allow Black men to properly—and perhaps even exclusively—masculinize Black boys. Drawing upon analytic lenses from the previously reviewed scholarship from Black masculinity studies, it becomes clear that this saviorist cultural project has the potential to reproduce male dominance and heteronormative regulation. Consequently, saviorist discourses on Black men demand close and critical consideration, and they receive that in this book.

The presumption that the right type of Black man can save Black boys has played an important role in shaping public discourses on Black male teachers. Like the saviorist discourses on Black men reviewed thus far, popular perceptions of Black male teachers have been driven by a hope in the transformative power of Black male adults who can model hegemonic masculinity and serve as attentive patriarchs in the lives of Black boys. In what follows, I turn to popular media discourses on Black male teachers to show how the savior trope shapes social constructions of Black men in teaching.

Popular Media Discourses on Black Male Teachers

Popular media outlets have played an active role in circulating a certain set of discourses about the need for more male teachers. In their separate reviews of news media coverage on men in teaching, Martino (2008) and Sternod (2011) explore how such coverage has positioned male teachers as role models who can uplift boys by re-masculinizing schools, or countering the feminizing influence of women teachers by asserting their patriarchal presence. Following those authors' lead, I now turn to the role of popular media outlets in casting Black male teachers as savior-like figures for Black boys. Along with examples from more traditional outlets like local and national newspapers and magazines like *Newsweek* and *The Atlantic*, I also point to websites and blogs that have posted articles and opinion pieces on the need for Black male teachers. Through the effortless sharing of URL links via email messages and social media posts, stories about Black male teachers from any of these sources can reach and potentially influence large and diverse audiences. As the proliferation and impact of various websites and blogs increasingly blur distinctions between traditional news outlets and alternative information sources in the digital age (Hermida, 2012), it is important to grasp how all of these media venues frame the need for Black male teachers to save Black boys.

Combining press clippings that I saved over the years with new sources that I found through web searches, I reviewed a collection of 50 articles, columns, and opinion pieces that discussed the importance of having Black men in the American teaching profession. These sources spanned mostly from 2005 to 2017, with one from 1999, 2002, and 2004 each, and five with no identifiable publication dates. Although numerous themes emerged during my review of these sources, four stood out as particularly relevant for my analysis of saviorist discourses on Black male teachers: the focus on the plight of Black boys; descriptions of how Black male teachers model masculinity for Black boys; the recuperation of Black manhood through depictions of Black male teachers; and the liability posed by women teachers and popular perceptions of teaching as women's work. In what follows, these four themes are explored closely.

The Plight of Black Boys

Like the saviorist discourses on Black male role models and father figures cited earlier in this chapter, popular media coverage on Black male teachers makes repeated references to the plight of Black boys. Numerous press articles and website essays cite the high drop-out and low graduation rates, low academic achievement indicators, and disproportionate rates of disciplinary sanctions and special education placements that signal Black boys' troubled participation in American K–12 schools (Bailey, 2013; Basinger, 1999; Beatty, 2013; Chideya, 2007; Irvin, 2015; Matus, 2005; McClain, 2016; Mehrotra, 2013; Nazaryan, 2015; Reckdahl, 2015; Smiles, 2002). Other pieces invoke the specter of gangs, drugs, and street violence (Facey, 2012; McClain, 2016; Nazaryan, 2015) as well as the likelihood of incarceration and unemployment (Bailey, 2013; Chideya, 2007; J. Graham, 2011; Nazaryan, 2015; Roberts, 2016) to underscore the myriad threats that young Black males face in American society at large. As these sources illustrate, a common strategy for legitimizing calls for more Black male teachers is to situate Black boys in a perpetual state of crisis.

Often, the mere mention of these perils suffices as an implicit warrant for recruiting Black male teachers to save Black boys. In some instances, however, authors employ stark language to emphasize both the severity of the dangers facing Black boys and the urgency of finding more Black male teachers. For example, in his article on the Oakland Unified School District's Manhood Development Program (MDP), an effort that hires Black male teachers and mentors to work with Black male students, Nazaryan (2015) provides a warrant for the program by stating, "We may as well state plainly what we all know: Black men are this nation's outcasts, marked like Oedipus for doom from birth" (para. 5). From this ominous pronouncement, Nazaryan proceeds to describe the fear of Black males in American society and mentions the greater likelihood of Black males being arrested and imprisoned. Likewise, in her opinion piece on the need for Black male teachers, Facey (2012) warns that "the gang members, drug dealers, and the prisons are waiting to devour the destiny of each lost black child" (para. 5). This warning bolsters her call for schools to recruit more Black teachers, particularly Black male teachers, to address this crisis. In similar fashion to Facey and Nazaryan, the leader of a Black male teacher recruitment initiative is quoted in one newspaper article as stating that " 'we thought maybe we could do something about preventing more black males from going to prison' " (S. Byrd, 2014, para. 28) by preparing more Black male teachers. All of these examples illustrate how the bleak social backdrops of the lives of Black male youth are frequently used to justify the call for Black men to enter the teaching profession.

In recent years, some appeals for more Black male teachers have referenced high-profile killings of unarmed young Black males to bolster their case. Specifically, some authors cite the murders of Trayvon Martin and Michael Brown to illustrate the precarious futures awaiting young Black males and to drive home the need for Black male teachers (Facey, 2012; Mitchell, 2015; Nazaryan, 2015; E. Taylor, 2016). The following passage from Mitchell's (2015) opinion piece reveals the urgency evoked through this tactic:

> No parent wants to face their child leaving home and not returning like the parents of Emmett Till, Mike Brown, Trayvon Martin and a whole host of others that did not make the national news. Black men teaching and role modeling at the elementary and special education level can mentor and teach these students at a young age on how to survive this society as a black man and instill in them confidence. If as black men we continue to turn the other cheek to this epidemic, then more tragedies and the prison industrial complex awaits [sic] our black boys.
>
> (para. 1)

In line with frequent descriptions of Black boys' tumultuous or dangerous encounters with street culture and the prison-industrial complex, authors like Mitchell invoke another peril, the slaying of unarmed Black male youth, to justify calls for Black male teachers who can prevent such tragedies through their presence and work in the classroom. Across all of the sources cited, the dire conditions of young Black males' lives help to position Black male teachers as change agents who are uniquely qualified to save Black boys.

Modeling Black Masculinity

With Black boys existing in a chronic state of crisis, Black male teachers represent the bridge to a brighter tomorrow. Throughout popular media discourses, Black male teachers are repeatedly cast as role models for Black youth, especially boys. Along with generic claims about the positive influence of supportive adult role models, numerous articles and opinion pieces highlight a particular set of characteristics associated with Black male teachers' embodiment and performance of Black masculinity. These characteristics distinguish Black male teachers in popular media discourses as savior-like figures for Black male youth, and they also indicate the type of Black men who can serve in a saviorist capacity.

An instructive example of how Black male teachers are imagined in popular media can be found in Richard's (2005) *Education Week* profile of a Black male elementary teacher named Hayward Jean. With initial plans to attend college on a tennis scholarship, Jean was drawn to teaching after learning about Claflin University's partnership with Call Me MISTER, a teacher preparation initiative targeting prospective Black male educators. In his second year of teaching at the time of Richard's profile, Jean, a third-grade educator, was the only Black man teaching at his elementary school. Through various vignettes of Jean in action, Richard describes him as a charismatic teacher with a deep commitment to children. That commitment extends beyond his classroom, as Jean can be spotted from time to time playing basketball with young people in local public parks. In school, his professionalism is reflected in his rigorous preparation for work and, importantly, in his appearance. Jean comes to work every day in dark, three-piece suits, and several pictures corroborate his professional appearance. As Jean's former supervisor recounts, some of the boys in Jean's class began wearing suits and ties to school, remarking that they wanted "to be like Mr. Jean" (p. 26). One photograph even shows Jean placing his suit jacket on a Black male student for providing the correct answer to a question. His standards for himself are so high that both his pastor and his female fiancé concede that he can be very self-critical at times. Nevertheless, Jean has made such a strong impression that the principal of a nearby middle school wishes she could clone him. For his dynamic impact on his students—some of whom, as the article notes, are without active father figures in their lives—Jean, in the words of Richard, "is a model of manhood" (p. 23).

This close reading of Richard's article is in no way intended as a critique of Hayward Jean or any other Black male teacher who has been referenced in similar popular media profiles. Indeed, Jean emerges in Richard's article as a dedicated educator who, like other upstanding teachers, deserves recognition for his efforts. The purpose of focusing on Richard's profile of Jean is to spotlight four representational strategies in popular media discourses that cast Black male teachers as models of Black masculinity for Black boys. One of those strategies is an emphasis on middle-class professionalism. In Richard's article, Jean's appearance in three-piece suits is crucial to how he models Black masculinity. By placing his suit jacket on a Black male student, and by inspiring other Black male students to come to class in suits and ties, Jean invites and motivates Black boys to "try on" a white-collar, middle-class Black male identity. The significance of such role modeling is captured in other articles and opinion pieces on Black male teachers that include pictures and/or written descriptions of Black men in suits or shirts and ties (Allen, 2015; Bailey, 2013; S. Byrd, 2014; Chapman & Colangelo, 2015; Dunu, 2016; Evans, 2016; Irvin, 2015; W. D. Jackson, 2015; Jarrett, 2015; Jones, 2005; Mehrotra, 2013; Miller, 2016; Torres, 2006) or in business casual attire that still exudes middle-class professionalism (Hawkins, 2015; House, 2017; Matus, 2005; Milloy, 2004; Roberts, 2016; Smiles, 2002; E. Taylor, 2016; Watson, 2016). As role models of middle-class futures for Black boys, Black male teachers are credited for demonstrating white-collar professional pathways to success (S. Byrd, 2014; Chideya, 2007; Evans, 2016), particularly pathways that extend beyond what are characterized as Black male youth's stereotypical and limited interests in rapping and athletics (Chideya, 2007; Chmelynski, 2006; Grey, n.d.; Mitchell, 2015; Nazaryan, 2015; Nicolas, 2014). Some pieces even suggest that the presence of Black men in the classroom may lead more Black boys to become teachers (Deruy, n.d.; Nicolas, 2014; Pitkin, n.d.). The unique capacity of Black male teachers to model middle-class professionalism is brought into relief by authors who lament that the paucity of Black men in teaching leaves Black male custodians, security guards, food service workers, and gym teachers as the only adult Black men that many students will see in American K–12 schools (Beatty, 2013; Hawkins, 2015; Nicolas, 2014). These men are distinguished from Black male classroom teachers, who are associated with more desirable white-collar identities and futures. In all, it becomes clear that the saviorist role of Black male teachers includes modeling a middle-class professionalism that can save Black boys by steering them away from prison and street culture and leading them instead toward white-collar futures.

Underscoring the appeal of middle-class professionalism, authors routinely mention the college or university alma maters and/or majors of the Black male teachers they profile. Interestingly, not only does this emphasize the desire for college-educated Black men to become teachers, but it also subtly reinforces the hegemonic masculinity required of these men, which marks a second strategy for representing Black male teachers in popular media. When the college majors and previous career paths of Black male teachers are mentioned in articles and opinion pieces, they are often in business, science, and other typically male-centered fields (Bailey, 2013; Z. Crenshaw, 2015; Grey III, n.d.; Hawkins, 2015; Matus, 2005; Milloy, 2004), thus mitigating the feminization of teaching by highlighting male teachers with traditionally male-identified academic and professional passions. A similar function is served by descriptions of Black male teachers' physiques and athleticism. Like the references in the profile of Hayward Jean to his dynamic presence and his involvement in sports (Richard, 2005), depictions of Black male teachers in other pieces describe these men's muscular physiques, deep voices, commanding classroom demeanors, and previous involvements in athletics (S. Byrd, 2014; Chideya, 2007; Hawkins, 2015; Jones, 2005; Matus, 2005; McClain, 2016; Reckdahl, 2015). The relative absence of contrary representational strategies—for instance, details of prior involvements in the arts, descriptions of less conventionally masculine physical features, or pictures of men sitting on rugs for elementary read-alouds—further suggests an attempt to avoid associations with femininity and women's work. Together, these examples reflect a recurring attempt in popular media to focus on Black male teachers who can embody and perform hegemonic masculinity.

Attracting Black men who can model hegemonic masculinity in the classroom is critical for enabling the saviorist project of uplifting Black boys. The importance of this project is driven home through a third representational strategy in popular media coverage on Black male teachers: a focus on their interactions and relationships with Black male students. As in Richard's (2005) profile of Hayward Jean, similar articles and opinion pieces highlight moments that convey the special rapport between Black male teachers and Black male students. In some cases, this rapport affords a unique ability to manage young Black males in the classroom. Nazaryan (2015), for instance, marvels at the sense of order commanded by Black male teachers in Oakland's Manhood Development Program for Black male students. In contrast to the classroom chaos he often witnessed elsewhere, Nazaryan notes that when MDP students became off-task, "the teacher looked somberly at the offending student and said, 'I need my respect.' And he got it" (para. 28). Other pieces similarly credit Black male teachers for having a unique disciplinary sway over Black male students (Matus, 2005; Roberts, 2016; E. Taylor, 2016), and some also laud these men for nurturing a special bond with Black boys. This

bond becomes apparent in descriptions of Black boys eagerly responding to and seeking the approval of their Black male teachers (Bailey,
2013; Basinger, 1999; House, 2017; Jones, 2005; Matus, 2005; Mehrotra, 2013; Miller, 2016; Milloy, 2004; Richard, 2005; E. Taylor, 2016)
as well as in accounts of Black male teachers expressing a deeply felt
responsibility for Black boys (Bailey, 2013; Dunu, 2016; House, 2017; E.
Taylor, 2016). A striking example of the latter can be found in a column
by House (2017), a Black male social studies teacher, who states the following after recalling a transformative heart-to-heart conversation with
two of his underperforming Black male students:

> Black male teachers have the ability to see themselves in their black
> students and can build a connection that, quite frankly, will be very
> hard for others to make. For this reason, it is imperative for black
> male students to be taught by black male educators.
>
> (para. 5)

The special connection claimed by House recurs across popular media
accounts on Black male teachers, and it gets visually reinforced through
accompanying pictures that show Black male teachers working specifically with Black boys (Basinger, 1999; Brooks, 2016; Dunu, 2016; Jarrett, 2015; Matus, 2005; McClain, 2016; Mehrotra, 2013; Miller, 2016;
Nazaryan, 2015; Pitkin, n.d.; Watson, 2016). By centering these interactions, popular media discourses remind the public that Black male teachers are role models who are uniquely qualified to manage, engage, and
ultimately uplift their Black male students.

The unique status of Black male teachers as role models for young
Black males is underscored by a fourth representational strategy in popular media coverage: the repeated characterizations of these men as father
figures for Black youth. In the profile of teacher Hayward Jean that was
cited earlier, the author labels Jean as "a model of manhood" (Richard,
2005, p. 23) for children who, in some cases, do not have active fathers
in their lives. Amidst deep-seated anxieties surrounding the absence of
fathers in the lives of some Black youth, Black male teachers emerge as
ideal surrogates who can model a normative masculinity. Numerous
popular media accounts legitimate Black male teachers as father figures
by noting the dearth of such men in Black children's out-of-school lives
(Brooks, 2016; S. Byrd, 2014; Evans, 2016; Jones, 2005; Lattimore,
2014; McClain, 2016; Miller, 2016). Some accounts even include anecdotes about Black students actually referring to Black male teachers as
"father" or "dad" (Hawkins, 2015; Mehrotra, 2013; Miller, 2016; E.
Taylor, 2016), thus invoking student responses to confirm Black male
teachers as surrogate dads.

References to the father figure status of Black men in the classroom often
underscore the significance of these men as role models for individual Black

students. Some sources, however, attach broader sociopolitical stakes to Black male teachers' roles as father figures. For instance, in her article on Jackson State University's partnership with the Call Me MISTER teacher recruitment program, Byrd (2014) writes, "And few would dispute that the breakdown of the black family unit—primarily the absence of fathers in the home—is a factor in many of the social ills impacting black children" (para. 16). Building on similar sentiments, Evans (2016), a Black male teacher in Chicago, writes in his blog piece, "Black male teachers fill the voids left by a social system that perpetuates a sense of fatherlessness and overall abandonment in many low-income communities of color" (para. 3). Both Byrd and Evans point to the disappearance of Black fathers as the root of Black social ills, thus positioning the Black male teacher as a remedy not only to the plight of Black youth, but to the crisis state of the Black community. Across all of these examples, whether as personal inspirations or community-level saviors, Black male teachers are accorded significant transformative power in their roles as Black father figures.

The four representational strategies described—depictions of Black male teachers' middle-class professionalism, hegemonic masculinity, interactions with Black boys, and status as father figures—are apparent in the profile of Hayward Jean (Richard, 2005) that was used to frame this discussion. Interestingly, there is a fifth strategy in that profile that subtly speaks to Jean's qualifications as a model of Black masculinity: the implication of his heterosexuality via the acknowledgment of his female fiancé. While Jean's profile was the only one in which I noticed such a reference to a Black male teacher's heterosexuality, none of the popular media sources reviewed for this analysis included any references, explicit or implicit, to a teacher's queer identity. Since Black male teachers were repeatedly perceived as models of hegemonic masculinity, and since hegemonic masculinity is a traditionally heteronormative construct, perhaps the heterosexuality of these men was an unspoken given. The presumption of heterosexuality and the invisibility of queerness certainly seem in alignment with the four representational strategies described in this section. As models of masculinity for Black boys, Black male teachers are explicitly marked in popular media discourses as examples of middle-class professionalism, bearers of hegemonic masculinity, role models who can handle, connect with, and uplift Black boys, and father figures for Black youth. These depictions echo other popular media representations of Black male adults as savior-like figures for Black boys, thus aligning Black male teachers with the larger cultural project of a saviorist Black masculinity.

Recuperating the Image of Black Men

Earlier in this chapter, when I introduced the concept of saviorism, I noted that savior-like discourses on Black male adults not only call upon these men to save Black boys, but they also work to valorize Black men themselves as upstanding and virtuous. Such is the case with saviorist discourses on Black men in teaching as well. Popular media coverage includes numerous references to these men as positive representations of Black manhood. Through a saviorist Black masculinity, the Black male teacher presents a moral and respectable alternative to the pathological and villainous Black male Other that haunts the American social imaginary. Consequently, popular media discourses on Black male teachers do more than envision the uplift of Black boys; they also recuperate the image of adult Black men.

The recuperative effect of saviorist Black male teachers is implied whenever these men are lauded for being role models. However, some popular media sources go a step further by explicitly naming Black male teachers' ability to recuperate the Black man's image. These include pieces that suggest that having Black male teachers can lead White children and other non-Black youth to challenge their negative stereotypes about Black men (Facey, 2012; Hawkins, 2015; House, 2017). Some pieces also imagine the power of Black male teachers to trouble stereotypes about Black men in American society at large. Typical of such pieces is Walker's (2016) op-ed for *Ebony* magazine, in which he opines that "teaching offers committed brothers the opportunity to challenge the stereotype that we are angry, dangerous and not willing to make sacrifices to improve conditions within the Black community" (para. 5). Other pieces claim that Black male teachers can counter negative stereotypes of Black men as thuggish, lazy, and criminal (Facey, 2012; W. D. Jackson, 2015), as well as disrupt narrow associations of Black men with sports and entertainment (Basinger, 1999; Chmelynski, 2006). In these ways, the hardworking, college-educated, commitment-driven Black male educator who emerges across popular media coverage is credited for confounding representations of Black males in America as irresponsible and dangerous.

For the Black male teachers who convincingly represent a virtuous and dependable Black masculinity, the praise that they receive contributes further to the recuperation of the image of Black men. For instance, in his *Washington Post* profile of a Black male elementary teacher named Bakari Haynes, Milloy (2004) proclaims that Haynes "works magic" in his classroom with Black boys and is "worth his weight in gold" (p. C01) for his good deeds. In an article from *The Atlantic*, a leader of the Call Me MISTER teacher recruitment program notes that when program alumni return to their hometowns, "They're treated with great reverence, a great respect. That's what we promote—they are now called Mister, and we're changing the stereotype of black males" (Reckdahl, 2015, para. 28). Lamenting the scarcity of Black male teachers in small towns, Grey (n.d.) states in his piece for *Your Black World* that "small towns rarely see African-American male teachers and that's why we as African-Americans need to praise and honor those who are doing outstanding work" (para. 3). Similarly, in his website opinion piece, Jackson (2015) states that instead of fearing Black male teachers, society should "praise them" (para. 23), and in a piece for *Our Black World*, site publisher Allen (2015) asserts that for Black children who have lost their way, Black male teachers are "a ray of light to guide them in these modern times of uncertainty" (para. 4). In his online reflection on being a Black male teacher, Taylor (2016) characterizes Black male teachers as "a guiding light and beacon" (para. 12) for Black youth. And in recognition of their good deeds, especially as father figures, Black male teachers, according to Lattimore (2014), should be recognized and celebrated on Father's Day.

Across all of these examples, the language used to praise Black men in the classroom is striking. From deserving "great reverence" and "praise and honor" to being a "ray of light" and a "guiding light and beacon" who are "worth [their] weight in gold," the adoration of Black male teachers marks a decided departure from the stereotypical derogation of Black men in popular American culture. By being upstanding men who serve Black communities and save Black children, saviorist Black male teachers generate a reverence that counters the vilification of Black men in America.

The potential for honorable and respected Black male teachers to recuperate the image of Black men may help to explain the language taken up in some recruitment and retention programs. Since the late 1990s, popular media outlets have reported on numerous efforts initiated by colleges and universities (Basinger, 1999; Z. Crenshaw, 2015; Fenwick, 2010; J. Graham, 2011; Reckdahl, 2015), school districts (Chapman & Colangelo, 2015; Hawkins, 2015; Piorkowski, 2015; Pitkin, n.d.; West, 2013), and even the federal government (Webb, n.d.) to attract more Black men into the teaching profession, and to support and retain them upon entering the classroom. The titles of some of these initiatives suggest recuperative aspirations behind the preparation of Black male teachers. For instance, the Call Me MISTER program, founded in 1999 in South Carolina to recruit Black men into elementary teaching, gets its title from a 1967 film in which Sidney Poitier famously plays a Black detective from Philadelphia who demands respect from southern White racists (Richard, 2005). The invocation of Poitier's iconic portrayal of a defiant Black manhood that triumphs over southern White supremacy, along with the creation of a program acronym standing for Mentors Instructing Students Toward Effective Role Models, aligns Call Me MISTER's teachers with an indomitable yet dignified Black masculinity. The titles of other recruitment and retention initiatives like Profound Gentlemen in the Charlotte-Mecklenburg Schools (Pitkin, n.d.), Project MODEL—Males of Diversity Exhibiting Leadership—at Bethune Cookman College (Basinger, 1999), and Brothers Empowered to Teach in New Orleans (Irvin, 2015) evoke images of Black male teachers as proud and distinguished men who are ready to be both teachers and leaders. Likewise, at Southern University in New Orleans, the Honoré Center, which focuses on preparing Black men for teaching, is named after a retired Black military general who emerged as a hero among Black New Orleanians after Hurricane Katrina (Reckdahl, 2015). The Center's participants are known as Honoré Men, and the Center itself is part of Southern University's Five-Fifths Initiative—a defiant riff on the racist and dehumanizing Three-Fifths Compromise of 1787—to support Black male students. Together, all of these program titles link the preparation of Black male teachers to the redemption of Black manhood. Even without further explanations of program logistics, the repetition of these program titles in popular media coverage symbolically recuperates the image of Black men vis-à-vis the proud and admirable Black male teacher.

An important caveat to this analysis is that the symbolic work performed by the titles of Black male teacher recruitment and retention initiatives may or may not align with these initiatives' pedagogical aims, programmatic details, and participant experiences. The latter set of factors can be difficult to glean from popular media coverage, and in some cases, even program websites and related sources may offer limited insights into how such initiatives are run on the ground. My focus here on the symbolic effects of the initiatives' titles recognizes that regardless of how these initiatives actually operate, their titles contribute to a consequential representational project in popular media discourses on Black male teachers. The images invoked by Call Me MISTER, the Honoré Center, and similar initiatives wed the proliferation of Black male teachers with the recuperation of the image of Black men. Since popular media coverage leaves the aims of these recruitment and retention initiatives largely unchallenged—and often features stakeholder perspectives that cast these initiatives in a positive light—the symbolic impact of their titles adds an important layer to current representations of Black men in teaching. The coverage of these titles in popular media, along with the praise for Black male teachers who defy negative stereotypes and uplift Black children and Black communities, illustrates how saviorist discourses on Black men in teaching work to redeem the image of adult Black men.

Women Teachers and Women's Work

Women's presence in the American teaching profession plays an integral part in popular media coverage on Black male teachers. Over and over again, articles and opinion pieces on the need for more Black men in the classroom build their warrant by citing the predominance of women, particularly White women, in the American teaching profession. These references to teaching as a predominantly female field are, at times, more than mere statements of fact. A close analysis of popular media discourses on Black male teachers reveals that women teachers and the image of teaching as women's work are sometimes imagined as impediments to the saviorist project of recruiting and retaining Black men to teach and uplift

Black children. Understanding the stakes of popular media discourses on Black male teachers requires an attention to the liabilities posed by the feminization of the teaching profession.

In articles and opinion pieces on the need for more Black male teachers, the predominantly female composition of teaching is often paired with the profession's whiteness to suggest an unpreparedness to serve an increasingly diverse student body. For instance, after noting the increasing majority of non-White students in American schools, Hawkins (2015) writes in *NEA Today*, "White women (76 percent) continue to make up the majority of those who teach, according to 2010 PEDS data, down slightly from 80 percent in 2004. Today's teacher candidates reflect the same demographic makeup—82 percent female and White" (para. 21). References like these are common in popular media sources on Black male teachers (Bailey, 2013; Deruy, n.d.; Hawkins, 2015; Jarrett, 2015; A. Johnson, 2007; Jones, 2005; Matus, 2005; McClain, 2016; Nazaryan, 2015; Pitkin, n.d.; Richard, 2005), and while they do not explicitly derogate women teachers, they do imply that the predominance of women in teaching—especially White women—is problematic for an increasingly multicultural student body.

Other references to women teachers cast a more explicit doubt on their suitability to work with Black youth. For instance, in his call for more Black male teachers, Causey (n.d.) asserts that these men "can bring a level of authority that women simply don't have in the classroom" (para. 2). After mentioning a viral video clip in which a Black male high school student threatens to slap a Black female teacher in the classroom, Causey rhetorically asks, "do you believe this young man would have been acting the same way if he had a strong black male teacher?" (para. 6). Similarly, Byrd (2014) and Roberts (2016) suggest that Black male teachers are more adept at handling classroom management than female teachers, and both Allen (2015) and Nazaryan (2015) suggest that Black male teachers might academically engage Black students, especially Black boys, more successfully than their female colleagues. To varying degrees, women teachers are treated across all of these examples as a liability, and Black male teachers—with their ability to connect with Black boys and manage the classroom—are cited as the remedy.

Along with occasional deficit perspectives on women teachers, popular media discourses on Black male teachers reveal ongoing angst toward the perception of teaching as women's work. Several pieces mention that the image of teaching as a job for women remains a barrier to recruiting more Black men (Bailey, 2013; Dunu, 2016; Hawkins, 2015; Matus, 2005; Mitchell, 2016; Richard, 2005). Some underscore this challenge by playing up the feminized construction of teachers' work. For instance, while describing the routines of a Black male first grade teacher, Hawkins (2015) notes that most prospective Black male teachers are not inclined to teach first graders "to count, wipe runny noses, huddle in a cozy corner of the classroom with new readers to share stories of Civil Rights leaders and turn the pages of Dr. Seuss' *The Cat in the Hat*" (para. 27). In a separate article on the Black male teacher shortage in New Haven, CT, a Black male high school teacher laments that his father still views him as a " 'glorified babysitter' " (Bailey, 2013, para. 49). Even Hayward Jean, the standout teacher from the earlier-cited profile by Richard (2005), recalls "laughing at his high school's homecoming queen after hearing she wanted to teach. 'I thought it was a last resort,' he confesses of teaching. 'I thought it was a women's profession'" (p. 25). And when discussing the image of teaching as women's work, a Black male junior high math teacher in one article concedes that "the number of women in the classroom can be enough to keep men from giving teaching as a career a first look" (Hawkins, 2015, para. 23).

All of these examples illustrate how feminized constructions of teaching are identified as impediments to recruiting more Black men into the profession. Despite fervent calls for more Black men to join the nation's teaching ranks, the perception of teaching as women's work persists for some as a deterrent to entering the profession. This concern over the feminized image of teaching provides an illuminating backdrop to how popular media discourses depict Black male teachers. If some Black men avoid teaching because of its status as women's work, then masculinizing public perceptions of the profession seems a sensible strategy for attracting Black male recruits. Seen in this light, the deficit language on women teachers and the pushback against teaching's feminized public image advance a larger project to masculinize the teaching profession for Black male teachers by distracting public attention from the participation of women.

Making Sense of Popular Media Discourses on Black Male Teachers

Earlier in this chapter, I identified two analytical premises that drive my considerations of Black masculinity politics. The second premise—disrupting patriarchal and heteronormative constructions of Black maleness is essential for enabling counterhegemonic Black masculinities—intimately shaped my review of popular media's treatment of Black men in teaching. All four overarching themes in the preceding review reveal repeated attempts to envision Black male teachers as patriarchal figures who can perform hegemonic masculinity in the classroom, thus echoing prior calls over the past century for male teachers to serve as pedagogical patriarchs who can restore a normative gender order in American K–12 schools. Just as other scholarly works have raised concerns about past waves of public interest in male teachers (S. Johnson, 2008; W. J. Martino, 2008; Weiler, 1989), analyses of contemporary appeals for more men in teaching must consider the deeper implications of the desire for male bodies— and, in this case, Black male bodies—to enter a predominantly female realm.

By repeatedly citing the plight of Black boys as context and warrant, the popular media discourses reviewed here privilege the recruitment of Black male teachers as an antidote to the social and educational woes of Black male youth. This singling-out of Black male teachers as the answer to Black boys' troubles speaks to an underlying logic of racialized patriarchy—one that invests an extraordinary amount of hope in the transformative potential of Black men. If American K–12 schools have damaged Black boys, and if those schools are populated by a predominantly White and predominantly female teaching force, then White teachers and women teachers are inherently suspect. It is the Black male teacher—the suit-wearing, management-savvy, masculine classroom patriarch—who has the capacity to intervene. Black male teachers are not only assumed to have Black boys' best interests at heart, but they are accorded the power to save Black boys from the debilitating grips of educational systems that have failed them, fatherless families that have neglected them, and a larger society that has demonized them. Over and over again, the popular media sources reviewed in this chapter spotlighted Black men who exemplified a unique pedagogical capacity to connect with Black boys, and who symbolized the saviorist aspirations behind calls for more Black male teachers. For these depictions to make sense, they must summon a widely accepted, racialized patriarchal logic that values Black men as saviors of Black boys and Black communities.

While saviorist discourses have generated unprecedented attention toward the presence and potential impact of Black men in teaching, they have done so by reproducing several dilemmas that may undermine school-based efforts to support Black students. Here, I highlight three. First—and as mentioned earlier in this chapter—some scholars have noted that the faith in savior-like Black male teachers often comes at the expense of concurrent considerations of larger-scale remedies for the structural determinants of Black youth misery (T. O. Jackson et al., 2013; W. Martino & Rezai-Rashti, 2012; Maylor, 2009). By championing the transformative pedagogical powers of individual Black male teachers, the popular media discourses reviewed above may reproduce unrealistic expectations of what these men can accomplish in the absence of systemic, policy-level efforts to transform the schooling experiences and life chances of Black youth. Second, the emphasis on Black male teachers as saviorist pedagogues for Black boys reproduces patriarchal blind spots in popular discourses on Black education. Important issues like Black women educators' legacy of transformative pedagogical work with Black children (Beauboeuf-Lafontant, 2002; Dixson, 2003; Dixson & Dingus, 2008), the potential for White educators to support Black youth (Landsman & Lewis, 2011; H. R. Milner, 2011; Vetter, 2013), and the educational experiences of Black girls (Blake, Butler, Lewis, & Darensbourg, 2011; K. W. Crenshaw, Ocen, & Nanda, 2015) all receive minimal attention in popular media coverage of Black men in teaching, thus siloing these teachers from a broader and more intersectional Black educational reform agenda. Third, while saviorist discourses locate an extraordinary amount of agency in Black male teachers, they often attribute much less to Black youth, whose primary roles in the previously reviewed popular media discourses are being awestruck by and indebted to inspirational Black male teachers. This arrangement is necessary for the saviorist narrative to make sense, but it seemingly ignores important work that recognizes Black youth's central role as change agents in their own lives (Baldridge, 2014; Ginwright, 2010; Ginwright, Cammarota, & Noguera, 2006). Together, these three dilemmas suggest that while popular media sources may bolster the image of Black male teachers, they also may work against efforts to strategically serve the educational interests of Black students.

The saviorist discourses reviewed in the preceding sections also pose dilemmas for Black male teachers. Across the numerous examples that were cited, Black male teachers emerged again and again as confident, upstanding, masculine men who could model a proper Black masculinity as in-school patriarchs. Several pieces nodded toward the potential challenges associated with the high expectations facing Black men in the classroom (Bailey, 2013; Brooks, 2016; Henry, 2014; Matus, 2005; Nazaryan, 2015; Walker, 2016), but these pieces were drowned out by the overall chorus of praise for the savior-like Black male teacher. Given the solid mold that has been cast by these saviorist discourses, what happens to those Black male teachers who do not fit within it? How do students, families, administrators, teacher educators, and other stakeholders respond to Black male educators whose gender performance falls short of or contradicts hegemonic masculinity? What mechanisms are in place to police, correct, and/or weed out those teachers who appear at odds with the racialized patriarchal expectations facing Black male pedagogues? And, how do these men make sense of all of this? What are their perspectives on saviorist discourses on Black male teachers, and how do they embrace, refuse, and/or negotiate these discourses in their daily experiences? The answers to these questions have significant implications for if, how, and how long Black men participate in the American teaching profession, and yet they are routinely overlooked in popular media discourses on Black male teachers.

Although this section of Chapter 2 troubles the depiction of Black male teachers in popular media coverage, it is not intended to dismiss the significance of Black men in teaching. As a former middle and high school Black male teacher who has supported prospective Black male teachers as a teacher educator, I believe wholeheartedly that Black male educators can make invaluable contributions to their students' lives, the institutional cultures of the schools where they work, and the communities within which those schools are situated. That belief is not contradicted by my critical reading of popular media coverage on Black men in teaching. My goal is not to devalue Black male teachers or dismiss public interest in recruiting and retaining them, but rather to look closely and think critically about the grounds upon which Black male teachers are validated in popular media. While these men can be productive participants in the cultures of K–12 schools, they can also be positioned under the right conditions as agents of dubious pedagogical, political, and ideological projects. The preceding review of popular media discourses aimed to support the former by troubling the latter. In the chapters to come, the narratives of my study participants will further illuminate the possible dilemmas created for Black male teachers by saviorist discourses on Black masculinity.

Scholarly Insights on Black Male Teachers

Popular media coverage of Black male teachers frequently reflects the common-sense rhetoric about Black men's place and purpose in American K–12 classrooms. By contrast, scholarly analyses of Black men in teaching provide opportunities to delve more deeply into these men's identities, pedagogical practices, and work experiences. While this scholarship is not completely divorced from the presumptions about Black men and Black male teachers that pervade popular media sources, it does include critical insights that help to complicate saviorist discourses on the role of Black men in the classroom. This book seeks to build upon and contribute to the growing body of work that advances more nuanced considerations of who Black male teachers are and how they participate in American schooling.

Recent scholarship on Black male teachers is indebted to the trailblazing research of Lynn (Lynn, 2002, 2006a, 2006b). Informed by the scholarship on Black educators as a whole, Lynn's work was among the first to feature in-depth explorations of the culturally responsive pedagogies and role modeling efforts of Black male teachers. In one example, Lynn (2002) drew upon interview data to describe how 36 Black male teachers across grade levels from the Los Angeles Unified School District saw themselves as role models and change agents. While Lynn's respondents described an ability to relate to Black students based on a common cultural background, they also made explicit references to their racial *and gender* identities when asked about the significance of role modeling. Lynn went on to note that the majority of respondents described themselves as father figures for young Black males in their classrooms and schools. As one respondent remarked, "As a Black man, I want to . . . make sure that these Black boys become Black men" (p. 126), which included being positive and responsible members of their families and communities, and avoiding the pitfalls facing young Black males in their neighborhoods. Other respondents voiced the desire to be role models for young Black men so that more of them would attend college, or because so many of them lacked positive male role models in their out-of-school lives.

In a more detailed profile, Lynn (2006b) delved into the culturally responsive pedagogies of three Black male teachers from Los Angeles. These teachers' pedagogies were characterized by, in Lynn's words, an "other fathering" mix of "tough love, discipline, and caring" (p. 2517), as well as by a sense of mission to raise the social consciousness of Black youth and to give back to the Black community through teaching. Lynn also noted that the three teachers' pedagogies drew readily from their personal experiences as Black men in Black communities, and that their pedagogies were intimately informed by their insiders' knowledge of Black students' daily lives, community experiences, and cultural backgrounds. Elsewhere, Lynn (2006a) further underscored the importance of Black male teachers' personal experiences by chronicling the life history narrative of one Black male teacher from Los Angeles. Among other insights, the narrative revealed that the narrator's encounters with Black male teachers during elementary school, middle school, and college not only helped him to successfully handle the struggles he faced as a young Black male, but they also inspired him to provide similar supports to his current students.

Since Lynn's work has played a notable role in shaping educational scholarship on Black male teachers, highlighting its key take-aways can help to underscore some of the themes that pervade the field. Two aspects of Lynn's work are particularly noteworthy in this regard: the location of Black male teachers within the culturally responsive pedagogical traditions of Black educators as a whole; and the characterization of these educators as role models and father figures for Black youth, particularly Black boys. Following Lynn's lead, several scholars have credited Black male teachers for their racially mediated sense of mission to serve Black children and transform the social ills facing Black communities (Bridges, 2011; A. L. Brown, 2009; J. Davis, Frank, & Clark, 2013; Hayes, 2014; Lynn & Jennings, 2009), and they have described Black male teachers' culturally responsive practices like incorporating Black history and social justice themes into their curricula, engaging hip hop music and culture in the classroom, and fostering trusting relationships with Black students (Bridges, 2011; A. L. Brown, 2009, 2011; Hayes, Juarez, & Escoffery-Runnels, 2014; Lynn & Jennings, 2009; H. R. Milner, 2016; A. Pabon, 2016; Simmons et al., 2013). Some post-Lynn analyses of Black male teachers have also continued to cast these educators as role models and father figures for Black youth, particularly Black boys (Alhassan, 2013; Bridges, 2011; Gatling, Gatling, & Hamilton, 2014; Hayes et al., 2014; C. W. Lewis, 2006; Newell, 2013; Tafari, 2013). By emphasizing the value of Black male teachers' contributions, these works have helped to provide a warrant for another strand of scholarship on the structural barriers to recruiting Black men into teaching, and the potential strategies for attracting and retaining them (Bianco, Leech, & Mitchell, 2011; Bristol, 2013; J. W. Brown & Butty, 1999; J. Davis et al., 2013;

J. Davis, Parker, & Long, 2015; C. W. Lewis, 2006, 2013). Although all of this scholarly literature is generally more rigorous than the previously reviewed popular media coverage on Black male teachers, it does echo some of the same claims—namely, that Black male teachers are potential role models and father figures for Black youth, and that school districts and teacher education programs need to recruit and retain more of them in predominantly Black classrooms.

While the scholarly literature on Black male teachers repeats some of the themes that pervade popular media discourses on Black men in teaching, it also offers some critical pushback. Most notably, several publications have explored the dilemmas associated with presuming Black male teachers as role models for Black children. Brown's work (2011, 2012), for example, identifies the diversity of experiences that vanishes under monolithic constructions of Black male teachers as role models, and it surfaces Black male educators' own critiques of how those monolithic constructions essentialize them as disciplinarians and enforcers. Similarly, Pabon (2016) critiques the essentializing perception of Black male teachers as "Black Supermen" (p. 933) who can save Black children, and Woodson and Pabon (2016) critically examine how Black male teachers are expected to perform—and can be marginalized for falling short of—heteropatriarchal notions of Black manhood. Earlier iterations of my scholarship have also contributed to this body of work by noting how role modeling discourses overshadow several dilemmas, including the potential resistance to Black male teachers as role models and father figures (Brockenbrough, 2012c), the challenges these men may face when serving as hypermasculine and authoritarian disciplinarians (Brockenbrough, 2015), their potentially fraught working relationships with women colleagues and bosses (Brockenbrough, 2012b), the surveillance of queer Black male teachers (Brockenbrough, 2012a), and the intraracial identity politics that can confound these teachers' relationships with Black students (Brockenbrough, 2013). Collectively, this scholarship does not summarily dismiss the potential value of Black male teachers as role models, but it does push stakeholders to raise questions—especially around Black masculinity politics—that often are overlooked in more surface-level popular media coverage on Black men in teaching.

Other scholarly works have problematized role modeling discourses on Black male teachers for diverting attention from deeper pedagogical concerns and from structural analyses of educational inequities. For instance, in their consideration of recruitment and retention issues, Pabon, Anderson, and Kharem (2011) challenge schools to move beyond limited perceptions of Black male teachers as role models and disciplinarians to focus more intentionally on developing their instructional abilities as culturally responsive pedagogues. Toldson (2013b) challenges the presumption "that black male teachers have a primary responsibility to foster the social development of black male students" (p. 20), urging instead for Black male teachers to be viewed as important for all students. Jackson et al. (2013) problematize the positioning of Black male teacher role models as remedies for the structural inequities that produce Black youth marginality, as redressing these inequities requires much more than the efforts of inspirational role models. Similar critiques of the limitations of role modeling discourses and the resulting inattention to structural reforms have been raised in a Canadian context by Martino and Rezai-Rashti (2012) and in an English context by Maylor (2009). Again, this scholarship does not disregard the significance of Black male teachers, but it does challenge the attribution of that significance to what are often oversimplified and limited interests in role modeling.

Scholarly perspectives on Black male teachers are particularly important given the saviorist discourses that continue to shape popular perceptions of these educators. As noted in this section, while a core body of scholarly literature has captured Black male teachers' potential contributions to their classrooms and to their students' lives, a growing strand of work has identified several dilemmas that may undermine Black men's participation in the profession. Given the struggle of popular media discourses to extend beyond saviorist accolades, it is crucial for scholars to expand the reach of critical analyses that balance an exploration of Black male teachers' pedagogical insights with an attention to the racial, gender, and institutional politics that complicate their pedagogical impact. This imperative is why I have chosen to revisit and update earlier iterations of my own scholarship, as well as examine previously unpublished findings, in this book. Prior analyses of my work on Black male teachers have appeared primarily in peer-reviewed academic journals that are difficult for non-academics to access. My hope is that this book, grounded in a new critique of saviorist discourses, will invite wider audiences to critically deliberate over the presence and purpose of Black men in the American K–12 teaching profession.

Saviorism and Knowledge Production on Black Male Teachers

The goal of this chapter was to provide a context for understanding how the intersection of blackness and maleness is a consequential one for Black men in the American teaching profession. Set against longstanding anxieties surrounding the fraught involvement of adult Black men in American society at large and in Black families in particular, popular discourses on Black male teachers have reproduced saviorist rhetorics that not only cast these men as the answer to the plight of Black boys but also attempt to recuperate the image of Black men vis-à-vis the responsible and respectable Black male pedagogue. Drawing upon critical perspectives from Black masculinity studies enabled this chapter to name and problematize the larger cultural project of Black masculine redemption behind saviorist discourses on Black men in teaching. As the push to recruit and retain Black male teachers increases across teacher education programs and school districts, so, too, does the need for analyses like those in this chapter—analyses that interrogate the cultural and pedagogical politics surrounding Black men's presence in the teaching profession.

As noted throughout this chapter, concerns regarding the plight of Black boys in the United States are at the core of saviorist discourses on Black male adults and Black male teachers. Black boys' collective state of crisis, evidenced by a range of disparaging social indicators, is framed in scholarship and popular cultural discourses as both the product of Black men's irresponsibility and the justification for their saviorist interventions. While this chapter has offered critiques of saviorist Black masculinity politics, those critiques do not obviate the need to address the very real and alarming predicament of Black boys in America. These youth, as previously noted, experience high drop-out rates from K–12 schools, high unemployment rates, overrepresentation in the school-to-prison pipeline, a range of health disparities, and related dilemmas. In response to these conditions, educational scholars have devoted considerable energies to examining the role of K–12 schools in the marginalization of Black boys. Specifically, scholars have sought deeper understandings of Black boys' low graduation rates and underperformance on academic assessments (Howard, 2014; Schott Foundation for Public Education, 2012; Tatum, 2005; Toldson & Lewis, 2012), their overrepresentation in special education (Noguera, 2008; Toldson & Lewis, 2012), their disproportionate encounters with school disciplinary regimes (Ferguson, 2000; C. W. Lewis, Butler, Bonner III, & Joubert, 2010; Noguera, 2008), and their overall struggles to negotiate their identities and participation in K–12 settings that continue to pathologize Black male youth (Howard, 2008; Howard, Flennaugh, & Terry Sr., 2012; McCready, 2010; Spencer, Fegley, & Harpalani, 2003). Other works have highlighted afterschool and mentoring programs (J. E. Davis, 2005; Fashola, 2005; Howard, 2014; I. Jackson, Sealey-Ruiz, & Watson, 2014), pedagogical strategies and resources (Johns, 2016; H. R. I. Milner, 2007; Sealey-Ruiz, 2011; Tatum, 2005; Warren, 2016), and policy recommendations (Howard, 2014; Johns, 2016; Schott Foundation for Public Education, 2012; Toldson & Lewis, 2012) with the potential to improve the educational experiences of Black male students. Collectively, these and many other works leave no doubt of the severity of Black boys' troubles in schools or the urgency for strategies to improve Black boys' educational opportunities.

While saviorist discourses on Black male teachers seek to respond to the plight of Black boys, they may unwittingly undermine efforts to address Black boys' needs. As discussed earlier in this chapter, popular media depictions of savior-like Black men in teaching often appear in the absence of considerations of more structural remedies for Black youth marginality. At the very least, such depictions risk reproducing unrealistic expectations of what individual Black male teachers can accomplish in their classrooms without the support of far-reaching policy reforms that ameliorate the effects of poverty, White supremacy, the prison industrial complex, neoliberal educational agendas, and other systemic injustices that shape Black boys' lives. At worst, public faith in a saviorist Black manhood could enable the recruitment of Black male teachers to serve as a celebrated but inefficient quick-fix for urban school districts looking to demonstrate a commitment to Black male students. Indeed, urban school districts can place adult Black men in classrooms as savior-like figures without disrupting district-wide cultures of policing Black boys, leaving these men in some cases to perpetuate rather than disrupt Black boys' marginalization in schools. Thus, while it is crucial to consider the role of Black male teachers in the educational experiences of Black boys, it also imperative to avoid the quick-fix traps of saviorist discourses.

Along with diverting attention from structural reforms, saviorist discourses on Black men in teaching present other potential dilemmas. As previously discussed in this chapter, the elevation of savior-like Black male teachers frequently imagines Black boys with little-to-no agency, as inspirational teachers are cast as the central change agents in Black boys' lives. Additionally, the focus on Black male teachers tends to overshadow the invaluable contributions of other pedagogues, especially Black women teachers, to the education of Black youth, and the spotlight on saviorist Black manhood in the lives of Black boys often leaves the plight of Black girls in the dark. Whether intentional or not, the fascination with savior-like Black male teachers can reproduce troublesome blind spots within educational reform discourses on Black youth.

Before concluding, it is worth noting that many of the examples of saviorist discourses cited throughout this chapter came from Black writers, artists, scholars, educators, and media outlets, illustrating the resonance of a saviorist Black manhood among a range of Black cultural stakeholders. Given previously referenced scholarship from Black masculinity studies on the legacy of patriarchy in Black cultural politics, the appeal of savior-like constructions of Black men is not terribly surprising. If anything, it indexes the arguably epistemological nature of recuperative Black masculinity politics in some strands of Black cultural and knowledge production. In a sociohistorical context where alterity, vulnerability, and abjection have long-constituted Black male subjectivity, the redemption of a patriarchal and hegemonic-like Black manhood seems, for some, to define the very nature of knowledge production about Black maleness. In many examples of saviorist discourses cited throughout this chapter—from books on raising Black boys to media portraits of admirable Black male teachers—the decision to examine the Black male condition appears already predetermined by the aim of rescuing it from the margins of patriarchal legitimacy. For those who understand knowledge production about Black males as an inherently patriarchal and masculinist recuperative act, a critique of saviorist discourses on Black male teachers may be anathema to the fundamental nature of scholarship on Black manhood. How to engage those audiences in scholarly inquiries that do not seek to redeem Black masculinity is a major challenge facing this book and analyses like it, and it is a challenge for which there is no quick and easy solution. I raise it here to provide a framework for grasping some of the resistance that may greet this book, and to further underscore what is at stake in critiques of saviorist discourses on Black male teachers. Such critiques must be approached not as detached and esoteric intellectual exercises, but as scholarly acts that may expose the potential vulnerabilities of a historically marginalized community and, thus, require sensitivity and care.

The sensitive nature of Black masculinity politics guides my analyses throughout the remainder of this book. Building on this chapter's critique of saviorist discourses on Black manhood and Black men in teaching, I devote Chapters 3 through 7 to a careful examination of the narratives of 11 Black male teachers from Brewerton, a large urban center in the eastern United States, who participated in my study on the experiences of Black men in urban teaching. For these 11 men, saviorist discourses influenced both their entry into the teaching profession and the expectations they encountered as Black men teaching in Brewerton's predominantly Black school district. However, as their narratives reveal, the saviorist expectations that often greeted these men did not always align with their own identities and pedagogies as Black male teachers. And, as I assert in my analyses of their narratives, it is in these moments of disconnect that the burdens and repercussions of saviorist Black masculinity politics become apparent. By centering the voices of my study participants, I seek to tactfully yet honestly highlight the challenges that saviorist discourses can create for Black male teachers. By doing so, my hope is to engage multiple stakeholder groups in a reevaluation of how and why we place Black male educators at the helm of urban K–12 classrooms.

Conclusion

The purpose of this chapter was to establish the frameworks and concerns that contour the analyses throughout the remainder of this book. Grounded in critical, feminist- and queer-influenced perspectives from Black masculinity studies, this chapter introduced my critique of saviorist discourses on Black men in the American teaching profession. Informed by longstanding anxieties around Black men's absence from Black families and communities—and the impact of that absence on Black boys in particular—saviorist discourses imagine Black male teachers as savior-like figures who can wield culturally resonant modes of patriarchal authority and hegemonic masculinity to manage, inspire, and ultimately save Black children, especially Black boys. After citing examples of savior-like constructions of adult Black men across numerous discursive sites, this chapter looked more closely at popular media accounts that have reproduced saviorist discourses on Black male teachers. That review surfaced four recurrent themes: the plight of Black boys as context and warrant for recruiting Black male teachers; Black male teachers as models of hegemonic masculinity for Black boys; Black male teachers' recuperation of the image of adult Black men; and Black male teachers as the foil to women teachers and the perceptions of teaching as a women's profession. Together, those four themes underscore the saviorist imaginings of Black male teachers that pervade popular American media and fuel calls to attract more Black men into the nation's classrooms.

Following the review of saviorist discourses in popular media coverage on Black male teachers, this chapter turned its attention to the educational scholarship on Black men in teaching. This scholarly literature has made invaluable inroads by chronicling Black male teachers' culturally responsive pedagogies which, in some cases, have included commitments to serving as role models and father figures for Black youth. However, an emergent strand within this body of scholarship has troubled both the construction of Black male teachers as models of hegemonic masculinity and the reliance on Black male teachers as antidotes to the structural inequities behind Black youth's marginality. Building on that work, the remainder of this book employs a critical lens on Black masculinity politics to explore the narratives of 11 Black male teachers who worked in an urban, predominantly Black school district on the east coast of the United States. The dilemmas of saviorist Black masculinity politics that surfaced in study participants' narratives are used to trouble existing and posit new ways of defining the roles of Black male teachers in urban schools.

Notes

1. I should note that some masculinity scholars assert that Black men cannot attain hegemonic masculinity. Hill Collins (2005), for instance, describes hegemonic masculinity as an extension of whiteness and thus unattainable by Black men. In my analyses throughout this chapter and the remainder of the book, whether Black men can actually attain hegemonic masculinity is not as important as the aspiration in saviorist discourses to have them model it. That aspiration marks hegemonic masculinity as something for Black men, including Black male teachers, to strive for and reproduce in Black boys.
2. Scholarly works on Black educators (Fairclough, 2007; Foster, 1997; K. A. Johnson, Pitre, & Johnson, 2014), women educators (Munro, 1998; Perlmann & Margo, 2001; Prentice & Theobald, 1991), and queer educators (Blount, 2005; Graves, 2009; Rofes, 2005) have investigated how broader cultural discourses on race, gender, and sexuality, respectively, have affected these educators' participation in the teaching profession.
3. See Hughey (2014) and Sirota (2013) for particularly insightful explanations of the traits associated with the savior archetype.

3 Call and Response

The Resonance of Saviorist Discourses

For Black men entering the American teaching profession, a popular perception of who they are and what they do already exists. As discussed in Chapter 2, saviorist discourses on Black manhood have pegged Black male teachers as role models and father figures for Black youth, especially Black boys, whose in-school dilemmas are linked in part to the absence of responsible adult Black men in their lives. Since these discourses minimize or overlook a number of factors that may complicate Black men's participation in urban teaching, this book strives for more nuanced depictions of how Black male teachers navigate American K–12 urban schools. This does not mean, however, that prevailing discourses on Black men in teaching should be ignored or dismissed. In fact, one major finding of this study is that participants' own identities and motivations were mediated in significant ways by saviorist discourses on Black male teachers. To understand what it meant for the men in this study to be Black men in urban teaching, one must explore the resonance, for these men, of the pervasive calls for more Black male teachers to save and uplift Black youth.

In this chapter, I begin to unpack the salience of saviorist discourses in the personal narratives of the men in my study. Specifically, I explore how the calls for more Black male teachers motivated study participants' entry into the teaching profession and informed their sense of purpose. Since most of this book focuses on the tensions and challenges that study participants faced because of saviorist discourses on Black male teachers, their early encounters with and ongoing meaning-making around these discourses provide important context for the chapters to come.

As a quick reminder, I noted at the end of Chapter 1 that when presenting study findings in this book, I had to strike a balance between reproducing some narrative excerpts verbatim while just summarizing key themes from others. This was necessary to make the presentation of findings from multiple and lengthy life narratives manageable within this book's word length limitation. The verbatim excerpts that do appear were chosen for their evocative nature, which hopefully will compensate for the narrative passages that are summarized instead of reproduced in this text.

The Call: "We Need More Black Male Teachers"

To understand why and under what circumstances Black men decide to enter the teaching profession, all 11 study participants were asked to recall messages about teaching that may have shaped their perceptions of the profession. A recurring theme that emerged in response to this inquiry was the emphasis on the specific need for more Black male teachers, especially from members of Black communities. This theme surfaced in the narratives of seven of the 11 study participants. The accounts offered by those seven men are described in this section.

The urgency for more Black men in urban K–12 classrooms was a message that study participants received from various stakeholder groups within Black communities. One participant, Felix, described the following reactions from members of his Black church family:

> I grew up in a . . . I have a church family and in my church there are a lot of teachers, a lot of educators. They were ecstatic. They were pleased to hear me going into the field. The initial reaction was, "Oh, that's wonderful. That's great. We need more Black teachers. Our schools need more Black teachers, especially Black male teachers." So anyone who was to find out that I wanted to teach was like, "Oh, you could teach anywhere you know. There's such a demand for African American male teachers who are teaching math or are teaching the sciences." So I was getting that reaction.

Another participant, Bill, also recounted positive reactions to his decision to become a teacher. While White college peers congratulated Bill on his intentions to enter the teaching profession, it was Black family members and friends who emphasized the specific need for more Black male teachers. Similarly, a participant named Mitch noted that while his White college friends congratulated him on his acceptance into a popular alternative teaching certification program, it was older Black members of his home community who specified the need for more Black male teachers. As Mitch stated, "It was just, 'Congratulations, I'm glad to see a Black man teaching.' It was always, 'They need more Black men teaching.' " Citing church members, family and friends, and community elders, Felix, Bill, and Mitch noted the explicit recognition of the need for more Black male teachers from members of their Black communities. Echoing the review of saviorist discourses in Chapter 2, all three were praised for their decisions specifically as Black men to answer the call to teach.

When asked to further unpack why older Black members of his home community had stressed the need for more Black male teachers, Mitch offered the following reply:

> I think the whole idea of a Black man represented a tough love, a hard . . . an influence that was just, I don't know. I feel like a female,

like a Black woman teacher, was kind of seen as like . . . as something like a pillow, something that was comforting. Not bad in any way, but like provided something that was a comfort, something that was kind of a rest. A Black male teacher was something like a pillar or a column, something that was just more rigid, that served another purpose. It was something that I think they felt was lacking, that there weren't just enough of. Like a lot of students, they need to be nurtured and coddled and things like that. That's definitely a necessity. But at the same time you need somebody to just . . . like just won't take shit, and kind of just be very hard line. I think that's the idea of what a Black man represents in the classroom and in the city.

Because it wasn't so much I was teaching, it was that I was teaching and I was going to Brewerton. Because that's what it was all. . . "I'm teaching next year." "Where you teaching?" "Brewerton." "Ooohhh!" So it was kind of like, "That's good. They need more Black men. You gotta be careful, you gotta be careful."

Mitch's reply provided intriguing insights into the deeper meaning he made of other people's reactions to his career path. In remarks by the older Black adults in Mitch's home community, the Black male teacher came to symbolize an authority figure who could restore order—not simply to a Black classroom, but to a Black classroom in an urban space like Brewerton. Building upon the warning to "be careful," Mitch went on to recall how some of his community members encouraged him to "just go crazy one day and show them how you mean business. Pick a chair up and just throw it out the window. Let them know." Unpacking the messages he was receiving from others, Mitch discerned the saviorist expectation that he, as a Black male teacher, could curtail the chaos of the predominantly Black urban classroom by performing an indomitable masculinity.

Like Mitch, another participant, Ira, unpacked the positive reactions to his decision as a Black man to become a teacher, leading to several interesting insights:

Ira: I got a lot of praises. Being an African American male, there's just this thing where people just say, "Thank God! Another African American . . . we need more African American male teachers." So I was getting a lot of that from family and friends, and colleagues. "It's a good thing that you're doing," you know. "We need more Black male teachers." So I was getting a lot of that.

Ed: Did they ever explain why? What was behind the need?

Ira: Um, I don't think anyone really explained why. I think there was basically an understanding that there is a lack of African American males in the schools that are predominantly African American, and it perpetuates, I guess, the whole coming from a single parent home that's predominantly just run by females, and the lack of presence

in terms of a male. It seems like that was basically where it was
coming from.

Ed: So it was almost so taken for granted that there wasn't a need to
make it even more explicit. It sounds like it was sort of understood
that you understood what was meant by that.

Ira: Yeah, definitely. Definitely. That's basically where it was coming
from. We need more Black male teachers—you know what that
means. Right, we need more Black male teachers to get our kids in
line, especially our boys. Especially the boys. To get them in line,
straighten them up.

Like Mitch, Ira inferred a deeper layer of meanings beneath the positive
responses to his decision to teach: Our children are being raised by single
mothers, they lack male role models at home, they are out of control in
school (especially the boys), and they need Black male teachers to get
them back on track. That Ira and Mitch picked up on and understood
these messages even when they were not explicitly articulated spoke to
their currency and pervasiveness. When others from within the Black
community complimented these participants by saying, "we need more
Black male teachers," saviorist logics on Black male teachers seemed to
have already supplied a rationale for why.

Other narrative passages further illuminated Black stakeholders' positive reactions to study participants' decisions to become teachers. Two
participants, Damon and Quincy, mentioned supportive feedback from
Black female teacher colleagues who welcomed them by declaring "we
need more Black male teachers." Additionally, Quincy described positive
reactions from Black fathers and other male guardians whose children
attended his middle school:

> Sometimes, for a lot of the dads that I've talked to, that does come up
> a lot because more of the dads have said, "It's good to see a Black male
> teacher here," and that kind of thing. And the dads who I have seen,
> or the uncles, they do say that a lot. But for the overall, I think it's, a
> lot of it is just a Black teacher, a young Black male teacher. It's like,
> "It's good to see you, a young Black male teacher, a young Black guy,
> coming in and teaching the kids," or whatever the phrasing may be.

As in some of the previously cited narrative excerpts, a detailed explanation of why it was good to see Quincy, a young Black male teacher, working at his school was not offered by the fathers and other men who spoke
to him. The rationale behind the praise apparently was understood. That
the praise was offered by fathers and uncles suggests a special investment
among Black male guardians in Quincy's presence in their children's lives.

Quincy was not the only one to mention positive feedback from Black
parents. Recalling a former teaching stint at a predominantly Black middle

school, Greg noted that he had frequently had waiting lists for students to be switched into his classroom because of parents' preference for a Black male teacher. Another participant, Ira, recalled positive reactions from Black parents, with a specific nod to responses from Black mothers:

> The [Black] parents love me in much the same ways in which people in the community view me. They look at it like, "Black male teacher, he can do something." Especially if it's a [Black] boy. "We need you. Can you talk to my boy? Is he going to be in your class? I want him in your class." Stuff like that, I get that all the time from parents. They look for the Black male teachers to, it seems like, to do things that parents should do, to be quite frank with you. But at the same time, just trying to get in their heads that, "Can you please somehow motivate him to step it up? To show him that it's okay to do what you do?" Sometimes that kind of attitude we get from the parents, and it's mostly like the female parents.

That the Black parents described by Ira envisioned him as a role model specifically for their Black sons, and that it was "mostly like the female parents" who did so, aligns these narrative excerpts with key features of the saviorist discourses cited in Chapter 2. As a Black male teacher, Ira sensed that he was positioned not only to save Black male students, but to do so for those coming from single-mother households, thus addressing the presumptive absence of Black male adults in their lives.

The narrative passages that were quoted or summarized throughout this section identified various stakeholders within Black communities— Black church members, Black elders, Black female teacher colleagues, Black parents—who, according to the men in this study, responded in supportive and appreciative ways to their career paths as Black men in teaching. All of these examples speak to the circulation of saviorist discourses in study participants' life narratives. Key here is the recurrence across participants' narratives of the refrain "we need more Black male teachers," or some close variation thereof, which underscored the urgency not of Black teachers or male teachers, but of Black male teachers specifically. At the very least, that refrain conveyed a respect and admiration for study participants as Black men engaged in a noble calling. Several examples, however, indicated that "we need more Black male teachers," when attributed to Black stakeholders, invoked a larger set of concerns for participants—namely, the absence of Black men in Black families and communities, the deleterious impact of that absence on Black children (especially Black boys), and the dire need for Black male teachers to enter the classroom and set things right. That these concerns were invoked as participants were being lauded for becoming teachers illustrates how saviorist discourses played an important role in encouraging their decisions to join the teaching profession.

The Response: Black Male Teachers on the Need for Black Male Teachers

With educational researchers, teacher education programs, school districts, popular media outlets, family members, friends, community members, church members, parents, and fellow teachers all espousing the need for more Black men in the classroom, it should come as no surprise that some Black men in the profession might concur with this resounding chorus. An analysis of the narratives collected in this study uncovered participants' own assertions of the need to attract more Black men into the teaching profession. In what follows, references to the narratives of six participants reveal how these men took up popular discourses on the need for more Black male teachers.

During their final one-on-one interviews, participants were asked to describe their hopes for what this study would ultimately accomplish. One recurring theme was this study's potential to advance efforts to recruit and retain more Black men in the teaching profession. Quincy, for example, expressed his hope that educational powerbrokers—or in his words, "those big boys upstairs making the decisions"—would review study findings to understand "what are these guys complaining about or concerned about that either prevents them from staying or makes them wanna quit?" Another participant, Karl, expressed his hope that the alternative certification program to which he belonged might draw upon this study to better understand and support its Black male cohort members. A third participant, Damon, emphasized the need to recruit Black male teachers, specifically young Black male teachers, because "they're so close to the education themselves that they can remember what's going on." He then went to on state:

> Even though I'm not from Brewerton, because I'm Black and I'm a male, I'm going to be able to do certain things in my school community, and my parents are gonna have a certain amount of trust and thoughts about me as [opposed to] a White teacher. So how can you utilize young Black men in the classroom to help build bridges between communities and help think about ways in which, you know, all these things they're saying are the problems of young Black men, how can they maybe provide some help toward that problem?

As in saviorist discourses, young Black male teachers were imagined in Damon's narrative as vital for addressing "the problems of young Black men." By focusing on the recruitment and retention of Black male teachers, all three participants echoed the calls to find more Black men to join and stay in the teaching profession.

Two more participants expressed their hope that this study would help draw Black men into teaching. One was Ira, who envisioned a young

Black male reading this text and trying "to get a better sense of what this is all about as they grapple with trying to understand how to be an educator." The other was Bill, who shared his hope that this study would aid recruitment efforts targeting prospective Black male teachers. Bill's response also emphasized the potential impact of such recruitment efforts on Black male students, as captured in the following passage:

> So I guess immediately, more immediately, I would hope that [the study is] able to understand what brings Black men to the profession in order to bring more Black men to the profession. And I guess as an outgrowth of that, how to encourage young Black men in general, not even necessarily into the teaching profession, but just how to encourage young Black men to do more with themselves. Especially living someplace like the Brew where I interact with so many young Black men who don't really have goals. Learning how to inspire that more. But I think that's more an outgrowth of having people in the classroom who do that, who inspire. So I guess that's just for me, ultimately I would want to see that. I guess because on some level, having Black males in the classroom in some way benefits at the very least Black male students—if not all students, at least Black male students. So I think the goal, at least as I see it, if we had more Black males in the classroom, then you'll have more positive role models to influence those Black male students who are in the classrooms. So I guess that would be the ultimate hope for me, long term. But more immediately, to figure out what it is that attracts Black males to the profession, in order to bring more Black males to this profession.

While Bill's short-term goal repeated the call to attract more Black men into the profession, his long-term goal targeted the specter of Black male underachievement, with the hope that an increased number of Black male teachers would address that educational crisis. By explicitly marking these concerns in his response, Bill invoked the anxieties toward the plight of Black male youth that undergird saviorist appeals for more Black male teachers.

One of the most intriguing calls for more Black male teachers came from Oliver. Raised outside of the United States, Oliver's ethnic identification produced a slight disconnect at times with American-based discourses on racial identity. However, when asked about his hopes for the potential impact of this study, Oliver interrogated American racial histories and masculinity politics as he offered the following call for more Black male teachers:

Oliver: I think that Black men should definitely be teachers of other Black men, and maybe girls to a certain extent. This is not to say that White men don't have anything to offer Black men. But

I think that because of the history of the Black male in society from *waaaay* back, it's important that Black students see the Black male teacher as an authoritative figure, as a power, as an intellectual power, and as someone who can pass something on to them, as opposed to them seeing the White male teacher as the only authoritative male figure. Again, based on the history, based on that history.

Ed: And so you hope that this study will push that point?

Oliver: Yes, I hope it will encourage more Black men to teach, one. And also that it will head in the direction where Black students, mainly male, understand that they have something to live up to and something to emulate. And that they should try to seek, possibly, professions in the teaching area so they can pass on— because teaching is passing on, isn't it, what you've learned. So I hope it will go in that direction, and that Black men will have more respect for other Black men.

Ed: Black men will have more respect for other Black men.

Oliver: Yes. For people in general but more so for Black men. Because I think, from what I've observed in the schools, particularly Black men still—young Black men and young Black minds— still think that White is right to a certain degree. And so they treat their Black male teachers with less respect than they do the White male teachers. And I'm not sure if it's out of fear or if it's out of brainwashing.

Ed: Or both?

Oliver: Or both, yeah. And that the images of Black men in their homes have been possibly so negative that they could only imagine that the grass must be greener on the other side. So that's my concern, my worry. So it's not that Black males should ignore or negate the teaching of White teachers, but just not regard them as being the only authority or the only light out of their darkness.

Oliver's comments were quoted at length because of the myriad issues that all converged in this exchange. First, for Oliver, the Black male teacher was a role model for "other Black men, and maybe girls to a certain extent" to emulate. As in the saviorist discourses on Black men in teaching that were reviewed in Chapter 2, the impact of Black male teachers specifically on Black male students came to the fore for Oliver. Second, Oliver's narrative passage, more than any other cited thus far, highlighted the relationships between race, masculinity politics, and respect. Other narrative excerpts included in this chapter certainly have conveyed the admiration that various stakeholders seemed to harbor for study participants as Black male teachers. But for Oliver, attracting more Black men into teaching was not just about receiving admiration and respect. Instead, it was about getting Black students, especially boys, to respect Black male teachers as much as they seemed to respect White men in the profession. Greater numbers of Black men in the classroom promised to bolster this group's stature among Black boys by challenging perceptions of "the White male teacher as the only authoritative male figure." Mirroring saviorist discourses on Black men in teaching, Oliver's narrative linked the recruitment of Black male teachers to the recuperation of their manhood, primarily by elevating it from the shadows of White male privilege.

An analysis of Oliver's comments must not lose sight of the critique he offered of White supremacy. By noting how White male teachers seemed to be positioned for Black students as the "only light out of their darkness," a deliberate play on words on his part, Oliver called attention to a racial hierarchy that he witnessed among teachers in Brewerton schools. However, by articulating his critique of White supremacy as a contest of sorts between White male and Black male teachers for the loyalty and respect of Black male students, Oliver imagined a male-centered universe that only briefly referenced girls and, despite the predominantly female composition of the teaching profession, made no direct mention of women teachers. In this regard, Oliver was certainly not alone; previously cited narrative excerpts from Bill, Damon, and Ira also centered the relationships between Black male teachers and Black male students. In doing so, these participants privileged the masculinist agenda found in saviorist discourses on Black male teachers. Collectively, the narrative excerpts referenced from Bill, Damon, Ira, Karl, Oliver, and Quincy echoed saviorist logics to assert the significance of their presence in the teaching profession as Black men.

Saviorist Discourses and Good Black Men

Wedding the legacies of Black teachers' race work and male teachers' re-masculinization of schooling, saviorist discourses on Black male teachers imagine men whose Black cultural sensibilities and hegemonic masculinity make them ideal pedagogues for Black youth, especially Black boys. As discussed in Chapter 2, these discourses cast a decidedly celebratory light on Black male teachers that starkly contrasts with more familiar stereotypes of Black men in America as criminal, irresponsible, and unwanted. Building on the previous chapter, the data shared here in Chapter 3 indicate the influence of congratulatory and affirmational saviorist discourses on the men in this study. Across multiple narrative excerpts, study participants recalled being lauded by various Black community members for their decisions as Black men to become teachers. The significance of the compliments and admiration that they received cannot be underestimated. In a society that repeatedly enacts a violent and unrelenting contempt for Black manhood, saviorist discourses on Black male teachers present an intoxicating counternarrative: Black men, we need you.

Saviorist discourses might also be understood as a moral compensation of sorts for the relative lack of financial rewards in teaching. Low teacher salaries, at least in comparison to other white-collar professions, have been cited quite often as a barrier to recruiting Black male teachers (Davis et al., 2015; Hawkins, 2015; Jarrett, 2015; Johnson, 2007; Matus, 2005). While this was not examined in the previous sections of this chapter, it is worth sharing here that eight participants—Bill, Felix, Greg, Karl, Mitch, Phil, Quincy, and Victor—recalled second-guessing their decisions to become teachers, or being questioned about their career decisions by family and friends, because of the relatively low pay and status of teaching. As indicated throughout this chapter, community interest in finding more Black male teachers garnered accolades for many study participants from Black community members. Given the constraints on financial rewards for teachers, "we need more Black male teachers" may function as an alternative enticement for wooing Black men into the classroom.

But perhaps the biggest insight that this chapter offers into saviorist discourses is the sense of meaning that they provided to the men in this study. Looking across study participants' personal narratives, it is clear that "we need more Black male teachers" not only encouraged many of these men to pursue teaching, but it also informed their own saviorist conceptualizations of their significance in the profession. In the chapters to come, I explore a number of challenges that arose as study participants negotiated the expectations of saviorist logics. Here, however, it seems important to emphasize the community contexts and virtuous intentions that mediated participants' relationships to saviorist discourses. A wide range of educational and community stakeholders, as discussed in Chapters 1 and 2, has searched desperately for Black men with an interest in teaching. By entering the profession, the men in this study were responding, at least in part, to pervasive concerns throughout Black communities about the future of Black youth. Their decisions to become teachers were not driven by some sinister plot to proselytize students with patriarchal, hegemonically masculinist, and racially essentialist values. Instead, these men joined the teaching ranks in the Brewerton School District to improve the educational opportunities and social futures of Black children and to make sincere contributions to the advancement of Black communities. Put differently, these men were, in fact, good and admirable men—not perfect or infallible, but still good and admirable—and they were trying to do good in the world by becoming urban teachers. Any critiques of saviorist discourses and their consequences must be balanced with this fundamental recognition.

A dilemma emerges, however, when we also recognize that saviorist discourses tend to reproduce a limited view of the experiences of Black male teachers, as discussed in depth in Chapter 2. In this chapter, excerpts from study participants' narratives offered glimpses into male-centered renderings of teaching and schooling that privileged the participation of Black male teachers. Among the concerns that were overlooked in such renderings were the positioning of Black male teachers as patriarchs in their classrooms, and the potentially detrimental impact of patriarchal power on Black students, female teacher colleagues, and Black male teachers themselves. These are just a few of the factors that can seriously complicate the experiences of Black men in the teaching profession but rarely get interrogated in saviorist discourses. Taking as a given that the men in this study were well-intentioned educators, the next few chapters look closely at how they described and negotiated the challenges associated with the saviorist expectations facing Black male teachers. My hope is to show how saviorist discourses, while affirming on the surface, can also be of disservice to Black men in the classroom.

Conclusion

The goal of this chapter was to convey the resonance of saviorist discourses among the men who participated in my study. Across multiple narrative excerpts, study participants recalled hearing "we need more Black male teachers" in response to their initial decisions to enter the urban teaching profession. When attributed to Black community members, this phrase signaled a saviorist hope in Black male teachers' capacities to both manage and uplift Black children in the absence of other Black men in Black families and communities. The saviorist logics behind "we need more Black male teachers" were also taken up by the teachers themselves, leading some to underscore their importance by centering their potential impact on Black boys. Collectively, the narrative accounts referenced throughout this chapter indicated how saviorist discourses attracted study participants to teaching and shaped their sense of purpose as Black male urban teachers. The capacity of saviorist discourses to recruit men like my study participants into urban teaching must be weighed alongside the dilemmas associated with saviorist Black masculinity politics that are explored throughout this book.

4 Great Expectations

Black Male Teachers as Disciplinarians and Father Figures

In a memorable scene from the Hollywood film *Lean on Me* (Twain & Avildsen, 1989), the embattled Black male educator Joe Clark, portrayed by famed actor Morgan Freeman, takes a wayward Black male student named Sams to the rooftop of Eastside High School. Sams is one of approximately 300 students who have just been expelled for a plethora of offenses including, in Sams's case, cutting class and smoking crack. Standing near the edge of the school's rooftop, Mr. Clark administers a much-needed dose of tough love, yelling caustically until a teary-eyed Sams promises to work hard and avoid trouble. The scene is one of the film's most memorable, in part because it is one of the few in which the merits of Joe Clark's actions—the subject of controversy in real life (Lentz, 1989) and at least some ambivalence throughout the film—are not called into question. Like the visual metaphor of the rooftop's ledge, the class-cutting and crack-smoking Sams, whose father has abandoned him, is teetering on the edge of destruction. Enter Joe Clark, an unapologetically stern disciplinarian who fills the void left by Sams's absent father, submits the repentant and compliant Sams to patriarchal authority, and sets the young male on the path to achievement. That the image of Clark's fatherly intervention with Sams appears on movie posters for *Lean on Me* speaks to its evocative power, as does an accompanying tagline: "Eastside High was a training ground for jail. Then Joe Clark took over. Now the kids are getting something they never had. A future" ("27 x 40 Lean on Me Movie Poster," n.d.).

My nod here to the symbolic cache of *Lean on Me* is more than just an attention-grabbing hook. As I discuss later in this chapter, two teachers in my study made direct references to the cinematic depiction of Joe Clark while describing their own negotiations of their roles as disciplinarians and father figures for their students. Other participants cited similar images as they wrestled with recurring pressures to serve as surrogate patriarchs for Black children. All of these examples point to the impact of saviorist discourses in the narratives of the men in my study. As I argued in Chapter 2, these discourses imagine Black male teachers as race workers and masculine role models whose life-saving interventions are vital for Black youth, especially Black boys. Often overlooked, however, are the various challenges that may emerge when saviorist expectations come to bear on pedagogical responsibilities. For the men in my study, the patriarchal notions of Black manhood associated with saviorist discourses on Black male teachers complicated their participation in predominantly Black urban schools. This chapter focuses on two related dilemmas that surfaced in study participants' narratives: the pressure to operate as authoritarian disciplinarians, and the expectation to serve as father figures.

Highlighting these two dilemmas marks an important step toward a more critical understanding of the experiences of Black male teachers like the men in this study.

Patriarchal Constructions of Black Male Disciplinarians

Student discipline has long been a complex and contentious concern in urban school districts across the United States (E. R. Brown, 2003; Lewis et al., 2010; Skiba et al., 2011), and the Brewerton School District, where my study participants were employed, was no exception. At the time of the study, school violence was a recurring challenge in Brewerton, especially in the city's high schools, providing fuel for the District's zero-tolerance policy on violent student misconduct. Metal detectors, security guards, and disciplinary deans were commonplace throughout Brewerton high schools, and student suspension and violent incident rates weighed heavily in annual high-stakes assessments of the District's overall performance. Against this backdrop, it was not surprising that school discipline emerged as a significant theme in the narratives of my study participants. However, in contrast to popular discourses like those reviewed in Chapter 2—which stressed the need for strong Black male disciplinarians to intervene in the lives of Black youth and which cast Black male educators in that very role—the men in my study offered insights that critiqued and confounded other people's expectations of their participation in the disciplinary cultures of Brewerton schools. Two themes from study participants' narratives were particularly noteworthy: their struggles to adopt the authoritarian disciplinary personas that others expected of them as Black male teachers, and their critiques of the disproportionate assignment of disciplinary responsibilities to Black male teachers. In what follows, these themes are explored in further detail.

"I'm Not the Belt Dad": Struggling to Adopt Authoritarian Disciplinary Personas

Popular perceptions of Black male teachers as well-suited disciplinarians for predominantly Black urban schools emerged across multiple participant narratives. These perceptions reflected patriarchal constructions of

Black manhood that presumed Black male teachers' capacities to enforce stern, father-like forms of authority in the classroom. For five of the 11 men in this study, the patriarchal authoritarianism expected of Black male teachers was a notable source of stress, anxiety, or frustration in their professional experiences, as revealed in several passages from their narratives.

For some study participants, the patriarchal authoritarianism that was expected of them clashed with their preferred classroom demeanors. One of those participants was Victor. When discussing his pedagogy, Victor used "laissez faire" and "organized chaos" to characterize both his laid-back demeanor and his constructivist leaning toward project-based learning that involved minimal-to-moderate interjections from the instructor. Both his personality and pedagogy clashed with the rigid approaches to classroom management and instruction that others expected of him as a Black male teacher, as he explained in this exchange:

Victor: I think the perception is a Black man has to be strong, has to be like this strong, firm, this kind of. . .

Ed: James Evans?[1]

Victor: Yeah, James Evans or the principal. . .

Ed: Joe Clark?

Victor: Joe Clark, you know what I mean? Yeah, so I think that's the perception and if you're real far off from that, people are kind of questioning you I think, a little bit.

In contrast to the patriarchal authoritarianism immortalized in the cinematic depiction of Joe Clark, Victor presented a more casual and flexible approach to running his classroom that contradicted popular perceptions of the firm Black male authority figure. Victor's departure from a more authoritarian norm was repeatedly marked as a deficit by fellow teachers at his school, as he described in the following excerpt:

> For some men or Black men, that stern, real hardcore approach works, but you can't force it. You can't force something that's not there. That rigid structure, drill sergeant approach is not me. The approach of organized chaos is more my style. But then the question becomes now, particularly as a Black man, people say, "Oh, you're a Black man and these are Black kids." So now my colleagues and peers are like, "Oh, by his room is a mess, he's out of order. What's going on in there?" Their perception is like, the kids are running things!

Victor added that critiques of his laid-back styles of instruction and discipline came under particular fire from Black colleagues. In his words, "The Black teachers are like, 'You got to get with these kids, you got to be hard on them. Life ain't going to be easy for these Black kids. They need to be prepared by you. That's our agenda.'" With the plight of Black youth cited as a warrant for strict classroom disciplinary practices, Victor's less rigid approach became fodder for Black peer criticisms.

As Victor continued to discuss his more laid-back manner of running his classroom, he also noted the pressures he felt from students to enact a more rigid disciplinary approach. In Victor's words, his students mistook his "softness for being weak." In addition, Victor noted how students' perceptions of him seemed to be influenced by the attitudes and strict disciplinary styles of his Black female colleagues:

Victor: So kids were getting those strong [Black] female teacher classrooms and then they would come in my class and then they would use, they'd kind of try to play the teachers against... "Oh, when we go to Ms. Yarborough's class we don't do this, but you don't got no control in your class." So that's what they'll start saying, "You don't have any control in your class." These are the kids. I'm like, "Are you guys prisoners? Am I supposed to control you? Don't you control yourself?" I put it back on them, but again that's the questioning, you know.

Ed: Is that coming from them, or do you think they're picking up on stuff from other adults?

Victor: I think it's two parts. It's part them and part . . . because they will go into other classrooms and, "Oh, you're not in Mr. Rollins' class. You might be doing crazy stuff, but don't bring that hot mess in here." They use hot mess. "You're with Mr. Rollins with that hot mess, don't bring that hot mess in here!" And again, Mr. Rollins' hot mess, is this organized? People don't understand the organized, even the students, they don't understand organized chaos. If the principal is struggling to understand it, my [Black female partner teachers] are struggling to understand it.

In this exchange, Victor revealed that students' reactions to his more relaxed pedagogical style repeated the critiques of the "hot mess," or the perceived lack of control in his classroom, articulated by Black female colleagues. Such moments appeared to simultaneously normalize authoritarian classroom management strategies and discredit less rigid approaches like the one pursued by Victor.

Unfavorable reactions to Victor's instructional and classroom management strategies were not limited to Black teachers and students. At several points in his narrative, Victor reported that his less rigid teaching style prompted some White colleagues to suggest that he consider teaching in the suburbs, at an urban magnet school, or at a university. While not dismissing Victor's pedagogy as a "hot mess," these White colleagues, in Victor's eyes, echoed assertions of his ill-fit with the teaching culture of their school. These comments, along with the narrative excerpts above, revealed the sense of marginality that Victor felt as a Black male teacher who enacted a non-authoritarian disciplinary style in a Brewerton school.

Bill was another participant whose approach to teaching and discipline clashed with others' expectations of him as a Black male teacher. Like Victor, Bill reported receiving dual messages that Black male teachers needed to be stern patriarchs in urban classrooms, and that he was falling woefully short of that expectation. In the following passage, Bill recalled how a Black female teacher coach at his school had stressed the need for him to adopt a firmer disciplinary style as a Black male teacher:

> So we were talking. I was just telling her some of the problems I was having in the classroom. She basically was like, "You're a Black male, and a lot of these kids don't have a Black male presence in their life. So when you're in the classroom, they expect for you to be firm. They expect for you to lay down the law. They expect for you to do all of this stuff." She specifically said because you're a Black male, they expect you to be firmer with them than they would expect from these other teachers.

In addition to recalling this feedback from his Black female teacher coach, Bill noted that during his pre-service teaching experience, another Black female colleague—in this case, a mentor teacher—had urged him to assume a sterner disciplinary approach as well. Bill went on to explain that while he could understand the cultural context behind the image of the Black male as a patriarchal disciplinarian, that image simply did not match his natural demeanor:

> Part of me understands what [my teacher coach] means because I think there's this kind of push for the Black male . . . he's almost viewed as a disciplinarian, you know what I mean. In *Code of the Streets* [by Elijah Anderson (1999)], it talks about the male as the head of the household, and what he says, you know, blah-blah-blah. He lays down the law and all this kind of stuff. But my issue, and I was telling her, it's hard for me to get into that mentality because I don't naturally . . . I get the impression that I'm supposed be an asshole of some type. I can be that when I feel pushed to it, but it's not my natural inclination to come into the classroom and be like a hard-ass. But it seems like I have to be like that from the beginning, I have to be this kind of lay-down-the-law, don't-ever-let-up, be-mean-all-the-time . . . At least that's kind of the impression that I get from a lot of my coworkers, and even from this particular teacher.

That Bill characterized this patriarchal approach to discipline as being an "asshole of some type" plainly marked his disconnect with this style. It also underscored his frustration with the expectations he was encountering, as captured in the following exchange:

Bill: It's not that I can't be a father or a father figure, but maybe I'm just not the lay-down-the-law type of father [*chuckle*], you know what I mean. Maybe the type of father figure that I envision being effective is not the one who goes to work, brings home the bacon, and disciplines the kids when they need it, but a different type of father. And the type of father that they need is not the type of father that I can be. Does that make sense?

Ed: Yeah. It sounds like you're saying you can be . . . like the talk-it-out type of dad versus let-me-get-my-belt.

Bill: Yes, yes. But it seems like they're saying, "No, you can't talk it out with these kids. You have to get the belt out. That's what they need, they need the belt." Well, you know, I'm not the belt dad [*chuckle*]. And if that's what you're expecting, I'm gonna disappoint you.

In this passage, Bill envisioned himself as an alternative to images of Black male teachers entrenched in patriarchal narratives of dominance. This alternative, however, was at odds with the "lay-down-the-law" persona, or "the belt dad," that his colleagues seemed to repeatedly demand of him. Hints of the potential impact of his exasperation emerged during a focus group session when Bill stated, "I'm not a disciplinarian to the extent that I would need to be if I were to continue to teach in the Brewerton public school system." Despite entering urban teaching specifically to work with Black youth, Bill's deviation from a patriarchal, authoritarian norm for Black male teachers led him to question his fit with the teaching environment that surrounded him.

Like Bill and Victor, Quincy was another study participant who spoke about the challenges of adopting a stern disciplinary style. As noted in the opening of Chapter 1, Quincy's deviation from an indomitable, hegemonic masculinity was ominously marked on his first day of teaching when a student characterized him as "kinda sweet" and "kinda soft," and predicted that he would not last very long at the school. Quincy went on to explain that other students had developed similar first impressions of him as "kinda soft" because of his departure from the confrontational disciplinary styles enacted by other Black male teachers at his school, some of whom would "punch kids and shove kids into lockers all the time, or smack them over the head with rulers, or whatever the case may be." According to Quincy, "It was not a surprise to see a kid get pulled aside, punched in the stomach a couple times, saying 'sit down.'" Situated in a school where some Black male teachers resorted to physical violence to enforce disciplinary order, Quincy's mild demeanor marked him as an aberration in the eyes of some students, thus hindering his ability to establish himself as a credible authority figure in the classroom.

Realizing his initial failure to conform to the rogue elements of his school's disciplinary culture, Quincy spent much of his first year as a Brewerton teacher trying to reinvent himself as an authoritarian Black male disciplinarian. In one-on-one interviews, Quincy recounted recurrent bouts for authority in his classroom that led to volatile exchanges with his students, particularly his Black male students. One example was his ongoing confrontations with a student named Harold:

Quincy: Okay, so there's a kid named Harold, and we would go back and forth. He would try to sleep in my class every day. I'd call his mom basically every day dealing with this and that.

Ed: He'd try to sleep?

Quincy: Sleep, yeah. Like lounge. Not just head down, but lounge on the desk, and it got to the point where every day he'd put his head down and lounge. I'd pull the desk away so his head would almost hit the floor. He'd stand up and pretend to, or act like he was going to try to fight me, and I'm like, "Harold, I already told you, if that's what you need to do, let's go ahead and do this. Let's get it out of the way now so you can go ahead and show how big a man you are, and I can show you that you're not going to beat me up no matter how big you think you are." Because he was big for his age, but I was like, "You're not going to beat me up, no matter what. Somehow, if I have to fight dirty, I'm going to win this fight. I'm not going to let you win." So we go through the posturing and someone's like, "Mr. Stinson, let's just take him into the hall, why don't you all just finish it up." So the whole class would see it. And I didn't want to back down and he didn't want to back down, and we'd go through the same thing every day.

Although Quincy reported that he and Harold never actually came to blows, this account, along with a few others like it, revealed the lengths to which Quincy went to secure his authority in the face of student insolence.

Most of Quincy's volatile bouts for authority in his classroom transpired during his first year as a full-time teacher in Brewerton. With the passage of time, Quincy had developed a critical and insightful perspective on why he had fallen so readily into verbal and near-physical skirmishes with students like Harold:

Quincy: When a student would challenge me, I'd say, "Alright, let's go. You wanna fight, let's go. Let's take it outside, do it right here." And I had no desire to fight the kid, but I had no desire to back down either. And I would always get into power struggles with kids immediately. Sometimes I'd jump on top of my desk and start shouting, weird things to try and act like no matter what, I'm still in charge here, you're not going to beat me. So when I look back on it, I'm like wow, I did some crazy things. And even sometimes kids would call me on it, and I'm like, my kids are calling me on it, saying, "Mr. Stinson, why are you doing that?" And it did take me until after Christmas that I started realizing that I got to figure out some other way of doing it.

Ed: But the answer to why you were doing that is. . .?
Quincy: Because I wanted to make sure that they understood that I'm not soft, you know what I'm saying. No matter what you say, no matter what you're dealing with, you can hit me, you can do whatever, it doesn't matter. I'm going to show up every day, I'm not going to back down, I'm not going to change the way I do things just because you try to make my life a living hell.

In a school setting where his calm demeanor departed from the belligerent disciplinary norms perpetuated by some fellow Black male adults, Quincy felt pressured to resort to more confrontational strategies to assert his leadership in his classroom, even as those strategies brought him closer and closer to the threat of altercations. Conceding that "I wanted to make sure that they understood that I'm not soft," Quincy's commentary offered a glimpse of the extremes to which student-teacher conflicts could extend when fueled by performances of patriarchal and domineering constructions of Black masculinity. Unlike Victor and Bill, who reported an ongoing disconnect with stern disciplinary personas, Quincy wholeheartedly attempted to adopt such a persona in his classroom. And yet despite his efforts, Quincy still found himself in a stressful and precarious position because of his early struggles to perform an indomitable Black masculinity as an authoritarian disciplinarian.

As noted, Quincy reported a school culture where some Black male peers routinely engaged in austere modes of disciplinary enforcement. Similarly, three other participants—Bill, Solomon, and Mitch—made references to older and more experienced Black male educators who exhibited stern disciplinary styles that contrasted with their own departures from or inexperience with such styles. Bill, for instance, described an older and more experienced Black male colleague who frequently used profanity and stern lectures to maintain control of his classroom, and Solomon contrasted himself to an older, veteran Black male colleague who was "the über authoritarian henchman." Mitch, who ultimately developed his own strict approach to discipline, recalled how an early and clumsy attempt to mimic the stern disciplinary techniques of an older, more experienced Black male colleague inadvertently instigated a fight between two students in his classroom. In all of these cases, the presence of Black male colleagues who convincingly performed authoritarian teacher identities increased participants' awareness of their own divergence from or initial struggles with such identities, and ultimately underscored the pressures to master these identities as Black men in urban teaching.

In sum, the participants mentioned in this section attested in various ways to prevailing perceptions in Brewerton schools of Black male teachers as patriarchal, authoritarian classroom managers. In the midst of a discipline-intensive urban school culture, five of the Black men in this study felt pressured to control student conduct by performing a very particular construction of Black masculinity in the classroom. As captured throughout this section of Chapter 4, the dominant image of the stern Black male teacher delimited a narrow approach to classroom discipline that not only clashed with some participants' definitions of themselves as teachers but also threatened their very legitimacy in the eyes of colleagues and students. These dilemmas warrant closer consideration in critical scholarship on Black men in the teaching profession.

"The Discipline Stop": Disproportionate Responsibilities for Disciplinary Matters

All five of the study participants referenced thus far described anxieties associated with initial or ongoing struggles to adopt authoritarian approaches to discipline as Black male teachers. For other study participants, it was their successful performance of stern disciplinary personas that became the source of tension in their narratives. Specifically, three men in this study critiqued the disproportionate responsibility for discipline that they seemed to carry as Black male teachers who could successfully handle student misconduct. Their critical perspectives, which often problematized peers' perceptions of the hypermasculinity of Black male teachers, are described in this section.

One of the study participants who troubled the disproportionate assignment of disciplinary responsibilities to Black male teachers was Karl. During an exchange in a focus group session, Karl was critical of fellow teachers at his school who repeatedly relied on his capacity to manage student behavior:

Karl: I'm in a small school, and I'm just thinking, I thought back to the time where I had a sixth-grade teacher who literally called me. Like this was on the day when I had like nine kids from other classes coming in and out of my room because I'm the discipline stop. [*All: laughter*] And she was like. . .

Ed: The discipline stop!

Karl: Yeah, that's how I feel sometimes. Like, y'all think I'm not teaching at this point? So she calls me and she's like, "Mr. Reardon, I'm gonna send Peter up to you." I'm like, "Why?" She's like, "Well, I want you to scare him." And I'm like, "Scare him?" But I'm like, Peter and I . . . he's a [younger] student and I'm like, "Peter's like my buddy, so if you want me to scare him it's not going to work because he'll just laugh at me." So she was just like, "Well, we really just need to do something to really just get something in." And I'm just like, is that the role that you see me as, when I'm probably the most effective teacher in the building? But, that's another thing. . . [*chuckle*].

Greg: The big, Black, scary guy.

Karl: Yeah. I feel like that's the role, if any, that people will want me as.

Karl's reference to his classroom as "the discipline stop" spoke to the disproportionate burden for discipline that he seemed to carry at his school. In Karl's view, his colleagues' overreliance on his disciplinary talents revealed a disregard for his own workload and failed to recognize his strengths in other aspects of teaching. Contrary to his view of himself as "probably the most effective teacher in the building," Karl sensed a narrow peer perception of him as an enforcer who could frighten ill-behaved students into submission. It was this perception that sometimes turned Karl's classroom into, in his words, "the discipline stop."

Another study participant who reported bearing a heavier load for disciplinary matters than his non-Black male colleagues was Greg. During a focus group session, Greg noted that a White female colleague consistently asked for his help with disciplining Black and Latino boys in her classroom. While Greg stated several times in his narrative that he did not mind assisting his colleagues with their classroom management issues, he did note during his final one-on-one interview that helping other teachers with disciplinary matters in their classrooms required him to "go into a zone" that he did not want to enter at times, particularly as his own students were usually well-behaved. This "zone" consisted of raising his voice and summoning facial expressions that would scare students, and it did not reflect who he truly was as a teacher and a person. As Greg noted of those moments, "I don't know what I look like, but I don't look like Mr. Poland because I don't feel like Mr. Poland." Thus, while Greg was willing to help colleagues with their discipline matters, he was also aware that doing so forced him to assume a persona that did not reflect his true demeanor as a teacher.

Like other study participants, Greg expressed his awareness of particular constructions of Black maleness that seemed to inform peer reliance on his disciplinary prowess. During a one-on-one interview, Greg

attributed his White colleagues' perceptions of him to common stereotypes of Black men:

> Well, I don't know if it's a positive stereotype, but it's a stereotype
> that all Black men can handle kids. You know, we're aggressive.
> We're the big, bad, Black, scary teacher. So I do get that, where a lot
> of the White teachers, if there's a problem going on in the classroom,
> they'll want me to handle it.

Greg also noted assumptions about Black male teachers among some
former Black female teacher colleagues, as captured in this excerpt from
a focus group session:

> I think they look at us as, in my own situation, as disciplinarians first.
> Like, you should be able to handle these kids. When I was teaching
> in a middle school, the female teachers would say—the Black ones
> would say—"Oh, we need some more Black men in here to handle
> these kids." And I would say, "Well, y'all not doing too bad a job
> right now," you know. [*Others: laughter*] But they just felt as though
> if there were more Black men, then we could handle more of the
> discipline. Other than the fact that, you know, we would be good
> role models, but I think that they look at me and other Black men as
> disciplinarians first, and then all the other things.

Greg later recalled that Black parents at that same middle school, assum-
ing the disciplinary prowess of Black men, used to vie for spots for their
children in Black male teachers' classrooms. Although Greg challenged
the notion that Black male teachers were the only ones who could "handle these kids," he still was aware of the enduring perception of Black
men in urban teaching as, in his words, "disciplinarians first."

One result of the heavy emphasis on discipline that Greg encountered
while teaching middle school was his decision to move to the elementary level. As he mentioned during a focus group session, becoming an
elementary teacher allowed him to focus much more on his actual pas-
sion for teaching:

> Being an elementary teacher, I absolutely love my job because I do
> my job every day. Ninety-eight percent of what I do is teaching.
> And that's one of the reasons why we become teachers, because
> we wanna teach kids. But when you have to deal with . . . you
> know, when I worked at [the middle school], it was like 80% of
> what I was doing was disciplining, and that was just not cool with
> me. So I put my foot down, but still I had to keep putting my foot
> down. But as an [elementary] teacher now, I do mostly teaching
> and I love it.

While many teachers may desire teaching assignments that do not require constant attention to disciplinary matters, not all of them perceive themselves as bearing a disproportionate responsibility for student discipline because of their racial and gender identities. In Greg's case, being seen as a "big, bad, Black, scary teacher" and a "disciplinarian first" drove him to look for teaching opportunities in spaces where those perceptions, while not absent, exerted less influence on his daily experiences as a Black male teacher.

While Greg and Karl problematized their status as schoolwide, disciplinary go-to men, a third participant, Damon, seemed both critical of and sympathetic toward that status. In a focus group session, Damon noted that while his disproportionate responsibility for student discipline was "unfortunate," it was also something that he had resigned himself to accept:

> I think as much as I don't wanna be the disciplinarian, I know that the kids will listen to me, even the ones that I don't teach. I kind of take on the role because there are some people who don't have management, that I need to kind of step up for. If my strength is the fact that I happen to be a Black male who has control over students, then I have to play that role, even if I don't want to. I have to be on my A-game because some kids, they will cause our whole little area to go amuck if I'm not there. It's unfortunate because there shouldn't be so much responsibility put on a Black male in the classroom just simply because we're Black males in the environments we teach in.

Although Damon ultimately complied with the discipline-related pressures he encountered as a Black male teacher, he still underscored a significant critique voiced by Greg and Karl as well. Despite seeing themselves as talented and caring instructors, these three men sensed a narrow peer reliance on them as enforcers of school disciplinary regimes, reflecting prevailing presumptions of Black male educators as naturally inclined disciplinarians. This limited view frustrated these men as schoolwide, discipline-related responsibilities encroached upon the time and energies spent on their teaching.

Black Male Teachers: Disciplining and Disciplined

Overall, eight participants offered critical perspectives on their struggles and/or frustrations with prevailing perceptions of Black male teachers as patriarchal, authoritarian disciplinarians. Working in a discipline-intensive urban school culture, the men cited thus far felt pressured to control student conduct by performing a very particular construction of Black masculinity in the classroom. For some, the dominant image of the stern Black male teacher clashed with their self-defined identities as teachers, and their struggles to conform to this image threatened their legitimacy in the eyes of colleagues and students. For others, this image demarked an essentialist lens among colleagues that overemphasized the disciplinary roles of Black male teachers. In all cases, these popular perceptions failed to fully recognize and accept study participants on their own terms as Black male teachers in the Brewerton School District.

The dissonance at times between how these men defined themselves as teachers and what others expected of them as Black men in urban teaching underscores one of the analytic premises of this book—the importance of interrogating how individual Black men agentically negotiate dominant constructions of Black male subjectivity. In this case, saviorist discourses on Black male teachers are the subject of interrogation. As I argued in Chapter 2, saviorist Black masculinity is frequently associated with a stern disciplinary authority that can save Black boys by preventing wayward behaviors and poor decision-making. Along with numerous representations of discipline-minded Black patriarchs across popular media (Chandler, 2013; Healey, 2012; Nigel, n.d.; Petok & Greener, 2001; Worley, 2011; Yorkin & Lear, 1974), saviorist discourses have positioned Black male educators as authoritative disciplinarians as well. Examples include films about tough Black male educators (Twain & Avildsen, 1989; Reynolds, 1997), television docu-series that enlist Black male educators as disciplinarians for Black students (Barbini & Kuntz, 2013; R. Brown & Armstead, 2012), and popular media coverage highlighting Black male teachers' disciplinary prowess with Black children (Byrd, 2014; Causey, n.d.; Matus, 2005; Nazaryan, 2015; Roberts, 2016; Taylor, 2016). Collectively, popular discourses have emphasized the central role of strong Black male disciplinarians in saving Black youth, and they have cast Black male teachers to star in that role.

Traces of these saviorist logics on Black male disciplinarians were evident across the narrative passages shared thus far, particularly from Victor, Bill, Karl, and Greg. These study participants described how their colleagues framed the authoritarian disciplinary practices of Black male teachers as essential for the educational success and social futures of Black students.

What becomes apparent, however, from the narrative excerpts reviewed in this chapter is that the emphasis on authoritarian discipline in saviorist discourses on Black male teachers did not accurately represent the nuanced perspectives of a number of the men in this study. From Victor, Bill, Quincy, Mitch, and Solomon, all of whom struggled at times to perform stern enactments of disciplinary authority, to Karl, Greg, and Damon, who bemoaned being pigeonholed by colleagues as "disciplinarians first," the men in this study confounded and critiqued the domineering disciplinary personas that others expected of them. This, of course, does not mean that all Black male teachers struggle to serve as strict disciplinary enforcers. In fact, as described earlier in this chapter, some study participants cited Black male colleagues in their schools who convincingly performed domineering disciplinary personas, and some described their own successful enactments of such personas as well. However, given the pressure for study participants to live up to authoritarian modes of disciplining, their narrative insights beg several important questions.

First, how might saviorist discourses, in effect, discipline Black male teachers into becoming domineering disciplinarians? I use "discipline" here to refer not just to the school-specific management of students, but to the more general processes of surveillance and punishment within systems of power that condition individuals to regulate their own behaviors and to view and understand themselves as regulated subjects (Foucault, 1995). With saviorist discourses, what appears as a validation of Black male teachers' innate abilities to manage Black students may also be a tool for forcing these men to conform to certain performances of masculinity and authority, lest they risk the opprobrium—or disciplining—of colleagues and students. The high stakes associated with controlling students' behaviors in Brewerton schools seemed to subject participants to this type of disciplinary surveillance. Across multiple narrative passages, the reactions of colleagues and students essentially policed participants' exercise of authority as acceptable or illegitimate. That this became a source of tension for such a range of study participants, from those who struggled to exhibit stern authority in the classroom to those who excelled at it, underscores the urgency to interrogate it further. Building on these study findings, future inquiries could illuminate how expectations of authoritarian enforcement—from popular discourses, from multiple stakeholder groups in urban schools, and from Black male teachers themselves—may discipline these teachers into conforming to a limited range of approaches to managing student behavior.

In addition to considering how Black male teachers may be disciplined by saviorist discourses and their reproduction of rigid disciplinary personas, future inquiries might also wrestle further with Black male teachers' roles in sustaining or troubling the broader, discipline-intensive milieu of urban schools. Numerous scholars have decried the reign of zero-tolerance policies in urban schools that have intensified the surveillance and criminalization of youth of color (E. R. Brown, 2003; Giroux, 2001; Lewis et al., 2010; Lipman, 2004; Skiba et al., 2011; Verdugo, 2002). As suggested in works by A. L. Brown (2012) and Ferguson (2000), and as echoed by several of the study participants quoted in this chapter, the Black male educator can easily be pegged in such spaces as an enforcer for racially punitive school disciplinary regimes. He is, in study participant Greg's words, "the big, bad, Black, scary teacher" whose Black masculine prowess can intimidate and subdue unruly Black children. In the discipline-intensive milieu of an urban school district like Brewerton's, how might the disciplinary practices of study participants and other Black male teachers exacerbate and/or disrupt the criminalization of students of color? Although the data collected for this study did not address this question directly, several narrative passages shared above did suggest that study participants found themselves in school settings where saving Black youth got reduced at times to controlling them. Consequently, some of the men in this study had to negotiate the tension between peer pressures to embrace authoritarian disciplinary practices and their own discomfort with dominating Black children. Given the high stakes associated with the implementation of zero-tolerance policies in Brewerton and other urban school districts across the United States, future research could look critically at the relationship between Black male teachers' disciplinary practices and the broader politics of race and discipline in urban education.

Finally, the insights on discipline from participants' narratives suggest the urgency for Black male teachers' own reckonings with their disciplinary identities and practices. That this study became a generative opportunity for thinking about classroom discipline underscored participants' desire to examine this topic, especially with other Black male teachers. Moving forward, future efforts by researchers, teacher education programs, and school districts to understand and support Black male teachers might consider the creation of spaces where these men can individually and collectively wrestle with their participation in the disciplinary cultures of urban schools. Such spaces could provide opportunities for Black male teachers to engage in deeper considerations of the pedagogical rationales for, and the affordances and constraints of, their approaches to discipline and classroom management. For instance, how might one's investment in culturally responsive pedagogy (Gay, 2010; Howard, 2001; Ladson-Billings, 2009; Monroe & Obidah, 2004), critical pedagogy (McLaren & Kincheloe, 2007), or another pedagogical camp shape the theory behind and execution of his disciplinary practices? What affordances and constraints accompany different approaches to classroom management and discipline rooted in different pedagogies? How might strategies like incentives (Kohn, 1993) or positive behavioral supports (Reinke, Herman, & Stormont, 2013) inform one's overall approach to discipline? And how might one's positionality as a Black man mediate whatever disciplinary strategies he engages in the classroom? These questions point to the types of deliberation that could enable Black male teachers to intentionally craft their own strategies for classroom discipline instead of merely responding to external pressures to perform the authoritarian disciplinary personas associated with a saviorist Black masculinity.

The Politics of Surrogate Fatherhood

The pressures facing the men in this study to operate as stern disciplinarians speak to an even larger cultural project driving the recruitment of Black male teachers. In Chapter 2, I reviewed a wide range of sources that have attributed the plight of Black boys to the absence of Black men from Black families and communities. Against this backdrop, Black male teachers have been imagined as saviorist surrogates in the lives of Black youth, especially Black boys. Not only are these men summoned to perform the hegemonic masculinity required to manage and discipline Black boys, but they are also expected to serve as father figures who can uplift these boys by modeling a responsible and caring Black manhood. The expectations for Black men in teaching to act as surrogate fathers, much like the expectations surrounding their disciplinary identities and practices, are pervasive but underexplored. Given the high stakes and high hopes attached to Black male teachers' father figure status, it is crucial for scholarly analyses to delve deeper into the politics of surrogate fatherhood for Black men in the American teaching profession.

To that end, the narratives of the men in this study provided rich and nuanced insights into what it might mean for Black male teachers to serve as father figures for Black students. Echoing depictions elsewhere of the fatherly and role model statuses of Black male educators, six participants pointed to deep emotional connections with Black male students as highly meaningful aspects of their work. Those connections are explored in depth in Chapter 7. But in addition to citing their special bonds with Black male students, the men in this study also revealed palpable anxieties surrounding the responsibility to serve as father figures—anxieties that have not been fully investigated to date in the scholarship on Black men in teaching. Two particular challenges emerged across participant narratives: Seven men expressed their own ambivalence towards the extra-pedagogical responsibilities associated with the role of father figure, and four described student resistance to the paternal nature of their teacher authority.

These themes are explored in this second half of Chapter 4.

"Not in My Job Description": The Extra-Pedagogical Responsibilities of the Father Figure

Across a number of participants' narrative accounts, the role of the father figure was associated with levels of personal and emotional engagement with students that did not always fit into participants' understandings of their responsibilities as teachers. Contrary to scholarly and media depictions of Black male educators' readiness and eagerness to serve in this capacity for Black students, seven of the 11 participants in this study articulated bounded conceptions of their job descriptions at times that questioned or eschewed what they marked as the extra-pedagogical responsibilities of being a father figure. These participant perspectives are explored in this section.

One of the participants who expressed a bounded conceptualization of his role as a teacher was Oliver. After describing Black students' resentment towards male teachers because of the absence of their fathers, Oliver explained in a one-on-one interview that he did not venture into discussions of such issues with his students because, in his words, "I think you get into areas that may get very dangerous. It's not in my job description. I don't feel I'm trained to do that." Situating personal and emotional investments in students' lives beyond the domain of his job description, Oliver articulated strict boundaries that precluded discussions about absentee fathers and Black students' other personal dilemmas for which he felt unaccountable as a teacher.

Similar sentiments emerged during a focus group session as participants were asked about popular perceptions of Black male teachers as father figures for Black boys. In his response, Victor pushed back against these perceptions by asserting the need for more mental health support for his Black male students, and not just more Black male teachers:

> I've been recently reflecting, looking at my male students. In addition to just having Black male teachers, we need mental health support. *[Others: Mmm-hmm]* I mean the issues that particularly a lot of my young Black males are dealing with, I can't help them. Even when you try to get rapport with like "what's wrong with you, son?," they just put all this against you. So even though I'm there, it's like I'm not even there. The ones that are real problematic, that I really wanna try to reach, or maybe . . . I don't know. I'm just at my wit's end. I send them to the counselor. And even then, that's not helping really because it's a large school, [large number of] kids and [small number of] counselors.

In this excerpt, Victor challenged presumptions of a father—son rapport between Black male teachers and Black boys by describing his limited capacity as a Black male educator to help these boys process their anger and other emotional issues that manifested in school.

Victor's remark sparked similar comments in the focus group from Oliver and Greg:

Victor: So you got across the gamut, all these issues [that boys are dealing with].

Oliver: But don't you think it's too much of a demand placed on the teacher to deal with all these issues?

Greg: Oh, I agree. I agree.

All: [*Inaudible, talking over each other*]

Victor: Yeah, but if we had some mental health help. . .

Greg: Some *serious* help, not just the school psychologist once or twice a week.

Victor: Right. Sessions, where these boys could go.

Greg: They come to school with all this baggage and then they look at us and say "well why isn't he learning?" You say, "well first of all, we have to unpack this baggage, figure out why he can't or she can't focus," you know. And that's a tough job to do, and I don't think as a teacher I should have to do that.

Oliver: I don't feel qualified to do that. And I think trying to unpack the baggage might do more harm than good . . . in some cases.

Responding to popular perceptions of Black male teachers as father figures for Black youth, the teachers in this exchange challenged the presumption that they could or should be able to mitigate the effects of the deep psychological scars exhibited by some of their Black male students. Along with bemoaning the lack of psychological support services made available to students in their school district, these men were also asserting the boundaries of their responsibilities as Black male educators.

Another participant who asserted the limits of his duties as a teacher was Mitch. When asked if he saw himself as a father figure for his Black male students, Mitch replied that he preferred a measure of distance from students that precluded the type of personal connections he associated with the father figure role. Declaring that "my job is to teach," Mitch distinguished his teaching duties from the willingness to probe into students' personal lives, which he ascribed to a school counselor. He then went on to suggest that he was more like a "cool uncle" than a father:

Mitch: I'm the cool uncle, that's what I am. I'm the cool uncle that you kind of wanna go hang out with, but you know he's still your uncle, and he still treats you like you're the child and you're the nephew. You guys might go out and play basketball and have fun together, and do all that kind of stuff. But if you do something that you're not supposed to do, he's still gonna correct you about it.

Ed: But uncle as opposed to father because. . . ?

Mitch: There's a much closer connection with a father. You go to your father for a lot of things that you're not gonna come to me about. And if you do, I will stop you immediately and say "do you need to go to the counselor? Because if what you're saying is what I think you're gonna say, then you need to go to the counselor." Honestly I could be that person, but I just . . . that's not me. I don't wanna deal with those types of things. It's a much greater investment emotionally and personally than I'm willing to undertake.

In this exchange, Mitch envisioned himself as an authority figure—the cool uncle—who maintained a studied distance from the more intimate details of students' private lives. The greater personal and emotional investment that Mitch associated with the father figure did not fit into his definition of his role as a teacher.

Like Mitch, Bill was another study participant who distanced himself from serving as a father figure. As noted earlier in this chapter, Bill was critical of the "belt dad" enactments of Black masculinity that were expected of him by some of his colleagues. Elaborating further on how he defined his role as a Black male teacher, Bill distinguished his teacherly duties from those associated with a parent. The latter, for Bill, entailed providing lessons on how to respect adults and behave properly—lessons for which he did not feel responsible as a teacher:

> Generally, this is the culminating statement. I'll spend half a class period trying to get kids to be quiet. You know, I'll have kids cussing me out and all this kind of stuff. And it's like, by the end I'm like "look, I'm not here to raise you. I'm not here to raise you. I'm trying to teach you something. If you don't have an interest in getting it, if you don't wanna be here, especially if you don't know how to be respectful enough to me, then I don't know how in this point in your life to instill respect for adults in you, if no one has been telling you to be respectful to adults for the first 14 years of your life. If no one has told you that you have to respect your teacher, or you have to respect authority figures." And there've been times when I've had to say to kids, you know, "I don't know what your parents taught you, if they taught you anything, but someone along the line should have taught you. And I'm not that person who is supposed to teach you from the beginning to respect your teachers." And I think some people would disagree with that. That in a lot of ways, teachers are supposed to be kind of moral upbringers. My job should not be to teach you how to behave, I don't feel. I don't feel like my job is to teach you how to behave.

In this excerpt, Bill attributed disrespectful student behavior to a lack of parenting ("I don't know what your parents taught you, if they taught you anything . . .") and eschewed responsibility for filling that parental void. Associating "raising" with instilling respect for teachers and other adults, Bill situated his job duties beyond the potentially muddied and contested terrains of a fatherly or parental role—one that would require him to enforce compliance in otherwise intractable students. Contrary to others' perceptions of teachers as "moral upbringers," Bill expressed his reticence in this passage to assume a parental responsibility for teaching good behavior.

Like the teachers referenced thus far in this discussion, two other study participants provided perspectives on the boundaries of their roles and responsibilities as Black male teachers. One was Quincy, who expressed notable ambivalence towards the prospect of serving as a father figure:

> Even though I always say "I'm not your father," for some kids that's the way they react to me because I'm that Black figure. And whether they have a father or don't, they still try to figure out, "Well what role is he playing in my life?" So because of that, sometimes I feel responsible in that role of trying to model one way that a Black male can be, or Black male role model, Black male father figure, whatever you wanna call it—mentor, whatever—can be. On the other hand, I feel a little overwhelmed, like why should I have to when there should be a lot of other folks doing the job?

Despite reassuring his students that he was not trying to be their father, Quincy sensed that some of them still precariously positioned him as such. While he felt motivated at times to take on this role, he also felt overwhelmed by it and, ultimately, not primarily responsible for it.

Ira, another study participant who acknowledged his status as a role model for urban Black students at several points throughout his narrative, also expressed slightly mixed feelings towards serving as a father figure:

> I don't totally welcome it [the expectation to be a father figure]. But at the same time, I don't view it as unfair either. I just look at it as part of the reality of teaching urban kids.
>
> You do have single mothers trying to raise boys who are impressionable with the ills in their community, and they do desire some African American male presence. It's just a reality, so I don't shun it, I don't look at it as unfair. [But] I'm not trying to step outside the box; I'm not trying to go too far. I'm not going to be Joe Clark knocking on your door. I'm not doing that, unless I feel it's totally serious, like red light, emergency, that kind of thing. But I haven't gotten to that point yet. But here, calling parents, requesting if it's okay to sit down and talk to a student about issues. I've been there. But definitely not like, "I'm going to pick you up and take you to a ball game" kind of approach.

In this passage, Ira revealed that he was certainly aware of and sensitive to the social and cultural circumstances of Black urban life that fueled public desires for Black male teachers to serve as father figures. However, in contrast to the popular cinematic depiction of Joe Clark in *Lean on Me* (Twain & Avildsen, 1989), Ira, like other men in this study, had clear limits to how much he would take on as a potential father figure for his students.

All of the participants referenced in the preceding discussion provided insights into the boundaries they imposed on their roles and responsibilities as Black male teachers. Repeated utterances of "not my job" or "not in my job description" underscored participants' assertions that it was not their professional charge to contend with the potentially messy emotional, psychological, and behavioral spillover from students' personal lives. Together, the narrative passages discussed revealed an important ambivalence towards a central hope within popular discourses on Black male teachers: the willingness of these men to serve Black children by blurring the boundaries between classroom pedagogue and surrogate Black patriarch.

"You Ain't My Daddy!": Student Resistance to Black Male Teacher Authority

Study participants' reticence toward serving as father figures was not the only obstacle to their potential status as such. Idealized perceptions of Black male teachers as father figures belied the struggles that could complicate study participants' encounters with Black students, especially during moments of disciplinary enforcement. Contrary to pervasive expectations of Black student responsiveness to Black male father figures, four participants cited their paternal-like, authoritative status as the very cause for student backlash. As revealed in the narrative excerpts that follow, Black student resistance to study participants' authority challenged presumptions of these men as ready-made father figures for Black youth.

One participant who spoke to this theme was Victor. In the following narrative excerpt, Victor contrasted student compliance with women teachers to student resistance to his authority, noting the striking choice of words used by students to articulate the latter:

> Our kids are used to the mother nurturing more so than they are to male nurturing, if I could just put it that way. So even when I'm trying to nurture kids, often it can be more easily rejected. But with a female—or when I say nurturing, maybe even admonishing a kid— the response is going to be different when a female does it, particularly if she's a Black woman. It's just going to be a different dynamic. Particularly with the boys, because they'll get the defensive "you're not my father, you're not . . ." But when a woman nurtures them, it's more "okay, well, she could be my mother. She's not my mother, but she could be my mother." But with the male, with me, it's clear. "You're not my father." You get that response readily.

For Victor, "you're not my father" signaled the divide between, on the one hand, his students' acceptance of Black women teachers' mother-like authority and, on the other, their resistance to him as a male authority figure. Later in his narrative, Victor offered a further explanation of the resistance he received during such moments:

Victor: Well, in the beginning of the year with me and my boys, most of the time everything is just kinda cool. First of all, some of them are kind of like in awe because they may not have had that many male teachers before. So it's like, "It's cool, we got a male teacher." After the honeymoon rubs off with the boys, particularly when you start setting limits and parameters, then tensions will start arising. Tensions will start arising with the boys. "You ain't my father!" This whole notion that "you ain't my father!" And you treat them like your kids, [but] this whole tension with the "you're not my father" kind of thing goes on with the boys more so than with the girls.

Ed: And what's that about?

Victor: What it's about is, the ones that are saying it in most cases lack a father. So because of the lack of the father, "You ain't my father, my father ain't here, you don't have nothing to say to me. Leave me the f . . . alone. My mom is the one that is doing everything, and I don't really have nothing to do with you men folks because my father wasn't around." I have less tension with the boys that have their fathers. There'll be normal tensions, but it's not like "you're not my father" tensions. It's more like "I'm a man, you're a man." It's more a man tension. They won't say "you're not my father."

In this exchange, Victor revealed that while tensions with Black boys were not limited to those who did not have fathers, the absence of father figures in some students' home lives marked a crucial distinction in his assessment. For Victor, "you're not my father" reflected the psychological and emotional baggage of Black boys who were struggling to deal with absent father figures in their lives. That this retort arose as he attempted to establish the parameters of his classroom environment suggests that the father figure, for his students, may have been a loaded framework for processing adult male authority. Despite his willingness to "treat them like [his] kids," Victor reported that his classroom management-related interactions with some Black male students foundered under the symbolic weight of surrogate Black fatherhood.

The potential baggage associated with the Black father figure was described by another participant, Quincy. Like Victor, Quincy reported that some students responded to his teacherly authority by saying "you ain't my daddy." In the following passage, Quincy explained how such moments transpired:

There were situations when I was like, "You need to sit down" or "you need to calm down and stop doing that." And they'd be like,

"You can't talk to me like that, my dad doesn't tell me what to do. You ain't my daddy, you can't tell me what to do." And some of them, I didn't know what their relationship was with their dad, if their dad lived with them or whatever. But to me, eventually I just had to let them know, "Whatever relationship you and your dad have is fine. I'm not trying to make any plans or changes or anything like that. But you're in this classroom, you gotta follow the rules of this classroom. So if you don't like that, that's fine, but we're going to have some problems. And whether or not you want your dad to come up here and talk to me about that. . ." "Well, my dad's gonna beat you." "Well, that's fine. Bring your dad up here; we'll deal with that when we come to that bridge. That may be. Your dad maybe has killed three people, I don't know, that's fine. But the point is, when you're in here, you gotta follow the rules of the classroom, and if you don't like the rules of the classroom, you gotta find somewhere else to go, and I'll make sure that we can figure some way to make that happen."

In this narrative excerpt, "you ain't my daddy" operated as a student counterstance to Quincy's authority as a teacher. It was when Quincy attempted to assert control over and set limits within the classroom that "you ain't my daddy" challenged his right to do so. Not only did this retort seek to discredit Quincy's authority by excluding him from the father figure role, but it was also followed by a threat to subject him to the wrath of the legitimate occupant of this role, the student's actual father. In his quest to establish dominion over his classroom, Quincy thus faced two challenges: student defiance of the legitimacy of his fatherly authority, and the threatened confrontations with other patriarchs. Both challenges underscored the complicated and contentious politics associated with the role of the prospective father figure.

Similar tensions around the paternal-like authority of Black male teachers surfaced in Oliver's narrative. For Oliver, urban Black family and community contexts proved key in explaining the student antagonism he witnessed:

I think female teachers don't have it as difficult as male teachers because a lot of these children are accustomed to having female authority figures. They're brought up by their grandmothers or their aunts or their mothers. So when a male figure tells the students to do something, they wanna know, "Well who are you to tell me to do something?" You know, that's the feedback I get. They're so accustomed to having women tell them to do things and following the instructions of women, whether it be their grandmother or whatever, because the father's not there. The father's absent. So all of a sudden it's 'who is this man telling me to do something, when I've never had a man telling me to do something before?"

In Oliver's view, his Black students' familiarity with women authority figures in their families, along with their resentment towards absent father figures, produced a resistance to his authority in the classroom—one that was not commonly experienced by his women counterparts. This excerpt provided yet another example of the animosity towards patriarchal Black male authority that, in the eyes of some participants, seemed to complicate their roles as adult Black male figures in the classroom.

Echoing other participants, Mitch also contrasted students' compliance with female teachers to their defiance of male teachers like himself. While describing his interactions with Black male students, Mitch noted,

> There's certain nuances you have to deal with with boys, especially as they start to smell themselves. And then they wanna be the cub trying to assert his authority, and you gotta rough him up a little bit and remind him he's still a cub.

Mitch used "smell themselves," a colloquialism for a sense of overconfidence, to describe a burgeoning cockiness among some male students that led to masculinist struggles for power in his classroom—struggles that led him to subdue those students by reminding them of their "cub" status. He went on to assert that such power struggles emerged specifically in response to male teachers and not their female colleagues, whose mother-like qualities seemed to make their authority more palatable for Black boys:

> If there's any particular thing they'll do, it's that the boys when they start, I don't know, growing pubic hair, get really buck and stuff. That's the only thing that I feel like is a universal thing, is that they will buck at a man before they buck at a woman. Which I think is another reason why certain things are successful for women in [classroom] management that aren't successful for men. The whole going off on a kid and like kind of just taking it over the deep end with the kid can work for a woman because a mother can do that. And they're kind of like, "Uuuugh, she's always gettin' on my nerves." But you just do it. You deal with it. Mothers nag, they do that.

Drawing upon longstanding comparisons of women teachers to mothers allowed Mitch to explain boys' deference to his female colleagues. In his own case, however, Mitch felt that being a male teacher made him the target of the burgeoning egos and masculinist competitiveness—or "bucking"—of his pubescent male students. Although Mitch did not make specific references here to his potential father figure status, his descriptions of male students' antagonisms toward him versus their acceptance of mother-like women teachers echo other participants' accounts of the contested nature of their paternal authority.

From boys "smelling themselves" to the possibility of fisticuffs with students' fathers, the preceding accounts offered examples of the some-times-precarious nature of study participants' authority over their students. For the teachers quoted in this section, student compliance with women teachers and student defiance of male instructors marked two important obstacles to the legitimacy of their authority: the predominance of women authority figures in the lives of their Black students, and the emotional and psychological resentment harbored by some Black students towards absent fathers. Contrary to the popular presumption of a culturally mediated rapport between Black male teachers and their Black students, the participants cited in this discussion revealed that their potential status as Black male father figures, rather than endearing them to their students, could trigger a palpable and problematic disconnect with the Black youth in their classrooms. These insights suggest the need for more critical examinations of the politics of surrogate fatherhood.

Discipline, Surrogate Fatherhood, and the Re-Masculinization of Urban Schools

As previously noted, the dual pressures for Black male teachers to serve as stern disciplinarians and surrogate father figures for Black youth are part of a larger cultural project. Both roles have repeatedly emerged in saviorist discourses that underscore the urgent need for Black male teachers who can discipline and uplift Black students, especially boys, in the relative absence of adult male role models in Black homes and communities. Since disciplining and fathering are linked to the same saviorist project, it makes sense that references to both overlapped in participants' narratives. From Bill's use of "belt dad" to identify authoritarian modes of discipline to reports of some students' use of "you ain't my daddy" to resist participants' disciplinary practices, several examples throughout this chapter illustrated the potentially paternal nature of disciplinary authority and the potentially disciplinary nature of surrogate fatherhood. Whether as disciplinarians, father figures, or some combination of both, study participants faced pressures as Black men in urban schools to establish and assert patriarchal control over their classrooms.

Both sections of this chapter captured some of the tensions associated with the patriarchal nature of study participants' positionalities as Black male teachers. One way to fully grasp the significance of those tensions is to view them through critical scholarly lenses on the re-masculinization of schools. Other scholars, as cited in Chapter 1, have troubled recurrent attempts to transform schools into spaces that more effectively reproduce hegemonic masculinity in boys vis-à-vis the influx of male teachers (S. Johnson, 2008; W. J. Martino, 2008; Sternod, 2011; Weiler, 1989). Applying that scholarship as an analytic lens to this chapter, the power struggles between study participants and Black boys can be understood as a product of that re-masculinization project. While positioning Black male teachers as father figures, masculine role models, and patriarchal authority figures may inspire some students, this study suggests that it may spark masculinist struggles for power with others. Fodder for this claim can be found in participants' accounts of Black male students' defiance of their authority, as well as in their descriptions of their own reassertions of patriarchal and masculine power over those students. The language used to describe these moments—"you're not my father," "remind him he's a cub," "my dad's gonna beat you"—further corroborates the masculinist nature of these power struggles. Across the narrative excerpts referenced in this chapter, study participants' enactments of patriarchal authority seemed to antagonize rather than inspire some of the Black boys in their classrooms.

Placing these study findings in conversation with the scholarship on the re-masculinization of schools may prove generative in at least two ways. First, it can underscore how study participants were positioned as agents of a much larger cultural project to re-masculinize schools. The review of saviorist discourses in Chapter 2 laid the groundwork for understanding the masculinity work expected of Black male teachers, and the narrative excerpts in Chapter 3 recounted how the teachers in this study were called upon by saviorist discourses to engage in that masculinity work. This chapter, like others to follow, goes a step further by describing particular aspects of study participants' masculinist participation in Brewerton schools, thus illustrating how these men were actually situated within a broader re-masculinization project.

Additionally, and perhaps even more importantly, aligning this study's findings with the re-masculinization scholarship can shed light on the threat of conflict, sometimes violent in nature, that may accompany attempts to situate and showcase masculine role models in schools. As context, masculinity's association with competition, invincibility, domination, and violence has been examined in the broader field of masculinity studies (Connell, 2002; Kimmel, 2013) and in masculinity studies scholarship in education (Kehler, 2009; Pascoe, 2007; Stoudt, 2006). Unfortunately, these critical perspectives on masculinity are generally absent from saviorist discourses on Black male teachers. Likewise, with exceptions like the previous iterations of my work (Brockenbrough, 2012a, 2012b, 2015), and works by Brown (2011, 2012) and Woodson and Pabon (2016), much of the scholarship on Black men in the American teaching profession has yet to fully engage these perspectives. From boys "bucking" and saying, "you're not my father, leave me the f . . . alone" to teachers engaging in in-class stand-offs with defiant students, this chapter highlighted masculinist confrontations with Black male students that challenged study participants' patriarchal authority and masculine credibility. While the descriptions of these confrontations were troubling, they also were not terribly surprising given the expectations that study participants faced to dominate students, especially Black boys. Instructing study participants to function as hypermasculine enforcers over Black boys within an already confrontational, discipline-intensive school district arguably inflamed the conditions for study participants' power struggles with Black male students. By engaging critical lenses on masculinity—lenses that recognize and trouble masculinity's association with domination and violence—scholars, school districts, and Black male teachers themselves can start to rethink how Black men are positioned within American K–12 schools.

Any attempts to rethink the positionalities of Black male teachers also must interrogate the complex politics of surrogate fatherhood. While this study provides a compelling warrant for thinking further about the father figure status of Black male teachers, it does not offer a clear conclusion on what the fate of that status should be. As discussed later in Chapter 7, six of the men in this study described deep connections to Black male students that mirrored scholarly and popular media depictions of Black male teachers as father figures. By contrast, the findings shared in this chapter indicated that study participants' paternal classroom presence was a possible trigger for some Black boys who were struggling to manage the absence of fathers in their lives. Add the ambivalence expressed by some of the men in this study toward being seen as surrogate fathers, and the potential fatherly status of Black male teachers becomes even murkier.

In the absence of clear conclusions on if and how to position men like my study participants as father figures, several questions come to mind that may guide future inquiries. For instance, what does it actually mean for a Black male teacher to serve as a father figure? What is the goal of this role, and what responsibilities come with it? How does it resemble or diverge from the role of a teacher, and how does it resemble or diverge from the roles of other father figures in students' lives? What are the constraints and affordances of situating father figures specifically within schools that may or may not align with the values and worldviews of students' families and communities? Given the dilemmas that were the focus of this chapter, how can Black male teachers serve as father figures without reproducing the patriarchal authoritarianism, hegemonic masculinity, and racially punitive disciplinary surveillance that are prescribed for Black men in urban schools? Also, how can Black male teachers serve as father figures not only for Black boys, but for other students as well? Thinking about supports, what are teacher education programs and school districts doing to help Black male teachers think about and negotiate their potential roles as father figures, and what should these institutions do when Black male teachers, like some of the participants in this study, cannot or will not fully assume that role in their students' lives? These are but a few of the questions that speak to the need for further and deeper deliberations on the politics of surrogate fatherhood for Black men in urban teaching.

How future discussions will unfold around the father figure status of Black male teachers is uncertain. There is, however, one critical insight from this study that clearly deserves consideration in those discussions: study participants' plea for more mental health supports for their students. This plea emerged in a focus group after participants were asked to discuss their potential roles as father figures for Black boys. Echoing scholarly critiques of the reliance on Black male role models to address structural inequities in the lives of Black youth (Jackson et al., 2013; James, 2012; W. Martino & Rezai-Rashti, 2012), participants in one of the focus groups for this study pushed back against the pressure for Black male teachers to heal students' emotional and psychological wounds, asserting instead that these issues warranted the services of mental health professionals. This critique of the lack of mental health supports in urban schools must not be overlooked. Whether Black male teachers take on or eschew forms of emotional support that some associate with fathering, that support cannot be in lieu of additional services from trained counselors and other mental health specialists.

While it is difficult to imagine widespread objections, at least in principle, to supporting students through the provision of in-school counseling professionals, it is not so difficult to anticipate pushback against many of the other implications that have emerged from this analysis. As I argued toward the end of Chapter 2, saviorist discourses on Black male teachers reflect how the epistemological nature of recuperative Black masculinity politics has come to define the very meaning of knowledge production about Black maleness in some strands of scholarship and popular discourse. Against that backdrop, the construct of the Black male teacher as a strong disciplinarian and father figure for Black students is rooted in deeply held beliefs about what it means to be a Black man, and what it means for Black men to work with Black children. To question his role as a stern authoritarian or his responsibility as a paternal surrogate may seem naïve, and possibly even dubious, to proponents of a saviorist Black masculinity. But in the end, my hope is that readers will listen first and foremost to the voices of the men who participated in this study. They were the ones who challenged prevailing expectations of their disciplinary personas, and they were the ones who complicated popular perceptions of themselves as father figures for Black students. Their willingness to speak their truths deserves to be taken seriously.

Conclusion

This chapter was the first to delve directly into the dilemmas of saviorist Black masculinity politics that emerged in study participants' narratives. Addressing widespread perceptions of Black male teachers as tough and abled disciplinarians, several men in my study described their struggles at times to adopt authoritarian disciplinary personas, and they noted how such struggles could lead peers and students to question their legitimacy and belonging as Black men working in Brewerton schools. Some participants also expressed frustrations with other teachers' reliance on them as Black male adults to act as schoolwide disciplinarians—a burden that encroached upon the time and energy spent by study participants on their own teaching. Despite popular discourses that presume and laud Black male teachers' natural disciplinary prowess, the preceding narrative excerpts troubled the hegemonic masculinity and brutish authoritarianism expected of study participants as Black men in discipline-intensive urban schools. The critiques that emerged in this chapter from analyzing participants' narratives may help to frame further deliberations over supporting Black male teachers' participation in urban schools without requiring them to control children by embodying domineering and potentially violent forms of Black masculinity.

Along with challenging popular presumptions of Black male teachers as disciplinary enforcers, this chapter also troubled saviorist discourses that imagine these men as father figures for Black youth. Repeated utterances of "not my job" or "not in my job description" across multiple study participants' narratives underscored a palpable ambivalence toward the blurred boundaries between classroom pedagogue and surrogate Black father. Likewise, "you ain't my daddy" and similar sentiments attributed to students indicated the psychological and emotional baggage that could complicate participants' status as father figures. While not precluding the possibilities of Black male teachers' father-like roles in the lives of Black youth, the analyses offered in this chapter suggest the need for much deeper considerations of the murkiness and complexities of the father figure role for Black men in urban teaching. Those considerations may become more likely if we question the saviorist logics shaping popular beliefs about Black male teachers.

Note

1. James Evans was the strict but loving Black father in the 1970s sitcom *Good Times* (Yorkin & Lear, 1974). Routinely, James would reach for his belt to signal a forthcoming spanking when his children disobeyed him.

5 Patriarchy Meets Women's Work

Encountering Female Power in the Workplace

The masculinity politics that pervade this book cannot be fully understood without exploring their fraught relationship to womanhood. Several examples of that relationship have already surfaced. As discussed in Chapter 1, the predominance of women in the American teaching profession by the early 20th century sparked subsequent calls to recruit male teachers to re-masculinize schools, and, as noted in Chapter 2, the profession's enduring image as women's work remains a barrier to those recruitment efforts. Also noted in Chapter 2, the prevalence of single-mother-headed households in Black communities is one factor fueling saviorist appeals for more Black men to enter teaching. And in Chapter 4, several men in my study cited pressures from Black women colleagues to be stern disciplinarians for Black students, while also noting students' greater receptiveness to women teachers' motherly disciplinary personas. Together, these moments from the preceding chapters underscore the inextricable links between the masculinity work of male teachers and the enduring—and at times resented—presence of women. To make sense of the narratives of the men in this study, we must also make sense of the complicated specter of womanhood.

To that end, this chapter revolves primarily around the following question: What happens when Black male teachers, dutifully answering saviorist appeals to embody and perform patriarchal modes of manhood in the classroom, encounter the gendered power dynamics and participatory politics of a predominantly female field? This question remains under-explored in the extant scholarship and popular media focus on Black men in urban teaching, and as this chapter reveals, that inattention may be a huge disservice to Black male teachers and their women colleagues. After a brief note on the sensitive nature of the data shared in this chapter, the analyses that follow are organized around three themes: study participants' inattention to male privilege; their conflictual encounters with women in the workplace; and their desire for more male-centered spaces and interactions. By exploring these themes, this chapter makes a critical scholarly contribution by highlighting the tensions in participants' narratives between patriarchal constructions of Black man-hood and participation in the women-centered professional spheres of teaching.

Gender Talk: Surveying Sensitive Terrains

After reflecting honestly and openly on male-female power dynamics dur-ing his first one-on-one interview for this study, Victor began his second interview by expressing apprehension about some of his prior remarks. As he stated:

Victor: [After the last interview,] the gender piece was like still resonat-ing with me. And I mean, in the interview, I hope I didn't say anything insensitive or anything like that, but also like, I'm still more keen . . . I guess I'm still struggling with the dynamic of the gender issues in the school because the profession is domi-nated, you know, there are more women teachers, administra-tors. And then you know, here I'm a male in that context. And then even the dynamics that I have with my students, vis-à-vis the dynamics, the interactions that they have with their female teachers. So that's an area that I'm just spending more time on my own just thinking about how it plays out, how the gender plays out in the classroom and in my practice and stuff. So that stuck with me from the interview.

Ed: I'm curious, though, what do you mean when you say you hope you didn't say anything insensitive in the first one?

Victor: Because sometimes I can just, you know, in speaking my mind or whatever . . . not insensitive or whatever, but did I really hit, did I really hit the issue.

Ed: Was there a particular theme that you thought, "Oh, that might cause . . ."

Victor: I was talking about the male body part and. . .

Ed: That a man has a penis [*chuckle*].

Victor: Yeah, and girls are like different. And it's not a racial thing, it's just . . . but, I'm still struggling with it myself. Maybe because I'm still struggling with that aspect myself. The racial piece I'm not really struggling with. It is what it is. Ok, we got racism and all those facets that we deal with, but I don't struggle with that at all. I mean, it's there and I know it's there, maybe I've just learned to deal with it. But this, the gender piece, male-female piece, I guess I'm still struggling with it.

Victor's concern regarding the reception of some of his comments served as an important reminder of the sensitive nature of gender rela-tions in teaching. Many of the excerpts throughout this chapter will show

how some participants spoke in frank terms about the challenges of being men in the predominantly female workplace of schools. As a researcher, I was intrigued by the gendered lens that such commentary afforded on participants' navigation of urban schools as Black men. However, Victor's remarks underscored the potential risks that he and other participants in the study were taking by addressing gender dynamics so forthrightly. Like other male teachers, the participants in this study were working in spaces where they were often outnumbered by female colleagues and sometimes supervised by female administrators. The perspectives that are explored in this chapter reveal that for some of the men in this study, negotiating the gendered participatory politics of the teaching realm was a complicated endeavor.

Despite some of the provocative language and views that surface in this chapter, none of the teachers in this study, from my standpoint as a researcher, addressed gender differences in an intentionally malicious manner. Their decisions to offer candid accounts on women in the workplace seemed due primarily to their need to voice their perspectives, and partially to my success in creating comfortable spaces for doing so. As this chapter's analysis unfolds, I hope that readers will appreciate the willingness of the men in this study to offer honest and thought-provoking perspectives on how they experienced gender dynamics with their women colleagues. I also hope that the study participants themselves, along with other readers, will see the analyses in this chapter as unique opportunities to consider how to more strategically negotiate possible tensions between male and female teachers in American K–12 schools.

The Inattention to Male Privilege

Data collection procedures for this study provided opportunities for participants to trace the salience of identity categories across the multiple spatial and temporal contexts of their life experiences. As participants' experiential narratives began to unfold in initial one-on-one life history interviews, seven of the men in this study expressed perspectives on gender identity that revealed a similar inattention to their access to male privilege. These perspectives are highlighted in the narrative excerpts that follow, and they provide an illuminating backdrop for later accounts of participants' negotiations of gender in the predominantly female domain of teaching.

The salience of Blackness and Black masculinity proved critical in producing a blind eye to male privilege among the men in this study. Six participants—Bill, Damon, Karl, Mitch, Quincy, and Solomon—viewed Blackness and sometimes Black maleness as the key determinants of their marginalized positionalities in society at large. Stressing the importance of Blackness and Black maleness as consequential markers of difference, all six attributed less significance to maleness alone as an identity category or a potential source of power. The following brief excerpts from individual participant narratives illustrate this pattern:

Quincy: I don't tend to think about being male in the abstract sense because when I'm walking around, I guess society as a whole views males as the main thing. So I could be wearing a dress and that could confuse them, but I'm still Black, you know what I'm saying.

Damon: I think that being Black is bigger than being a male. Because I feel like as much as there's gender bias and et cetera, et cetera, ultimately, no matter what I am, you can physically look at me, automatically [snaps finger], "Black. He's Black."

Karl: I think being a Black or African American person is something that stands alone outside of the actual gender issue. I feel like being a Black person in America, that usually comes before gender. [I identify as] "Black" and then "Black male."

Bill: I think about sexist theory and how, you know . . . but I don't think I think about my maleness. I don't think about it as being an advantage or disadvantage. I just don't think I think about it.

Solomon: Whereas the Blackness puts me in a state of less power, the maleness puts me in a state of more power. So I'm not as concerned about my maleness.

Mitch: Culture [i.e., being Black] is something I think about a lot more, and it's much more a salient topic personally than gender is to me.

These comments capture a recurring theme throughout the narratives of the six participants. In contrast to the prominence of Blackness and Black maleness in their identities and racialized worldviews, little to no attention was devoted to maleness as an independent category of identity. Although the White supremacist surveillance of racial differences heightened these men's awareness of their Blackness and Black maleness as axes of marginalization, their access to male privilege generally received minimal attention as they articulated their worldviews and sense of selves as Black men in America.

In addition to a relative inattentiveness to maleness as a source of power among the six participants, two participants articulated frameworks for understanding gender differences that seemed to further occlude potential critiques of male privilege. One of those participants was Mitch. While explaining his views on gender during his first study interview, Mitch noted that "liberated women" tended to object to his more traditional desire to date women who were willing to cook. When asked to elaborate on this, Mitch provided the following overview of the functionality of gender roles:

> I think that gender roles are a necessity to society. I think they provide some sort of stability to a society, and that they kind of evolved in that way. They evolved as just a necessary thing to provide stability, just as a lot of other things. There are just like a lot of other systems of government, just keeping groups of people in check. It's not something that's necessarily a problem . . . I'm not saying that there's me, you know, going and taking out the trash and cutting the grass is better than you cooking. I feel like they're equal. I just feel like I'm not gonna let a woman that I'm like, if I am in a relationship—because this usually is the realm of relationships—I would never let my woman cut the grass or take out the trash. I never let her do anything like that. I'm not against her doing it. I don't feel like it's not something they can do. I just feel like, you know, there's things that men should do, there's things that women should do.

In this passage, Mitch framed gender roles not as a tool of sexist subjugation, but as a functionalist system for providing societal order and stability, much like systems of government. Although he went on to acknowledge the greater status frequently accorded to male roles in American society, Mitch distinguished the hierarchal character of gender roles from what he viewed as their utility in establishing social order. Concluding ultimately that "there's things that men should do, there's things that women should do," Mitch's perspective delineated and justified clear boundaries between the roles and responsibilities of men and women.

Another study participant who articulated a framework for understanding gender difference was Victor. In contrast to his belief in the socially constructed nature of race, Victor viewed gender differences as biologically rooted and stable, as he explained during his first one-on-one interview:

> With blackness and whiteness, that is a construct, but with male and female, it's not a construct. I mean, I got a penis. You know what I mean? And she's got a vagina. It's just like real, real clear. But after that, ok, after that there's a lot of gray areas. I mean, as far as roles that females can play, roles that men can play, you know, there are gray areas.
>
> But then fundamentally, we're different. I really do believe fundamentally, males and females, we're different. Our wiring, our hormones, our everything. But on the racial thing, I don't see the differences as stark like that. Those differences are constructs otherwise,

but the male/female thing, I don't see it as a construct. I mean, and they say, "Oh, well, we're socialized to be feminine, or we're socialized to be this and this." But then some of it is just wiring, you see it in kids and in their play. So that's, yeah, you get into deep stuff.

In this passage, Victor's references to male and female genitalia grounded gender difference in biological terms. Briefly noting the potential for some "gray areas," Victor ultimately returned to biologically rooted grounds to explain his view of the inherent differences between men and women. Although the premise of his biologically deterministic framework diverged from Mitch's functionalist paradigm, Victor ultimately arrived at the same conclusion: There are fundamental and justifiable factors that differentiate men and women.

All seven participants who were quoted in this section repeatedly expressed an acute awareness of the systemic nature of White supremacy throughout their narratives. This palpable racial consciousness stood in stark contrast to their general inattentiveness to the presence and consequences of male privilege, as exhibited in the preceding narrative excerpts. That this blind eye to male privilege initially surfaced in participants' first one-on-one interviews, which focused broadly on their life narratives as Black men, suggests that a wide expanse of lived experiences beyond teaching conspired to obfuscate maleness as a node of power for these men. Nevertheless, because teachers' lives beyond the classroom influence their identities and pedagogies within schools, study participants' inattention to male privilege across multiple experiential contexts offers a crucial backdrop for understanding their negotiations of gendered power dynamics in the teaching profession.

Conflictual Encounters With Women in the Workplace

As noted earlier, Black male teachers' collegial relationships with women in the workplace have received little attention in the extant scholarship on Black men in teaching. Addressing this void, six participants in this study offered descriptive accounts of conflictual relationships with women colleagues. Most of these accounts revolved around antagonistic encounters with women in leadership positions, and a few spotlighted particular tensions with Black female colleagues and administrators. This section of Chapter 5 offers excerpts from and descriptions of these accounts.

Oliver was one of the study participants who recalled contentious dynamics with women administrators. During a one-on-one interview, Oliver described his ire for a female assistant principal who, in his view, had overstepped her bounds one day by interrupting his class and challenging his authority in front of his students. While providing this description, Oliver also offered a broader treatise on women in positions of authority, as captured in this exchange:

Oliver: I find that there are some women that feel so insecure that they have to oversee men who are strong, as I told you in my case with my assistant principal, that they figure, well, "I am the boss here and because I'm the boss . . ." and this kind of thing, and I don't fall for that nonsense. If it's not right, I'm not doing it, you know what I mean? So I find that the women's rights, and the women wanting to be bosses and lead and those kinds of things, has sort of like gone over the top a little bit in that they figure that in order to lead, that they need to be bosses, and that's not necessarily the case. Whatever the term boss means, you know.

Ed: Does it mean they have to be masculine?

Oliver: Aggressive. But you see, I don't necessarily associate that with masculinity, but that they have to be aggressive and have to be, you know, be the aggressor. And I get the feeling that a lot of women love whipping men and love castrating men, you know. And that turns me off. You're not going to cut my balls off [chuckle].

Oliver referred to the incident with his assistant principal again during a focus group session, using strikingly similar language to vent his frustration:

I find that lots of women in authoritative positions—principals, assistant principals, and so on—they get that position and they think that, you know, to be an assistant principal I must cut a man's balls off or something to prove their point . . . I definitely think that women who are in authoritative positions in the school district or in school have this thing with strong men. I think we as men have to stand up and say you're not [inaudible]. You could be [Brewerton's superintendent], you don't come and tell me what to do in my classroom in front of my students.

In both of these passages, Oliver employed the castration metaphor to demonize the power of women in leadership positions. Stating that these women felt like they had to "cut a man's balls off or something to prove their point," Oliver attributed women administrators' overly assertive leadership styles to their own insecurities as authority figures, especially in the presence of "strong men." Furthermore, suggesting that women's rights and women's desire for leadership have "gone over the top a little bit," Oliver framed women administrators' exercise of power as excessive—so much so, in fact, that this power had become emasculating. Through his own contention that he would not stand for the emasculating use of women administrators' power, Oliver seemed to assert and protect his own masculine integrity in the face of an insecure female power gone amuck. During his final one-on-one interview, when asked which emergent themes from the study had left a lasting impression on him, Oliver cited his critiques of "female leadership in schools" and the "overly aggressive women in the school district," and he expressed some surprise that other participants in his focus group, in his view, had not been as troubled by these dilemmas as he. For Oliver, gender unequivocally mediated his lens on female leadership as excessive and emasculating.

Frustrations with women in authority positions were also voiced by Victor. At several points in his narrative, Victor described and critiqued perceptions among his Black female colleagues that he and other Black male teachers were reluctant to listen to women supervisors. After challenging that perception, Victor provided a broader portrait of the tensions between women administrators and male teachers, as captured in this exchange during a one-on-one interview:

Victor: So this whole chauvinism, feminism aspect and its impact on men, that's . . . yeah, the whole role of feminism, the feminists . . . feminism, what impact it's having on, you know, relationships between Black men and Black women. I think in your research. . .

Ed: That's something to tease out?

Victor: Yeah. Like what role does this feminism thing have?

Ed: And what are you defining as feminism?

Victor: Women feeling empowered. Women having, women being empowered . . . you know, women being in power. Which there's nothing wrong with them being in power, but alright, if you're in power, but then . . . I don't know, it's hard. Yeah, just women being in power and what . . . women being in power when still men are the ones that have the power. And this tension that it causes, that it's causing. Like, for example, the female administrator, there's this notion that she always has to constantly prove herself, so there's this tension. Like she's proven herself and then this man is not listening to her, so then there's this tension or this dynamic around that.

Ed: Sort of preventing her from successfully proving herself?

Victor: Yeah, which she already has. Like, "You're the administrator, you have the power. Use it. Do your thing. I'm not stopping you." But there's sometimes the perception that you're stopping them or you're not listening to them, going against them.

This passage revealed an intriguing tension in Victor's perspectives on female leadership. Toward the end of the excerpt, Victor insisted that despite perceptions to the contrary, he willingly acknowledged the power of women administrators and did not attempt to stand in their way. However, Victor also framed the inherent contradiction of "women being in power when still men are the ones that have the power." This echoed a sentiment that Victor expressed at another moment in his narrative, when he stated that women struggled to grapple with authority because "sometimes they get it mixed up because they see power still associated with the penis." A recurrent thread and source of tension in Victor's narrative was that women might occupy positions of authority, but power still resided in what women lacked: the phallus.

Equally revealing from the excerpt were Victor's hesitations. His repetition of "feminist" and "feminism" conveyed a level of uncertainty and/or discomfort that prompted me to ask him for clarification. In the middle of the exchange when Victor paused and stated, "I don't know, it's hard," his own exasperation with the tensions he was describing came to the surface. Throughout this passage, it was apparent that Victor was torn between two opposing influences: his frustration with being perceived as a malicious threat to female authority, and his ambivalence toward the legitimacy of that authority. This contradiction produced a palpable level of angst toward his encounters with women administrators in his school.

As demonstrated so far, Victor and Oliver had broader theses on the excessiveness and illegitimacy of female administrative power. Other participants offered accounts that focused more on tensions with specific female administrators but nonetheless produced revealing insights into their perspectives on women in leadership. For instance, repeated clashes with his White female principal were a recurrent theme in Karl's narrative. In a one-on-one interview, Karl stated, "My principal is a yeller. As soon as she starts yelling, boom, I cut her off. I don't even process what she's saying. I'm just like, this bitch is yelling at me. Like, what is her problem?" Frustrated references to his principal as a "bitch" arose at other moments as well. For instance, during his final one-on-one interview, as he recapped a particularly antagonistic argument with his principal at the end of the school year, Karl vented, "She's a bitch . . . You're harassing me. Get the hell out of my face, sloppy bitch. I hate her." Although many of Karl's critiques of his principal primarily targeted her antagonistic communicative style and abrasive rapport with teachers—issues that commonly emerge as sources of strife between teachers and administrators—his exasperated and repeated references to his principal as a "bitch" indicated gender as a mediating factor in his disdain for her.

It was during a focus group that Karl explicitly speculated about the roles of gender and race in his principal's treatment of him:

Karl: I think one little thing I've found, and I've been thinking about this a lot lately because me and my principal have just been going at it the last couple of months. I feel like she's kind of afraid of me a little bit, and because she's afraid of me, she approaches me very, like, with attitude . . .

Greg: Mmm-hmm.

Karl: . . . and very much . . . and it's to the point where like, one time I literally had to say *[in an offended tone]* "who are you talking to?" and walk away from her before I cussed her out. When I see her with other people, I really don't think her tone is the same. And I'm a pretty easy-going person. I'm not nice when I'm mad, but she . . . I don't know. I just feel like she approaches me in a way that might be different if I wasn't a Black male.

Karl's perception of his principal's unique antagonism toward him as a Black man pointed to gender, along with race, as a mediating factor in their ongoing strife. His speculation that his principal was afraid of him also suggested his sense that her own insecurities were undermining her authority as a White female school leader.

Like Karl, Greg described a strained relationship with his White female principal. In fact, it was after one of Karl's accounts of his principal's prickly demeanor during a focus group session that Greg also broached this topic, leading to a discussion of strategic, masculinist responses to excessive uses of authority by women administrators. The following is an excerpt from that discussion:

Greg: My principal, a White woman, she speaks . . . a lot of the staff members have said they don't like the way that she speaks to them. And I said, "Well why do you allow her to speak to you in such a way?" And she's never spoken to me in such a way. There was only one incident where she raised her voice and *[chuckle]* . . . We were on the phone and I said *[raises his voice]*, "Excuuuse me?" And she paused and then she *[All: laughter]* lulled a bit and then, you know, went on with the conversation. But I don't know *[All: laughter]*, I don't know if it's because I'm a Black man—I think so—that she doesn't speak to me in such a way.

Ed: Was that just an instinctual reaction, or did you do that intentionally?

Greg: Who, mine? Oh no, I did it intentionally, intentionally, to let her know you got the wrong one. Like, wait a minute.

By raising his voice to "let her know you got the wrong one," Greg seemed able to wield a Black male assertiveness to dissuade further disrespect from his White female principal. This account prompted other participants in the focus group session to prod Greg for tips on how to handle confrontational moments like this with women administrators, to which Greg responded by encouraging the use of "bass" in one's voice. In this exchange, a masculinist posturing emerged as a tactic for countering excessive assertions of power by women in leadership positions, further underscoring the potentially contentious nature of these encounters for the men in this study.

Like Greg, Quincy also described a masculinist posturing in response to women administrators. During the same focus group session, following Greg's suggestion to put "bass" in one's voice when responding to out-of-line women administrators, Quincy offered this account of how he managed his relationship with the mostly Black female administrative team at his school:

> It's weird because I don't have a lot of these interactions. Anytime [the female administrators] have ever tried to get out of sorts, they instantly apologize without me having to say anything. Like I just kind of look at them like "there must be something wrong going on here." So, you know, they'll be like "Oh I'm sorry." My female colleagues—Black, White, whatever—they get it all the time, you know what I'm saying. Anytime there's a little power trip issue like that, it's instantly popping off like that. But for me, as I said, anytime they even get a little bit out of sorts, either they'll apologize instantly right there, or they'll come back and apologize five minutes later or whatever . . . It just is that instant kind of "oops, I did something wrong, I need to check myself." And for me I just kind of stand and say, "Alright, it's fine with me, just don't do it again."

In this passage, Quincy's strategies for keeping women administrators at bay revolved around a strategically masculinist posturing of his own. The flash of his "there must be something wrong going on here" look, as well as his "just don't do it again" demeanor during women administrators' apparent lapses of judgment, echoed Greg's use of his deep voice to establish boundaries with his female principal. In both cases, masculinist posturing was cited as a tactic for placing excessive female power in check and for reasserting male power in the face of higher-ranked women administrators.

Although some of the tense encounters described thus far occurred with White women in positions of authority, it was the excessive exercise of female power, more than White womanhood, that fell under scrutiny in participants' accounts. By contrast, two participants attributed difficult interactions with Black female administrators and teacher colleagues to deep-seated tensions specifically with Black women. One of these participants was Mitch. In the following exchange during a one-on-one interview, Mitch discussed his frustrations with the nagging authoritative style of the predominantly Black female leadership team at his school:

Mitch: I'm always late with turning in stuff. Paperwork, all that other, you know, the rigmarole of being a teacher, all that kind of stuff. I'm always late with it. Always. Very rarely do I turn it in on time. Even less rarely do I turn it in early. And they're always like, "Mr. Abrams, when are you gonna get this done, Mr. Abrams? You gotta get this done. Mr. Abrams, stop fucking up. Get your shit done." And they'll say that to me. They'll be like, "Get your shit done. I'm not gonna play with you. You need to get your shit done."

Ed: These are Black women saying this to you?

Mitch: Yeah. "I'm not gonna sit here and play with you. You know what you need to do. Stop, get it done." And that's how they approach me most of the time. They treat me like I treat my kids, and I react like my kids react. I'm just like quiet and I'm like "Okay, yeah." Then, "Okay yeah, what? Are you gonna do something, or are you just gonna say okay yeah?" "I guess I should do . . ." "You should or you're going to?" [*Mitch imitates "assertive Black woman" voice throughout this*]

Mitch's description of the badgering style of Black female administrators mirrored his characterization of his Black female teacher colleagues, as captured in this exchange:

Mitch: As a Black male I'm a little bit more laidback than the Black woman. The Black female is kind of going to keep her foot like in your back. She's going to keep it. She's going to nag you to death until you fix it and is never going to let up. Like there's no let up there . . . The Black woman's gonna come to you and tell you, "Move. What are you doing? Didn't I just tell you that you're supposed to be over there? Get over there!"

Ed: So to what do you attribute that difference?

Mitch: Being a Black woman, I guess. I don't know. Black men are just laid . . . I think it's just a guy thing really. The male thing, just being kind of more even-keeled than the hormonal woman, where you kind of just [*imitates nagging noise*], [inaudible] their estrogen.

Observing that "the Black female is kind of going to keep her foot like in your back," Mitch ascribed a domineering and excessive authoritative style in this excerpt to his Black female colleagues, one that mirrored his accounts of the relentless nagging of Black women in his school's leadership team. That he then ascribed his colleagues' overbearing style to "being a

Black woman" and being "the hormonal woman" offered essentialist nods to the sources of gender difference and supplied further evidence that Mitch sometimes found the presence of his Black women colleagues challenging.

Victor was another participant who spoke to the difficulties of negotiating collegial relationships specifically with Black women. Like Mitch, Victor described a relentlessly nagging interactional style displayed at times by his Black female colleagues, and he even speculated that a "bad hair day" or menstrual cycle may be to blame for his colleagues' unpredictable "mood swings." Although Victor often espoused biologically rooted notions of gender difference, his lens on the tensions he encountered with Black women colleagues extended beyond biological explanations. At one point, Victor invoked a sociohistorical analysis of the widespread friction between Black men and Black women:

> I'm not a sociologist, but there have been noted tensions in research where, first of all, you have the Black man. I mean, going back to the whole slavery notion where the Black men were separated and then after the separation, you may even have been forced to mate with somebody who wasn't necessarily your love interest. So these tensions, and then further tensions with the whole welfare thing, where men would have to leave the house. So you know, there are just these tensions with Black men and Black women, they're larger. And then Black men, on ourselves, we feel a little like we, the perception that we're disempowered and we're being emasculated. I mean, our issues of our own Black . . . maybe even our own insecurities where some of our own insecurities make the way we deal with women, perception or reality, like we won't listen to them because we've already been emasculated. We feel that we've been emasculated, so why listen to them? So I think those bigger issues play out in the workplace, play out even in relationships.

In this passage, Victor pointed to the broad historical legacies of White supremacy and capitalist oppression as contexts for the complicated relationships between Black men and Black women, both in society at large and within schools. Interestingly, against this broader backdrop, Victor also implicated Black men's own anxieties around masculinity as potential contributing factors to tensions with women. In fact, by situating gender relations within the historical narrative of Black oppression, Victor was able to consider the possibility that Black men's own insecurities around emasculation might lend some truth to Black female colleagues' perceptions of Black men's aversion to the advice of women. The sociohistorical contextualization of Black gender relations thus produced an important momentary shift in Victor's narrative on the encounters between Black men and Black women. However, this shift was short-lived, as his frustrations with women colleagues and administrators returned to center stage in subsequent narrative accounts.

In sum, women in the workplace, especially those in positions of authority, exerted an undeniable presence across the narratives of the six study participants cited in this section. The preceding narrative excerpts revealed participants' perspectives on the excessiveness and illegitimacy of women administrators' authority, the capacity of masculinist posturing to counter that authority, and the sometimes-challenging nature of working specifically with Black women administrators and colleagues. A key theme cutting across all these narrative accounts was the assault on and defense of male privilege. From defending themselves from the indignities of an emasculating female authority to reasserting their masculinity in the presence of female power run amuck, the consolidation of male privilege underlay participants' responses to women of authority and influence in the workplace. These contentious encounters revealed the gendered politics of participation in the teaching profession as a crucial theme to explore in the lives of the Black male teachers in this study.

Male-Centered Interactions and Space

Participants' perspectives on gender in the teaching profession were brought into further relief as they spoke about the possibilities of more connections with other men who were employed in schools. In all, eight participants expressed some interest in having access to more male-centered interactions and spaces within the teaching profession. This shared interest is described next.

Ruminations over working with male principals, especially as an alternative to contending with female administrators, were one way in which participants expressed their interest in connecting with other men in urban schools. While chronicling his stressful past with women administrators and colleagues during a one-on-one interview, Victor wondered aloud about the prospect of having a male principal:

> I've heard people say, "Oh, it's wonderful when you have a male principal. It's totally different. I like working for a male principal." I've never even had that experience at all, so I don't even know what that is like. It would be interesting to have that experience, to have a male administrator and see the difference, to have something to compare to.

Like Victor, Karl also expressed curiosity about what it would be like to have a male principal. Raising this prospect during a focus group session sparked the following exchange:

Karl: Something else I thought about, too. Terrence Carlisle who's at. . .
Greg: Oh yeah. He was my principal.

Karl: Yeah, I wanted to ask you about that. Thinking about that there are very few Black male principals even, I was curious to know, do you feel like having him as a Black male was any different, or was that a bonus, a positive? Because I had strongly considered trying to transfer there. I know the kids are . . . it's a wild neighborhood.

Greg: Mmm-hmm.

Karl: But I was hoping that under his leadership, it might be a little different. So I don't know, maybe you could speak to that.

Greg: He's very positive towards Black males. Black male teachers, he seeks out [as] leaders. He expects a lot from you, being a Black male. He was good. I just got tired of the students . . . But he was a good principal. He didn't want me to leave, so that says something.

Ed: You felt wanted.

Greg: Yeah, he put all his men in positions. He moved out the women, which I thought was kind of wrong, but he was in charge, and I was a Black male so I didn't really. . . [*All: laughter*]

Ed: "It worked for me."

Greg: He put all his strong Black men in leadership positions. So that's kind of the mentality that he has.

In this exchange, the prospect of having a Black male principal represented, for Karl, a more supportive alternative to his contentious relationship with his White female principal. Greg's account of his prior experience with a Black male principal not only supported Karl's speculation but also depicted a radical shift in the gendered power dynamics that were being discussed by participants in the focus group, as Greg's former Black male principal decided to "move out the women" and put "his strong Black men in leadership positions." Importantly, although Greg noted that this decision worked to his advantage as a Black man, he also went on to state that he thought this decision was "kind of wrong" on the part of his former principal. That he benefited from an apparent consolidation of Black patriarchal power did not mean that he wholly approved of it. However, this implicit critique did not undermine the overall thrust of this exchange: In a school district where women occupied a number of administrative positions, the male principal represented an intriguing alternative to female leadership.

The possibilities of male-centered interactions also surfaced in ruminations over the creation of male-centered spaces within schools. This theme was articulated most explicitly by Victor, who talked at length about his sense of isolation as one of the few male teachers in his school. What Victor envisioned was a more stable space where men in his school could come together on a consistent basis, as he described in this passage from a one-on-one interview:

> At our school, right, the ladies' bathroom was nice. It was a place to go and hang out or whatever. They fixed it all up nice and everything. And I asked the dudes, "Man, our bathroom is horrible. Why don't we do something to make our space . . ." Just having a decent bathroom for the men to go in and chill, you know, to get away. That would have just been cool. Because the ladies had a little space. They could just go and they could chill in their bathroom. I mean, in our bathroom, you would just get in and get out of there because it was just horrible. So that would be one of the key things I would do; I would make the bathrooms a haven for men. Go in there, read the newspaper, chill. And, I don't think I would make it specific to Black men because we, I think through our struggles, we've learned how to negotiate and mediate the racial issue. But like I said, there's still these gender things that I'm still grappling with, and if I had other guys and we could come around and have lunch or just bond or have space. Like I said, it can be isolating sometimes, being a male teacher in a school. So if the men kind of knew that "alright, this was our space and we could be there," I think that would be cool.

In this excerpt, Victor cited his isolation as a male teacher on a predominantly female faculty, along with his ongoing efforts to grapple with gender differences, as cause for creating a male space within his school. Such a space would potentially mitigate the isolation and gender tensions that male teachers experienced by providing a respite from the challenges of crossgender encounters and a haven for male connections and bonding. While the men's bathroom served as an example in the preceding passage, Victor's conceptualization of male spaces in other narrative excerpts ranged from casual but consistent discussions among male teachers over lunch to schoolwide programming that would bring together male teachers, male students, and their male guardians. That Victor envisioned such a space in the passage as serving male teachers regardless of race underscored the salience of gender as an axis of difference in his teaching experiences.

Given Victor's desire to connect with male colleagues, his participation in a focus group session with other participants was a standout experience for him during this study. In this regard, Victor was not alone. Of the nine teachers who participated in the focus group sessions for this study, seven—Bill, Damon, Greg, Karl, Oliver, Quincy, and Victor—identified the focus groups as a standout aspect of the study during their final interviews, often noting that they had rarely, if ever, experienced similar opportunities to share their perspectives with other Black male teachers. Four of these men (Bill, Damon, Greg, and Quincy) stated that they would have preferred even more focus group sessions, and Damon suggested hosting a larger summit-type gathering for Black male teachers. Victor reported that he described his focus group experience to other male teachers at his school in hopes of sparking interest among them in holding similar gatherings. In addition to the seven participants mentioned, Solomon, who also participated in a focus group session, stated that he wished his focus group experience had been even more engaging, given his desire to connect with fellow Black male educators. Although the focus group experience was not as satisfying as Solomon had hoped, his remark still echoed the desire for more opportunities to interact with other Black men in the profession.

In all, the prospect of working with male principals, the desire for male-centered spaces in schools, and the feedback on the focus group sessions for this study underscored participants' interest in having more interactions with fellow male educators. These male-centered spaces and connections were conceived as potential escapes from women in the workplace as well as opportunities to bond with and possibly support other male and Black male teachers. As with the previously cited accounts of contentious encounters with women colleagues and administrators, the ruminations on more male-centered spaces provided further evidence of the significance of workplace gender politics for the men in this study.

The Deliberate and Nuanced Nature of Anti-Patriarchal Work

This chapter presented study participants' accounts of the conflictual gendered politics of participation in Brewerton's teaching ranks. A major reason for the significance of these accounts is their absence elsewhere. In scholarly and popular discourses on Black men in the American teaching profession, potentially antagonistic negotiations of power across gender lines have not come into view as clearly as they have in this chapter. The absence of such perspectives is striking given the predominance of women in teaching, the competitive and egocentric nature of hegemonic masculinity (Connell, 2002; Kimmel, 2013), and the contentious power dynamics between teachers and administrators of all races and genders in many school districts across the country (Lipman, 2011; Schniedewind & Sapon-Shevin, 2012). Taking these factors into account, either the men in this study are anomalies—an isolated, conflict-prone subset of sexist male educators to be reprehended—or the saviorist celebrations that shape how we talk about Black male teachers come equipped with patriarchal blinders. This book predictably presumes the latter. Building upon this book's second analytic premise, that anti-patriarchal perspectives are needed to enable new ways of envisioning Black manhood, this chapter indicates that Black male teachers' attitudes toward and interactions with women in the workplace may warrant much closer attention.

Patriarchal gender ideologies in the narratives of the men in this study were particularly palpable in participants' reactions to the dubious offense of female authority. The epithets toward women in power, the descriptions of hormonally induced female flippancy, the equation of female authority to emasculation, the phallocentric definition of female authority as inherently flawed, and the masculinist posturing to attenuate the reach of female authority cast the influence and leadership of women in schools, when unchecked by male-imposed constraints, as affronts to patriarchal sensibilities. While there is certainly cause to encourage study participants to reconsider how they perceived and interacted with women in the workplace, their reactions arguably were logical extensions of saviorist discourses on Black male teachers. As described in Chapter 3, many of the men in this study reported praise and encouragement from Black community members for their decisions as Black men to enter into urban teaching. Underlying that praise and encouragement was a saviorist logic that lauded these men for taking on the hard work of disciplining and uplifting Black children, especially Black boys. If saviorist discourses function as a tool for recruiting Black men into teaching, and if those discourses lionize rather than problematize patriarchal depictions of Black manhood, then it makes sense that some Black male teachers might expect to be revered not only by the Black students they are saving, but by the women educators who need Black men's assistance. It also makes sense that some of these men, including the ones identified in this chapter, might struggle with women whose school-based authority could undermine their patriarchal sense of selves. Like the complicated politics of disciplinary authority and surrogate fatherhood that were examined in the previous chapter, study participants' frictional encounters with women in authority underscore the need to rethink saviorist discourses on Black male teachers, as these discourses arguably contributed to the dilemmas described in this chapter. By failing to trouble saviorist discourses, we may miss opportunities to prepare Black male teachers for critical engagements with the politics of male participation in a predominantly female profession.

Against the broader backdrop of participants' contentious encounters with women in the workplace, several accounts homed in on specific tensions with Black women colleagues and administrators. Critical perspectives on such tensions are arguably another casualty of saviorist discourses on Black male teachers. As discussed in Chapter 2, these discourses have overshadowed the presence, power, and accomplishments of Black women educators by championing the rarity of and the urgency for Black men in the classroom. As Black women's contributions to the education of Black youth have taken a relative backseat to the more emphatic appeals for Black male teachers, so, too, have considerations of how Black men in the profession might honor and strategically negotiate their relationships with Black women peers. This chapter suggests that future work about and with Black male teachers should critically examine the racial and gender politics that emerge between Black male and Black female educators, especially in predominantly Black educational settings where Black women may outnumber and outrank their Black male peers, and where Black women educators may have already established their own gender-mediated pedagogical traditions and institutional cultures to effectively address the needs of Black students.

Given the inattention in saviorist discourses to the potential conflicts between Black male and Black female educators, it was important to bring those conflicts to light in this chapter. However, it is crucial to note that in narrative passages not included in this chapter, some of the men in this study indicated the supportive roles of Black women colleagues and administrators in their careers. Mitch and Solomon, for instance, credited Black female teachers and administrators for helping them to develop effective disciplinary strategies, and Damon recalled the respect he received from Black female teachers once he developed a reputation for having effective classroom management techniques. Damon also characterized some of the Black women on his faculty as "aunties" who performed a familial style of mentoring with him, and Victor described some of his Black female colleagues as sister-like. That some of these participants also recalled tensions with Black women colleagues and administrators illustrated the complicated and shifting relational dynamics between these men and the Black women in their workplaces. Moving forward, it seems critical that future work on Black male teachers not simply reproduce antagonistic discourses on Black gender relations, but draw instead upon both the loyalties and tensions that may exist between these educators, as well as upon their shared commitment to Black students' academic achievement, to envision their constructive collaboration in schools across gender lines. While critical dialogues between Black male teachers and non-Black women colleagues and administrators are important as well, I am intentionally emphasizing opportunities for Black men and Black women in teaching to connect with each other and work through possible tensions. Given the difficulty of gender justice work, Black educators' shared legacy of and commitment to empowering Black children may provide an extra incentive for engaging in uncomfortable yet critical dialogues.

Of course, such dialogues alone will not be enough. In addition to working through potential tensions with Black women and other women colleagues and administrators, teachers like the men in this study must find spaces and opportunities for their own introspective work on gender. As described in this chapter, inquiries into definitions of and attitudes toward gender identity across the life span revealed a general inattention to male privilege, essentialist constructions of gender difference, and phallocentric notions of power among seven of the men in this study. That the majority of participants spoke in some salient manner to the influence of patriarchal discourses beyond their teaching experiences indicated that these discourses permeated the multiple social contexts of these men's lives and filtered into their navigations of predominantly female professional spaces. Consequently, their tensions with women in the workplace were not born in the workplace. Rather, these tensions stemmed from and reproduced patriarchal gender ideologies that had shaped study participants' identities and worldviews long before teaching.

Combined with this book's earlier examination of the patriarchal logics ingrained in saviorist discourses on Black male teachers, this chapter's analysis of the depth and reach of patriarchal gender ideologies in participants' lives suggests an important task for teacher education programs and other stakeholders that prepare and support Black men in teaching: facilitating deliberate and nuanced explorations with Black male teachers of their encounters with, and possible investments in, patriarchal gender ideologies as Black men. It is the unique complexities of Black male teachers' experiences with gender that require such explorations to be both deliberate and nuanced. Citing the men in this study as examples, narrative accounts on women in the workplace clearly exhibited participants' patriarchal sensibilities, thus warranting deliberate attempts to engage study participants in critical reflections on gender and power in teaching. However, participants' accounts also revealed the psychosocial stresses stemming from their struggles with what they characterized as the emasculating effects of female administrative power. Furthermore, participants' accounts revealed their professional vulnerability as teachers working in school environments where administrators frequently used their power to curtail teacher autonomy, where women occupied a number of those administrative positions, and where the prevalence of women colleagues lent additional influence to women's perspectives, concerns, and judgments. Add the fact that some of the women administrators in participants' narratives were White, thus affording their access to White privilege, and the power dynamics at play become even more complicated.

Together, all of the factors listed above point to the need for nuanced understandings of how Black male teachers can be marginally situated within schools despite male privilege, and how that marginalization presents particular psychosocial stresses for Black men in the profession. This is not to say that a critique of patriarchy should be abandoned or accorded less priority. Rather, this is an appeal for future scholarly analyses and support efforts focusing on Black male teachers to wed a deliberate and critical stance against patriarchal gender ideologies with a nuanced attention to the unique professional and psychosocial challenges that may affect Black men in the profession. Fortunately, there is already a rich body of work in Black masculinity studies that can frame such efforts (Byrd & Guy-Sheftall, 2001; Carbado, 1999a; Drake, 2016; Mutua, 2006b; Neal, 2005, 2013). Insights from this work may prove especially helpful for wedding critiques of male privilege with recognitions of Black male teachers' precarious and contingent access to patriarchal authority.

The importance of facilitating Black male teachers' critical reflections on gender and power in the profession raises a final set of concerns regarding the creation of male-oriented spaces in teaching. As described in this chapter, the men in this study expressed a desire for more male-oriented spaces—a desire which, in some cases, was informed by frustrations with the predominance of and confrontations with women in the workplace. Glimpses of the affordances of such spaces surfaced during this study's two focus groups, both of which became generative settings for exploring participants' unique experiences as Black male teachers in Brewerton. However, it was during one of those focus groups when several participants shared strategies with each other for masculinist posturing in response to women administrators' overreaches of authority. With the proliferation of recruitment, preparation, and retention initiatives specifically for Black men in teaching—some of which, as discussed in Chapter 2, seem to reproduce saviorist logics in their titles—the affordances and constraints of all-male spaces to facilitate anti-patriarchal consciousness-building among Black male teachers deserve careful consideration. As this chapter suggests, it may not be enough for such initiatives to simply place more adult Black male bodies in K–12 classrooms. Rather, the success of male-centered teacher preparation spaces and recruitment/retention efforts may depend in part on how well they prepare male teachers, Black and otherwise, to accept and negotiate an anti-patriarchal presence in a predominantly female profession.

Conclusion

This chapter opened with a nod to the sensitive nature of the terrains that were about to be explored. It was important for me to implore readers to critically engage the issues that emerged throughout this chapter while not vilifying the men in my study, whose honest disclosures created unique opportunities to interrogate the effects of patriarchy in the lives and work of Black male teachers. As revealed across one-on-one interviews, patriarchal gender ideologies stemming from lifelong socialization experiences had produced a general inattention to male privilege among many of the men in this study. With that blind eye toward male privilege as a backdrop, this chapter then explored participants' perspectives on contentious workplace relationships with women, especially those in positions of administrative power. Accounts of excessive and illegitimate female administrative authority, masculinist responses to undermine that authority, and tense exchanges specifically with Black women administrators and colleagues depicted emasculating assaults on male teachers and counter-maneuvers to reconsolidate male privilege. Given the domineering impulses of American masculinity, the predominance of women in K–12 schools, and the friction in many urban districts between teachers and administrators, contentious dynamics between other Black male teachers and their female colleagues and administrators are not difficult to imagine. Hence, the analyses in this chapter suggest that the gendered politics of participation in urban teaching, which have been noticeably absent from saviorist discourses, warrant close attention in future scholarship on Black male urban teachers.

In contrast to recurrent frustrations with women in the workplace, access to more malecentered spaces and connections in the urban teaching profession emerged as an idyllic alternative across multiple narratives. Study participants conceived these male spaces and connections as affording reprieves from stressful interactions with women colleagues and bonding time with and support from other male educators. Combined with the accounts of contentious encounters with women peers and administrators, the ruminations on male-centered spaces provided further cause for more interrogations of Black men's negotiations of the gendered politics of participation in urban teaching. As argued, such work will need to juggle anti-patriarchal sensibilities with a sensitivity to Black male teachers' potentially marginalized status in the teaching force. The success of critical scholarly analyses and support efforts focusing on Black male teachers may depend heavily on how well they wed a deliberate and critical stance against patriarchal gender ideologies with a nuanced attention to the unique professional and psychosocial challenges that may affect Black men in the profession.

6 The Voices (and Silences) of Black Queer Male Teachers

All of the chapters in this book challenge conventional ways of thinking about the presence and purpose of Black men in the American urban teaching profession. However, this chapter, with its focus on Black queer male (BQM) teachers, may be more disruptive than others.

Dating back to at least the mid-20th century, homophobic cultural discourses in the United States have demonized queer men as improper role models for and pedophilic threats to the nation's children (Davis, 1961; Rofes, 2005). Echoing these anti-queer discourses throughout American society at large, heteronormative constructions of racial authenticity and respectability within Black American cultural contexts (Hill Collins, 2005) have similarly cast Black queer men as a danger to Black youth. Such perceptions are evident in Black church discourses on queerness and its threat to children (NewsOne Staff, n.d.; Server, 2012), homophobic reactions to representations of Black queer fatherhood (Nichols, 2014), and Black queer men's own accounts of Black cultural anxieties toward their influence on children (Riggs, 2006; Simmons, 1991). These backdrops help to explain the absence of Black queer men from the saviorist discourses reviewed in Chapter 2. Whether in the literature on how to raise Black boys or in popular media appeals for more Black male teachers, Black queer men have been decidedly invisible. Amidst recurrent warnings to protect children from the lure of adult queer male sexuality, the Black queer man as a caring adult for Black youth runs counter to homophobic logics within Black American culture and American society more broadly, making him, for some, simply unimaginable.

This chapter seeks to make the unimaginable imaginable by analyzing the narratives of five queer men who were among the participants in this study. Like the other study participants, these five men entered urban teaching to make a difference in the lives of Black youth. However, as their stories unfolded across one-on-one interviews, the closet emerged as a significant and often risky backdrop for these five men's negotiations of power, credibility, and membership in Brewerton schools. This chapter explores how these five queer men negotiated the closet, and it raises several issues that are crucial for understanding the terms and stakes of BQM educators' participation in urban educational spaces.

A quick note on terminology: This chapter uses "queer" to denote same-sex desires and identities, as well as transgender and other gender identities and expressions, that are marked in similar fashion as deviant or nonconforming by heteronormative power structures. See Johnson (2005) and Rodriguez (2003) for further explanations of this deployment of queer. For the five men who are the focus of this chapter's analysis, queer is used specifically to describe their same-sex desires and identities, as none of the men in this study claimed a transgender or nonbinary gender identity.

Context: Black Queer Men in Teaching

The five study participants who take center stage in this chapter were situated at the intersections of blackness, maleness, and queerness in teaching. As previously discussed in this book, scholarship on the American teaching profession has attributed a legacy of culturally responsive pedagogical work and racial uplift to Black educators, and it has explored the dilemmas associated with male teachers' negotiations of patriarchal authority and hegemonic masculinity in the classroom. The narratives featured in this chapter present an opportunity to consider how the politics of queerness in American teaching may intersect with these two legacies.

Marked in the Western cultural imagination as perverts and sexual predators who pose a threat to childhood innocence, queer teachers have been the targets of recurring efforts in the United States to purge the teaching profession of queer interlopers (Graves, 2009, 2015; Griffin & Ouellett, 2003). Against this backdrop, the literature on queers in teaching has chronicled queer teachers' sense of isolation and vulnerability, their experiences with harassment and violence, and their fear of being accused of inappropriate sexual advances toward children (Endo, Reece-Miller, & Santavicca, 2010; Evans, 2002; Griffin, 1991; Jennings, 1994; Kissen, 1996; Sanlo, 1999). Some scholarship also has described the variety of strategies employed by queer teachers to manage others' awareness of their sexual identities within schools. While these strategies may include partial or full disclosures of queer teachers' identities to students and/or colleagues (Griffin, 1991; Kissen, 1996), scholarly literature suggests that they more frequently entail silences around one's queer identity, a separation of one's queer personal life from one's professional persona, and the deliberate use of heteronormative styles of dress and behavior to evade homophobic suspicions (Connell, 2014; Evans, 2002; Griffin, 1991; Kissen, 1996; Rofes, 2005). Given pedophilic depictions of queer teachers in the West, these strategies may also include a studied caution toward interactions with queer youth who are seeking support from queer teachers (Griffin, 1991; Kissen, 1996; Russell, 2010; Sanlo, 1999). Together, the scholarly literature cited has captured queer teachers' ongoing struggles to negotiate the terms of their participation within the homophobic milieus of Western teaching professions.

In addition to bearing witness to queer teachers' traumas within homophobic institutional and cultural contexts, some scholarly works on queers in teaching have situated these educators as potential agents of a gay liberationist progress narrative. Within this narrative, the declarative act of coming out and the concurrent and/or subsequent connection to a visible gay community enable the closeted gay subject to emerge from a space/time of relative powerlessness, affirm his gay identity, and become better equipped to advocate for anti-homophobic change.[1] Russell (2010) has noted the pressures presented by Western gay liberation discourses for queer teachers to come out of the closet and serve as role models for queer youth, and she has cited several works by queer educators and researchers that actually apply these pressures on queer teachers. Like the works cited by Russell, Jennings (1994, 2005) has decried the closet for discouraging queer teachers from confronting homophobia in schools while also celebrating those who have nonetheless summoned the courage to come out, and Griffin (1991) and Sanlo (1999) have placed a particular emphasis on queer teacher visibility as an antidote to queer student misery. Underscoring the importance of identity affirmation in gay liberationist narratives, Griffin (1991) and Jackson (2007) have stressed the anti-homophobic agency of queer educators who successfully affirm and integrate their queer and teacher identities, and Jackson has even developed a linear stage model for gay teacher identity development that ultimately produces socially conscious queer educators. Griffin (1991) and Endo et al. (2010) have described queer teachers' increased advocacy efforts within schools after connecting with groups for queer educators, and Blount (2005), Graves (2009), and Harbeck (1997) have cited the fate of queer teachers as a harbinger of the broader gay rights movement. All of this literature contributes to a broader discourse that situates the plight of queer teachers within gay liberationist narratives of struggle. Silenced and immobilized by the dictates of the closet, it is through coming out that the queer teacher emerges across this literature as a viable agent of anti-homophobic change.

Although the scholarly literature on queer teachers has made invaluable contributions to educational scholarship on identity, pedagogy, and power in the teaching profession, it has offered few considerations of the possible intersections of blackness and queerness. Some empirical studies on queer teachers' experiences have included White subjects only (Evans, 2002; Jackson, 2007; Sanlo, 1999), while others have offered little or no analysis of race in the lives of their minority of non-White participants (Griffin, 1991; Mayo, 2008; Russell, 2010). One exception is Kissen's study of queer teachers (1996), which explores racial minority participants' professional experiences as anti-racist advocates for students of color, as well as their personal experiences with racism in gay communities and homophobia in communities of color. Also, DeJean (2008), whose study on queer teachers included White participants only, acknowledges the urgency of recruiting a more diverse pool for future research endeavors. However, neither Kissen nor DeJean offers insights into how race might shape Black queer educators' connectedness to a queer teacher identity or an anti-homophobic pedagogical agenda. A noteworthy corrective is offered by Connell (2014). Not only does Connell complicate the gay liberationist emphasis on coming out, but she also discusses how racial identities and cultural ties to racial minority stakeholder groups informed how the queer teachers of color in her study navigated their professional experiences. But beyond Connell's work, the bulk of scholarship on queer teachers as a collective has supplied few insights on the intersections of race and queerness for Black or other queer of color teachers. Since similar blind spots also exist in the literatures on Black teachers and male teachers that were reviewed in Chapter 1, scholarly insights into the experiences of Black queer men in teaching have been noticeably scarce.

Given the gaps identified in the extant literatures, the publication of an earlier iteration of this chapter (Brockenbrough, 2012a) marked a significant turning point in the scholarly recognition of Black queers in American K–12 teaching. Since then, several pieces by other scholars have slowly yet steadily advanced scholarly inquiries into the experiences of Black queer teachers. Of those works, one by Hayes (2014) and one by Woodson and Pabon (2016) have included an attention to BQM teachers in American K–12 schools. Hayes's work explores how one Black and two Latino queer male teachers engaged the culturally responsive teaching traditions of Black and other teachers of color, while Woodson and Pabon's work analyzes how heteropatriarchal expectations complicated the experiences of three Black male teachers, including one Black transgender man. Complementing the attention to Black queer men, Love (2016) investigates how a Black lesbian custodian and Boy Scouts troop leader at an Atlanta elementary school used her female masculinity to mentor Black boys, and Ford (2016) explores how seven Black lesbian teachers in the southeastern United States emphasized the role of honesty in how they defined, represented, and refused to deny their Black lesbian personhood as teachers. Other works—Msibi's (2013) study of how South African Black queer male teachers negotiated their identities, McCready and Mosely's (2014) consideration of how to make space for Black queer teachers in teacher education, and pieces that have explored the perspectives of Black queer educators on the collegiate and university level (Alexander, 2006; Lewis, 2012, 2016)—have not specifically focused on American K–12 teaching, but they still have contributed significantly to the recognition of Black queer educators in educational scholarship.

The gradual recognition of Black queer educators' presence, identities, and pedagogies has been no small feat. Stuck in the shadows of heteronormative and White-centered discourses on teaching, Black queer educators have been all but absent from the scholarly record. Bringing them to the fore has required the coterie of scholars cited above to courageously and strategically disrupt dominant modes of knowledge production—on teaching, on gender and sexuality in schools, on Black and queer educational liberations—that have depended on Black queer erasures. The scholarship on Black queer teachers has made critical intellectual disruptions, making it an important body of work. It currently stands, however, as a small body of work, leaving ample room for more inquiries. This includes further analyses that address the experiences of teachers like the five men featured in this chapter. With a relative dearth of scholarship available on BQM teachers in American K–12 teaching, this chapter makes an important contribution by situating my earlier work on BQM teachers within a broader interrogation of saviorist discourses on Black male teachers. Doing so not only brings a new analytic framework to bear on the data revisited in this chapter, but it also creates a strategic opportunity to disrupt modes of knowledge production that exclude Black queer men from what we imagine for, about, and with Black male teachers.

Conceptual Framework: The Closet

Analyses of the closet from the scholarly field of queer studies inform the conceptual framework for this chapter's examination of the experiences of BQM teachers. Numerous authors within queer studies have described the closet as the effect of socially and historically produced arrangements of power in the West that wield political, economic, cultural, and ideological resources to define and pathologize queer subjects (Brown, 2000; Connell, 2014; Ross, 2005; Sedgwick, 1990; Seidman, 2002). Amid an arsenal of punitive technologies for maligning, ostracizing, harassing, incarcerating, attacking, and even eliminating queer deviants, the closet is the accumulation of complex modes of concealing and denying queerness that have emerged in the face of heterosexist and homophobic oppression. Unfolding across myriad social, institutional, and interpersonal contexts, its far-reaching effects make the closet "a condition of social oppression" (Seidman, 2002, p. 54) that attempts to reinscribe the oppositional relationship between heteronormativity and queer deviancy, as well as delimit the boundaries of individual and collective queer possibilities. As Connell (2014) argues, while some scholars have troubled the closet as a heuristic for understanding contemporary queer life, the ongoing consequences of antiqueerness in American K–12 schools continue to make the closet a salient framework for scholarship on queer teachers. In this chapter, analyses of the closet in queer studies provide a crucial backdrop for understanding BQM teachers as queer subjects who, like other queers, must contend with the systemic grasp of homophobic oppression on queer lives, and who may do so by engaging various strategies for concealing or disavowing their queerness.

This chapter's conceptualization of the closet also draws upon efforts in queer studies to trouble binaries like secrecy/disclosure and invisibility/visibility that commonly are signified in references to the closet—i.e., that one is either "in" or "out." As Fuss (1991) famously noted, a problem with the rhetoric of the closet is that "most of us are both inside and outside at the same time" (9). The simultaneity to which Fuss referred speaks to critical perspectives in queer studies on the disciplinary techniques of the closet. By making queer aberration a consequential phenomenon, the arrangements of power that orchestrate the closet have produced a heightened awareness, or "spectacle" (Sedgwick, 1990), of queer secrecy, allowing them to enforce the suppression of queerness while concurrently shining a taunting spotlight on the act of queer hiding. Even if the closet door is ostensibly and dutifully closed, the queer subject is not necessarily immune to external campaigns to acknowledge the door's presence and function. Consequently, in addition to marking the sociohistorically produced pressures to conceal queerness, the closet functions as a contested site where the impulse for queer secrecy and disavowal coexists and collides with attempts to make queerness visible and, thus, more accessible to homophobic surveillance and derision. Instead of absolute distinctions between "in" and "out," the closet is constituted at once by degrees of silence and disclosure, degrees of ignorance and knowing (Sedgwick, 1990). Furthermore, as socially produced nodes of power, the degrees of secrecy and exposure that constitute the closet can be modified by multiple actors within a given social context, making the negotiation of the closet a collective social enterprise. For this chapter, understanding the closet in these terms enables analyses of those moments when the queerness of closeted BQM teachers is not only denied, ignored, or silenced, but also questioned, hinted at, or acknowledged. What happens during those moments—the degrees of queer secrecy and exposure that are produced and then renegotiated—can reveal how the closet functions variably across time and space to shape the personal and professional fates of BQM teachers.

Exploring Black Queer Narratives

Five of the 11 men in this study were queer. While these five participants spoke about their queerness in one-on-one interviews, no disclosures of queer sexual identities occurred during focus group sessions. Furthermore, as discussed later in this chapter, some of the five participants only tentatively acknowledged their queerness in one-on-one interviews, producing moments in their narratives that, while incredibly instructive,

Table 6.1 New Pseudonyms for Analysis of Queerness

Participant	Identification
Davis Cass	Gay
Leo Icarus	None provided
Maxwell Sid	Gay
Peter Ulrich	Not heterosexual
Ray Jackson	Homosexual

clearly reflected some discomfort. These factors led me to create a new set of pseudonyms for the five participants whose experiences are explored in this chapter. These pseudonyms, along with how participants identified their sexual orientations, appear in Table 6.1. In addition to the use of new pseudonyms, some details from participants' narrative accounts have been omitted to further protect their anonymity. While these measures may prove somewhat disorienting for readers, and while they unfortunately inhibit connections between the following discussion and participants' narrative excerpts elsewhere in this book, it is my hope that readers will be sympathetic toward the intent of these additional protective measures.

Across the narratives of the five men who are referenced in this chapter, three themes illuminated their negotiations of the closet as BQM teachers: their closeted participation in this study; their expectations of the classroom as a closeted space; and the closet as the site of teacher-student power struggles. I will now turn to an exploration of these themes.

Closeted Participation in This Study

While participation in this study provided a unique opportunity for respondents to reflect upon and speak about their experiences as Black men in the teaching profession, it also produced unanticipated tensions around queer disclosures. As noted, no queer disclosures occurred during either of the focus groups conducted for this study. Additionally, the in-depth interviews for this study were sites where the participants negotiated shifting degrees of closetedness. What follows are some examples of these negotiations from one-on-one interviews with participants.

Pre-study social interactions with each of the five BQM participants suggested a level of openness about his sexuality that I as a researcher assumed would carry over into the study. This assumption quickly faltered during the first in-depth interviews when participants were given the opportunity to name and describe identities besides Blackness and maleness that played significant roles in defining who they were. For instance, after making several vague references to "my sexuality," Peter, when asked how he labeled his sexuality, stated that he did not have such a label. When subsequently asked how he would generally describe (rather than specifically "label") his sexuality, he responded, "Not heterosexual." Similarly, a second participant, Ray, made several references to his sexuality without specifically marking it as queer. When asked how he labeled his sexual identity, he, too, stated that he did not have a label, explaining his disregard for "gay" as a marker of cross-dressing gender confusion. Eventually, Ray expressed slightly less discomfort with "homosexual," but nonetheless voiced a continued aversion to labels when he stated, "I will not say that I am not homosexual, but I will not say that I am gay."

Although their aversions to labels initially made more specific knowledge about their sexualities inaccessible, Peter and Ray ultimately allowed "not heterosexual" and "homosexual," respectively, to facilitate explorations of their queerness. Contrastively, another participant, Leo, resisted providing such language, thus maintaining barriers around more intimate knowledge of his queerness. During the first interview, after Leo made no mention of his sexuality as an identity that defined who he was, I attempted to tactfully raise the topic, as captured in the following exchange:

Ed: You and I met in a cyberspace where certain people congregate.
Leo: Mmm-hmm.
Ed: Does that sort of figure into how you see yourself?
Leo: Nope.
Ed: No. Interesting.
Leo: Mmm. . . *[Pause]*. Sort of. Sort of.
Ed: Can you elaborate a bit on that?
Leo: There's always this connotation of being always sharp, together, on-point, excellent. Just a tad above the rest. And I think I fall into that.
Ed: So you exhibit those characteristics that are associated with this particular population? Being sharp. . .
Leo: Professionally, yes.

After several minutes of using references to "sharp style" as a proxy for queerness, Leo stated that he did not have a label for the subject to which he and I were referring, and he added, "I don't let it define me. It's a part of my character. It's a part of my make-up. It's not an overwhelming part of my make-up, but it's a part of my make-up." When asked how he would label that part of his make-up, Leo responded, "Honestly, I'm still working on that. Still defining that answer."

Unlike Peter and Ray, who balked at labels but nonetheless made references to their sexuality, Leo resisted any direct references to his sexuality. Instead, he found terminological proxies that enabled him to explain the minimal significance he attributed to his queerness while never explicitly marking queerness as such. In their second in-depth, one-on-one interviews, Peter and Ray revisited themes around their sexualities, offering insightful details into how homophobia influenced their relationships with students. Leo, on the other hand, did not. Additionally, while varying levels of queer disclosures occurred with all five queer participants in one-on-one interviews, no such disclosures occurred during focus group sessions as queer participants discussed their teaching experiences in the presence of other study participants. All of these factors exemplified the closet as a negotiation between degrees of silence and disclosure that manifested differently across this study. In contrast to pre-study encounters, speaking formally about their experiences as Black male teachers produced pressures for some participants to conceal their queerness.

This reticence to name queerness, which stood in stark contrast to willing explorations of Blackness and maleness during study interviews, suggested an inherent conflict for some participants between their (semi-) private experiences of queerness and their public identifications as both Black men and Black male teachers. It also spoke to a hierarchy of sorts between their racial and sexual identities. During one-on-one interviews, four participants—Davis, Maxwell, Peter, and Ray—stated that their sexualities, while significant, were not as influential as Blackness in shaping their sense of self. For these men, racial markers ultimately took precedence over indicators of sexual identity and difference. This hierarchy helps to further explain the contrast between some participants' willing examinations of Blackness and their dodgy articulations of queerness in this study.

Expectations of the Classroom as a Closeted Space

None of the five Black queer participants in this study were openly queer in their classrooms, and this was due in part to their own reported expectations that the classroom would and/or should operate as a closeted space for queer teacher sexuality. Ray, for example, remarked that it would be inappropriate to bring his queerness into the classroom. Similarly, Leo explained that he did not express his queerness in school because it doesn't have anything to do with the classroom. "Certain things I want [to have an] influence, certain things I don't want [to have an] influence. So I know what to keep in the classroom, I know what to not keep in the classroom." For both Ray and Leo, the classroom was understood as an inappropriate space for articulations of their queer sexual identities.

Expecting the classroom to function as a closeted space for queer teacher sexuality led some teachers to police possible signs of their queerness. For instance, Peter described an attention to attire, noting how certain styles of dress enabled him to exude a more masculine image that was less likely to fall under homophobic surveillance. Likewise, Davis described an attention to attire, as well as to speech:

Davis: Just little things, especially in the classroom, like making sure I'm dressed in a certain way, making sure these jeans are just not too tight, or certain speech that because I only talk to gay people, I'll use fluidly and then all of a sudden think, "Did I really just say that?"

Ed: Like what? Can you think of a slippage?

Davis: I remember last year, I got so mad at one of my classes, and they just made me go off. And I was just like, "I am not the one." I just lost it. . .

Ed: You started reading![2]

Davis: And then, it was funny. Three weeks later, this little girl was like, "Y'all better not mess with Mr. Cass, he is not the one." *[Laughter].* I thought, "Nooo! Nooo!"

Although this recollection amused Davis, it nonetheless revealed his awareness of the classroom as a space in which a teacher's queerness must be concealed. Entering the classroom required the regulation of ways of being that, while acceptable in queer spaces outside of school, could be marked as unacceptably queer in the classroom. Unlike Ray and Leo, Davis did not convey an explicit conviction that classroom articulations of queer teacher sexual identity were wholly inappropriate. Nonetheless, the knowledge that the classroom would ultimately present pressures to conceal queerness led all the teachers mentioned above to monitor the potential signs of their own queerness in the classroom.

The Closet as the Site of Teacher-Student Power Struggles

The most provocative accounts of the closet emerged in descriptions of power struggles between teachers and students. In an underresourced urban school district where stress and conflict abounded, the tenuous balance between secrecy and disclosure of BQM teachers' sexualities became a fertile terrain for student contestations of teacher authority. Based on participants' narratives, students had the power through a variety of speech acts—from homophobic innuendos to direct inquiries into teachers' sexual identities—to produce a heightened visibility of BQM teachers' suspected queerness. The strategies that BQM teachers employed to avoid and/or address such speech acts revealed the closet as the product of an ongoing battle of wills in the classrooms and hallways of Brewerton schools. Furthermore, these strategies pointed to the pressures that BQM teachers faced to perform their identities as Black men in particular ways in front of a predominantly Black student body.

While none of the Black queer men in this study had disclosed their queerness to students, a number of narrative passages revealed how BQM teachers could become targets of student homophobia despite efforts to conceal their sexualities. For instance, an anecdote shared by Ray illustrated how one student had attempted to undermine his authority by challenging the silence around his queerness:

Ray: Like the other day, there's a boy, this one who made it an issue, and I put him out of my class and he begged me to come back to class. He yawned in class [*Ray demonstrates dramatic yawn*]. I said, "You could at least put your hand to your mouth." And you know what he turned that into? "What you say you're going to put in my mouth?" You know, so. . .

Ed: Go [*as in telling the student to go, or to leave the classroom*].

Ray: He did go. But I'm saying, he wanted to start something out of it. Of course everybody chuckled because they realized the sexual connotation. And I put him out, and I explained to the principal why I put him out, and I want to see a parent before he comes back to class.

In addition to this specific instance, Ray also reported that male students had called him "faggot" in the past and had made remarks like "ooh, he's gonna come and get you from behind," once again as antagonistic responses to his assertions of teacher authority.

Other responses by BQM teachers to students' homophobic speech acts further illuminated the closet as a site of teacher—student power struggles. In the anecdotes that follow, Maxwell recalled dramatically contentious interactions with students over the visibility of his queerness:

There are a whole bunch of kids who just call me faggot that I don't even teach. And one of them, he called me a faggot, and I was like, "You're gonna be fat, dumb, and fuckin' ugly for the rest of your life." And I blew the shit out of him, like just railed him a new one in the hallway in front of everybody. And then he ended up sending me [an email] message saying, "A-yo, you fuckin' faggot, you gay as shit." I went to the administration, I did what I had to do [*i.e. reporting the student's actions*].

Another incident recounted by Maxwell echoed the confrontational nature of student speech acts that attempted to expose his queerness, and it once again revealed the potentially volatile tenor of teacher responses:

Maxwell: Again, most of the kids who have called me a faggot are kids who've done it out of real anger. I think that I've had three [students this year call me faggot]. And I think two of those three kids that did it to me were new students to the class who kind of didn't get the agenda and know what the fuck was going on. But then, other than that it's been kids like out in the hallway. "Look at that faggot walk down the hallway." I saw this kid, he was like, "You faggot." And one of my other teachers happened to be with me, and she cursed him out. I didn't even say a word. She was just like, "Yo, your mother tricks on 9th Street. When you get her to handle that, you can say stuff to us."

Ed: That's what the other teacher said?!
Maxwell: Yes.

These excerpts from Maxwell's narrative are obviously disturbing. While the aim of this analysis is neither to defend nor critique those who were involved in these encounters, it is difficult to ignore the apparent normalization of disrespect, at least during the interactions recounted above, that surfaced in the caustic language of students and teachers, and that surely compromised the safety of all. That said, the tone of the preceding excerpts is also instructive. Despite Maxwell's desire to empower Black youth, students' homophobic speech acts had the capacity to interrupt that work by jeopardizing his safety and authority as a queer participant within an adversarial school culture. His colleague's "defense" of him in the second excerpt further underscored the antagonistic dynamics at play between teachers and students and, thus, the urgency of diffusing students' attempts to attack Maxwell by exposing his queerness.

The accounts from Maxwell's narrative revealed the reversal of insulting speech acts onto students as one strategy for reestablishing his authority and security as a BQM teacher. In other narrative passages, Maxwell discussed the performance of a masculinist, "hood" (or Black urban) persona as yet another response to homophobic encounters with students. This persona drew upon what Maxwell poignantly described as a "fuck you" coping strategy that he had developed during his own adolescent confrontations with homophobia, and that used external projections of bravado to mask his internal bouts of doubt and insecurity as a Black queer male. From his vantage point, his students' knowledge of his upbringing in a Black urban community helped to make his masculinist, hood persona an effective tool for reestablishing his authority, as he explained during a one-on-one interview:

Like today, one of my students said to one of my neighbors—like because I went ballistic, I had an anxiety attack at work—and before my anxiety attack when I was wilding-out on them, one of the girls went up to one of my co-workers and was like, "Yo, he got straight ghetto on them kids in there." So again, as much as there's that "oh he may be gay," at the same time I hold my boys up against the wall and like, "yo I'm not playing with you." I'm rough with them and I'll wild-out on them in a "bunk whatever you think about me" kind of way. Let me remind you where I'm from.

In this passage, Maxwell described an aggressive form of disciplinary authority that typified the culture of many Brewerton schools. As discussed in Chapter 4, the pressure for Black male teachers, queer or otherwise, to perform this style of discipline is cause for concern. This chapter, however, seeks to identify strategies that BQM teachers employed in response to the institutional cultures in which they participated. In this excerpt, Maxwell pointed to the performance of a masculinist persona—one that combined physical contact with boys and a hood authenticity—as one of those strategies.

Like Ray and Maxwell, another participant, Peter, reported being the target of student speech acts that attempted to publicly mark him as queer. However, his responses to these speech acts unveiled a set of strategies that differed significantly from the ones described by Ray and Maxwell. For instance, one day during the after-school program at his school, Peter had a conversation with a boy who would repeatedly make taunting remarks about his queerness:

> He always has comments about my sexuality. And I actually sat down with him Thursday, this past Thursday. I sat down at the table and I said, "Do you think I'm gay?" And he said, "Nah, I don't think you gay. I just be messin' with you, I just be playin' with you." But then we had this long conversation. He was like, "But do you have a girlfriend?" I was like, "But really, why does it matter? Why is it important to you?" He was like, "You don't do things like a straight person would do," or something like that. I was like, "Well, like what?" He was like, "You never talk about your girlfriend or anything like that." I was like, "So I should talk about my girlfriend all the time? That would make me more . . ." So he was trying to explain it to me, but he couldn't really. But it led into this conversation, and that's a question I get a lot from kids: "Are you married? Do you have kids?" I've had kids who would come out and make little comments about "am I gay," you know. And they're pretty straightforward. They're like, "You gay?" *[Laughter]*. And generally that's what I do. I laugh. I'm like "whatever," and I just kind of brush it off and go on.

While Peter brushed off student inquiries into his sexuality at certain times, his exchange with this particular student during the after-school program revealed an attempt to engage the young man in a critical consideration of homophobia. In a similar vein, Peter described how he facilitated an awareness of homophobia when responding to another student who repeatedly quipped "that's so gay" whenever he disliked something:

> So Frankie, the boy who says that everything is gay, I think that he's at least aware. Because what I had to do was start calling him out on things. So every time he'd say something in class like "I don't feel like doing no work," [I would reply] "You don't feel like doing no work? That's gay!" *[Laughter]*. "That's gay, you don't wanna do no work." So now I do that all the time. Well, I don't do it as much anymore, but for like maybe a week or two, I did that with everything that he would say. I'd be like "that's gay!" He was like, "I don't have no pencil." "You don't have no pencil? That's gay!" *[Laughter]*. So everything he said, I would come back at him with that. So now, I know every time he's getting ready to say it, like he thinks about. I can see him like . . . he'll look at me and, you know what I mean. So I know that he's at the very least thinking, and I know that other kids in class are also.

Both excerpts above demonstrated Peter's attempts to diffuse homophobic student speech acts by transforming them into anti-homophobic teachable moments. While these teachable moments did not necessarily transform students' homophobic attitudes, they did help some students to at least monitor their homophobic comments in class, while encouraging others to begin to think more critically about queer issues.

In other interview excerpts, Peter described class discussions in which students raised questions about queer issues and/or homophobia. Peter reported that while he was careful to not initiate such discussions—so as not to generate further unwanted speculation around his own queerness—he was quite willing to facilitate these discussions when student-initiated. Doing so not only created opportunities for whole-class interrogations of gender, sexuality, and homophobia, but it also facilitated supportive connections between Peter and a handful of queer students. Peter described a BQM student who, while in Peter's words, was "very deep in the closet," would still stop by his classroom to discuss the struggles he was experiencing with his sexuality. Similarly, Peter described the in-class participation of a Black queer female student who eventually outed herself in class and repeatedly shared her perspectives during class discussions, due in part to the environment that he had established in his classroom. These accounts of his queer-friendly classroom culture revealed his willingness to allow space for the exploration of queer issues while strategically not presenting himself as an advocate for such discussions. Furthermore, they offered additional examples of his engagement in anti-homophobic pedagogical work as a closeted BQM teacher, specifically when that work entailed supporting Black queer students.

While Peter presented several examples of in-class examinations of queer identity and homophobia involving the entire class, he ultimately thought that one-on-one interactions with students around such issues had the most potential for affording critical reflection. Peter reported that in the absence of the pressure to perform a publicly virulent homophobic persona in front of peers, students still expressed homophobic views but were able to engage in thoughtful and more respectful considerations of identity and power. Interestingly, it was as he reflected on these one-on-one interactions that Peter considered the possibility of outing himself to students:

Peter: Sometimes I really wish I could just . . . I really wish I could be very open with some of my students, especially particular students I feel would benefit from it. And I just, you know, I haven't, and I'm very hesitant to. But there are times when I really. . .

Ed: Can you give me an example?

Peter: So, Ricky, when I was talking to him after school on Thursday, I really wanted to tell him, "Well, I am gay," and been able to have a conversation with him. Because I don't think that he would've changed his interaction with me. I think if anything else, it would've opened a very interesting dialogue, and a very interesting . . . I don't know. I feel like he would've learned a lot, and I feel like it would've been a good opportunity for him to ask questions and get answers. I really wanted to say that to him, just to see. And I guess there's ways I could have done it, kind of hypothetically. You know, "Well what if I were gay?" You know what I mean, and sort of had that conversation. But there are times when I feel the urge to say something, but I don't.

Ultimately, for Peter, the risks of outing himself outweighed the potential benefits. Still, that such a consideration emerged in connection to his one-on-one interactions with students attested to the potential of such interactions, in Peter's eyes, to critically engage his students in thoughtful dialogue.

Given the contentious backdrop of teacher—student interactions, it was not surprising that most of the student speech acts described in study participants' accounts were aimed at exposing BQM teachers' queerness and, thus, contesting their authority as teachers. Some speech acts, however, were fueled by the opposite intent. In cases where students felt loyal to BQM teachers who were under homophobic siege, these students would sometimes offer counter-claims to their peers' accusations. For instance, Peter reported that some students who favored him would provide unsolicited counter-claims of his purported heterosexuality:

I have a lot of kids who defend me without me saying anything. "Nah, Mr. Ulrich ain't gay! Mr. Ulrich got a girlfriend." *[Chuckle].* You know. They'll be like, "Mr. Ulrich married." And I don't know where it comes from, because I don't put it out there.

Maxwell offered a similar example of student counter-claims. In one instance, Maxwell recalled, "One girl [said], 'Everybody says you're gay, but you and I know deep down inside that you're not gay, and you just joke around too much.'" Perhaps even more telling was the reaction of the students in one of Maxwell's classes upon learning that one of their peers had emailed a homophobic message to their teacher: "I told my kids about this message that was sent to me. And the kids were like, 'Who the fuck sent that to you? Are you serious? I need to know who it is. We're gonna go get him.'" For Maxwell and Peter, despite the student speech acts that targeted their queerness, some students were willing to offer counter-claims of these teachers' heterosexuality—and in the case of Maxwell, some were even willing to exact revenge on a peer for his homophobic speech act—in order to express loyalty to these teachers.

Ray, Maxwell, and Peter offered provocative examples of the closet as a nexus of power struggles with students. By contrast, not only did Davis report that his students never expressed suspicions of his queerness, but he also described student inquiries into his alleged heterosexual romances with female colleagues:

> The kids are always like, "Do you got a girlfriend? Who's your girl-friend?" And this girl that's applying for [a teaching job] a couple of weeks ago came in and she observed my classroom. She's a cute little Black girl, and they were just like, "Is that your girlfriend?" And they would always say . . . I was really close to the teacher that was next to me last year. "You going with Ms. Nelson?" They all started these convoluted stories of how I was cheating on Ms. Nelson with another teacher in the building. Then we went on a field trip and they saw me eating lunch with another teacher, and they walked up to her and were like, "You better get off Ms. Nelson's man." So I mean, it's sort of all in fun, but I feel like when you inquire about stuff like that, it's in fun but you kind of really wanna know at the same time. So I mean, I just kinda never really talked to them about that. They'll be like, "Do you have kids?" "No, I don't have kids. I have y'all, that's all I need." *[Laughter]*.

In stark contrast to the accounts offered by Ray, Peter, and Maxwell, Davis described elaborate student speculation around his perceived het-erosexuality. This type of student speculation was perhaps due to his gender performance. A former college athlete, Davis's tall and muscu-lar build fit conventional notions of masculinity that apparently did not incite student suspicions of queerness. Stories about his college athletic career piqued the interest and admiration of his male students, and occa-sional bouts of horseplay with male students helped to establish his phys-ical prowess, as he recalled during a one-on-one interview:

> My first year, I made sure that there were times when I asserted myself physically. In the back of their minds, they [his students] knew

that not only was I mentally in control but physically as well. Like Desmond for example, he'd say that he was going to beat me up, like just joking. So I used to go out in the yard sometimes during lunch, and I would play football with them. He was threatening me again during the game, so I picked him up and stuffed his head in the trash can *[chuckle]*. I had his feet literally hanging out of a garbage can, and I made him apologize *[chuckle]*. And all the kids were like "AAAAAHHHH!!!" It's just kind of like testing those waters and seeing where your position is. I feel like with men in general, there's always kind of like, you know, let's feel each other out to see what the dynamics of this relationship are gonna be.

While unfolding during lighthearted moments of horseplay with his male students, Davis's deliberate demonstrations of his physical prowess still enabled him to perform a masculine teacher persona that playfully yet strategically established his dominion over his students, particularly the boys. That persona seemingly protected him from the homophobic student surveillance experienced by other BQM teachers in this study.

In sum, all of the excerpts referenced in this section of Chapter 6 revealed the closet as a consequential site of power struggles within schools. By heightening the visibility of a BQM teacher's presumed queerness, students could place his authority in jeopardy; by defending a BQM teacher's presumed heterosexuality, students could reconsolidate his legitimacy and belonging. For queer study participants, the closet, as described earlier in this chapter, was a site where queer secrecy could collide with homophobic surveillance, producing degrees of queer invisibility and exposure that were negotiated daily with students. Study participants' savvy in managing the threat of queer exposure emerged as a vital survival strategy in their careers as BQM teachers.

Reckoning With the Black Queer Closet

The narrative accounts of the BQM teachers in this study echoed a key assertion throughout the literature on queer individuals in the teaching profession: Homophobia can cast a dubious shadow over the lives and careers of queer educators. Despite the inclusion of sexual orientation in the Brewerton School District's anti-discrimination policies, the threat of being marked as queer—especially by students—could place a heavy burden on the BQM teachers in this study to determine how to contend with homophobic surveillance. Like other works that have built the case for anti-homophobic educational reforms (Kosciw, Greytak, Giga, Villenas, & Danischewski, 2016; Meyer, 2010), this study indicates the need to radically transform the anti-queer institutional cultures of American K–12 schools by engaging students, teachers, and other stakeholders in respectful and critical deliberations over homophobia and its effects. Anti-discrimination policies may offer legal safety nets, but they also may do little to interrupt the day-to-day encounters with homophobia described by the Black queer men in this study. The experiences of queer educators, Black and otherwise, are not likely to improve until schools complement policy-level protections with genuine, ground-level initiatives that directly target the homophobic dynamics of teacher-student encounters and other aspects of everyday school culture.

While the need to tackle homophobia in districts like Brewerton is clear, the role of teachers like the men in this chapter in such efforts is not. With gay liberationist underpinnings, the literature on queers in teaching, as noted earlier, has repeatedly idealized the openly queer educator. According minimal attention to the lives of Black queer educators, this literature has yet to fully interrogate the resonance of a politics of outness for Black queers in the teaching profession. By contrast, a body of work situated in the field of Black queer studies has troubled the salience of gay liberationist notions of outness and closetednness among Black queer individuals (Allen, 2011; E. P. Johnson, 2006, 2008; McCune, 2014; Ross, 2005; Snorton, 2014). In particular, these works have revealed that the desire to sustain ties with and receive support from Black communities, even when those communities harbor levels of antiqueerness, can complicate or even outweigh the purported benefits of a seemingly White-oriented, gay liberationist politics of outness for some Black queers. These perspectives from Black queer studies provide an illuminating backdrop for the narratives of the five BQM teachers in this study. As discussed in this chapter, all five BQM participants were closeted in their classrooms, and four of the five reported prioritizing their Black identities over their queerness. For these men, openly queer self-identifications were not necessarily desirable or even possible once their own backgrounds and senses of self as Black queer men, and their locations within and commitments to Brewerton's predominantly Black schools, were taken into consideration. Scholarly efforts and school-based initiatives that attempt to disrupt homophobia in urban schools, while necessary and just, may not obviate the closet in the lives and work of BQM teachers like my five queer study participants.

It would be problematic, of course, to assume that all BQM teachers are closeted. Future studies centering BQM teachers who disclose their queerness in schools could make invaluable contributions to the scholarly literatures on queer educators and Black male teachers. Nevertheless, given the anti-queer legacy of the American teaching profession and the queer erasure from both scholarly and popular discourses on Black men in teaching, it is not unreasonable to suspect that the closet will remain intact for now in the professional experiences of many BQM teachers. Hence, another possible direction for future research is to reexamine the relationship between the closet and the agency of BQM educators. This reexamination might challenge notions of the closet as a space and moment of powerlessness in the literature on queer teachers by illuminating the racially mediated, agentic acts of BQM teachers that are afforded by degrees of queer secrecy and invisibility. Peter's case is one example of this potential analytic focus. Despite the degrees of secrecy he attempted to maintain in his classroom and in his responses to some interview questions, Peter described the creation and pursuit of explicitly anti-homophobic teachable moments with Black students. Braving the inquiries and taunts, Peter found ways to talk to students, and to get students to talk to each other, about queerness and homophobia in thoughtful ways. At the same time, the closet allowed him to avoid the more intense censure that he anticipated in response to openly queer self-identifications in his predominantly Black, urban classroom. Peter's story provides one example of how the closet may actually operate as a site for anti-homophobic resistance and transformation in a Black educative setting, while nonetheless offering a degree of protection for BQM teachers working with minimal supports in queer-hostile spaces.

Other reconceptualizations of the closet are possible through analyses of the narratives of Davis and Maxwell. For Davis, the closet allowed him to secure his Black masculine image, as his narratives revealed a self-conscious manipulation of masculine gender performances in order to evade homophobic surveillance within the classroom. For Maxwell, while he was not as successful as Davis in avoiding the homophobic scrutiny of students, he still was able to wield an authentically Black urban identity that could temporarily secure his closeted status and reestablish his authority in the classroom. In both cases, these teachers arguably used the closet to perform racially mediated acts of agency. Unlike the case of Peter, these acts were not connected in any obvious fashion to anti-homophobic struggle, but they nonetheless revealed pedagogical agendas in predominantly Black educational settings that were effectively served by the closet.

To be sure, none of these reconceptualizations of the closet should be divorced from considerations of the signs of queer abjection that remained. Leo, Peter, and Ray's reticence to label their sexualities, Maxwell's description of his "fuck you" coping strategy, and Maxwell and Ray's contentious encounters with students' homophobia were among several indicators from participant narratives that the closet was far from idyllic for these men. Yet some of these cases still suggest that queer abjection was not the only manner in which these men experienced the closet. By exploring the relative (in)security and (dis)comfort of the Black queer closet, future research on BQM teachers could continue to critique the reproduction of Black queer marginality in K–12 schooling while also developing deeper understandings of how the closet may enable BQM teachers to survive in—and under some circumstances, subvert—homophobic school cultures.

That the closet may facilitate BQM teachers' survival in anti-queer school environments suggests one more crucial implication that, while implicit in this discussion thus far, deserves explicit recognition: the Black queer closet's relationship to Black masculinity politics. The patriarchal authority and hegemonic masculinity that pervaded the examples of saviorist discourses reviewed in Chapter 2, and that also informed study participants' narratives on disciplinary authority and gendered power dynamics in the workplace in Chapters 4 and 5, respectively, surfaced yet again in participants' accounts of the closet. The failure at times to convincingly perform hegemonic masculinity is what made Ray, Peter, and Maxwell occasional targets of students' homophobic speech acts, and the ability to convincingly perform that brand of masculinity allowed Maxwell to recuperate his authority while also enabling Davis to avoid anti-queer suspicions altogether. If the closet produces degrees of queer exposure or invisibility, then participants' performance of hegemonic masculinity was essential to managing the closet in their favor.

The relationship between masculinity and the closet in the narratives of the men in this chapter raises an important question about what to make of the complicated nature of the Black queer closet. A throughline in this book is that an authoritarian, domineering, and sometimes combative Black masculinity can be of disservice to Black male teachers, their colleagues, and their students. While the closet, as argued above, may provide protection for and afford the agency of teachers like the five BQM study participants, it may also require the performance of a hegemonic masculinity. For BQM teachers like the men in this study, how do we weigh the potential affordances of the closet against the potential ramifications of the masculinity required to produce it? The complex tensions between power and vulnerability in BQM study participants' narratives make this a difficult question to answer. Future research could make invaluable contributions by exploring this question in more depth, across more educational settings, and with a greater diversity of BQM study participants.

Finally, the relationship between the closet and Black masculinity in study participants' narratives begs us to consider the potential implications for broader discourses on Black male teachers. As noted earlier in this chapter, Black queer men have been noticeably absent from saviorist discourses on Black men and Black male teachers. Works by a handful of authors (Connell, 2014; Hayes, 2014; Woodson & Pabon, 2016) have joined the earlier iteration of this chapter (Brockenbrough, 2012a) in acknowledging the presence and perspectives of BQM teachers, but these works still represent a small portion of the larger corpus of work on Black men in teaching. The slow uptake of queer-inclusive perspectives throughout this field of study suggests that dominant discourses on Black male teachers continue to be invested in constructions of Black masculinity that depend on queer invisibility. Producing more queer-inclusive inquiries on Black men in teaching could disrupt queer invisibility and trouble the consequences of heteronormative masculinities for

Black male teachers, queer and otherwise, and their students. However, the narratives cited in this chapter raise concerns about the impact of such inquiries for BQM teachers. Namely, scholarship and support initiatives that nobly attempt to be more inclusive of BQM teachers may risk increasing the visibility of a group that relies upon—and possibly even prefers—its invisibility. Consequently, future inquiries that seek to trouble the heteronormative limits of saviorist discourses on Black male teachers may have to juggle the scholarly desire to surface the voices of BQM teachers with the ethical realization that these teachers may not share a similar investment in dismantling their classroom closets.

Conclusion

Throughout the educational scholarship on queers in American K–12 schools, a gay liberationist logic that casts the closet as a space of queer abjection decries the closet's impact on queer educators. It is the openly queer educator, free from anti-queer silence and shame, who embodies the promise of anti-homophobic change in this body of literature. Eschewing conceptualizations of the closet as an in/out binary, this chapter embraced an understanding of the closet as degrees of queer invisibility and exposure that are negotiated by the queer subject and other actors within a given social context. For my five queer male study participants, degrees of queer silence and invisibility marked their participation in my study, as well as their perceptions of the classroom as an appropriately closeted space. But it was in descriptions of the power relations between study participants and students that the most provocative accounts of the closet emerged. Set in conflict-ridden Brewerton school cultures, queer participants' narratives detailed how students had the power through a variety of speech acts—from homophobic innuendos and epithets to direct inquiries into teachers' sexual identities—to produce a heightened visibility of BQM teachers' queerness. Queer study participants' efforts to avoid and/or undermine such speech acts revealed the closet as the product of ongoing negotiations of identities, loyalties, power, and belonging that could expose or occlude queerness in the classrooms and hallways of Brewerton schools.

When considered in conjunction with queer study participants' identities and commitments as Black male teachers, the closet emerges as a site not only of queer abjection, but of Black queer agency as well. As conveyed across several narrative excerpts, degrees of queer invisibility enabled the queer teachers in my study to engage in agentic acts—from encouraging anti-homophobic reflections among Black students to pursuing other pedagogical agendas as Black male teachers in predominantly Black school settings—while dodging or enduring the anti-queer surveillance that surrounded them. By recognizing queer study participants' racially mediated aims, this chapter demonstrates how the Black queer closet may reproduce queer silences while simultaneously affording various forms of agency for BQM teachers. Since the extant body of scholarship on Black queer educators remains relatively small, future research could make invaluable contributions by further exploring how BQM teachers understand and exercise their agency. Additionally, since participants' abilities to perform hegemonic masculinity affected their negotiations of the closet, future inquiries could also delve deeper into the complicated relationship between Black queer agency and Black masculinity politics in the experiences of BQM urban teachers.

Notes

1. See Black (2017), Marcus (2002), Savage (2011), and Signorile (1993) for examples of this liberationist narrative, with its emphasis on the detriments of the closet and the transformative effects of coming out.
2. "Reading" is a performative style of verbal assertion and truth-telling in BQM culture. See E. P. Johnson (2008) for a fuller description.

7 "The Whole Black Thing Helps, Too"

The Affordances of Culturally Responsive Pedagogies

So far, excerpts from the narratives of the men in my study have been used to illuminate negotiations of Black masculinity politics that may burden the experiences of Black men in urban teaching. With saviorist discourses on Black manhood frequently overshadowing the dilemmas that Black male teachers may encounter in urban classrooms, spotlighting some of those dilemmas is a critical intervention in this book. It is important, however, to also recognize that the experiences of Black male teachers can encompass more than just trials and tribulations. My study participants' narratives may have unearthed prickly encounters and contentious power dynamics with colleagues and students, but they also identified the pedagogical insights and successes that characterized these educators' experiences in their classrooms, echoing both scholarly and popular media depictions of Black men in the teaching profession. Any rendering of my study participants' experiences would be incomplete without their accounts of their strengths and accomplishments as Black male teachers in Brewerton schools.

In this chapter, my study participants' pedagogical insights on educating and empowering Black youth take center stage. Those insights are situated throughout this chapter within the culturally responsive pedagogical traditions of Black educators. As noted in the review of scholarly literature on Blacks in the American teaching profession in Chapter 1, culturally responsive pedagogy recognizes cultural background as a significant mediator of students' learning and engagement within educational spaces (Gay, 2010; Ladson-Billings, 2009; Milner, 2011; Villegas & Lucas, 2002). This recognition, in turn, informs curricular content, instructional techniques, classroom management and engagement strategies, and modes of care that attend to students' culturally mediated participation in learning environments (Dixson, 2003; Gay, 2010; Ladson-Billings, 2009; Milner, 2011; Monroe, 2009). In this study, ten of the 11 participants described instructional interactions and interpersonal relationships with Black Brewerton students that mirrored the collective culturally responsive pedagogical traditions of Black educators. Across multiple narrative passages, study participants' lived experiences, worldviews, and loyalties as Black adults in America repeatedly emerged as significant mediators of their culturally responsive pedagogical work. In what follows, their accounts of their culturally responsive pedagogies are organized around four recurrent themes: curriculum content and discussions; discipline and classroom management; language, culture, and attire; and the special connectedness with Black male students.

Curriculum Content and Discussions

Even as neoliberal educational reforms have intensified the surveillance of teachers' compliance with state-mandated curriculum standards (Schniedewind & Sapon-Shevin, 2012), teachers' personal identities, cultural backgrounds, sociopolitical worldviews, and pedagogical beliefs continue to play powerful roles in shaping their classroom cultures and their students' learning experiences. The teachers in this study were no exception in this regard. Reflecting on teaching experiences under increasing curricular and instructional constraints within the Brewerton School District, five participants provided notable accounts of how their identities, cultural backgrounds, and racialized worldviews as Black male teachers informed their additions to existing curriculum content and their strategies for discussing race-related topics with Black students. The excerpts shared in this section reveal how these participants understood curriculum content and discussions as important facets of their culturally responsive pedagogies.

Two of the participants who described culturally responsive curriculum adaptations were Greg and Bill. In a one-on-one interview, Greg explained how being a Black male teacher motivated him to counter the lack of positive Black images on television and in other media by adding inspirational images of African Americans to in-class writing exercises. In another one-on-one interview, Bill described his incorporation of song lyrics by popular Black musical artists to help Black students grasp certain literacy concepts and skills. In the following excerpt, Bill explained how he would complement the poetic texts in the mandated literature curriculum with song lyrics by popular recording artists like the rapper Young Jeezy:

> There's a lot of things that they have to read, whether I think it's, you know, great poetry or not great poetry. But I also try to bridge the gap between those things and where I know they're coming from to make some things clearer. So we might have to do a sonnet by Shakespeare, but we might start off by doing some Young Jeezy. We might do some Young Jeezy lyrics in order to make a connection to the kids, and then to maybe get . . . So for example, tonight their homework is to find some lyrics of their own. We're talking about scanning, and how you scan lines of poetry and so on and so forth. So they have to bring

in some of their own lyrics, right, that they have scanned themselves and practiced scanning themselves, and then we'll use that tomorrow to talk about finding rhythm and finding rhyme and things like that. And then we can read something like Shakespeare, and hopefully the process of scanning and the process of finding certain things. And the poem becomes easier because at least they have some type of bridge to that.

As conveyed in this excerpt, drawing upon rap lyrics was, for Bill, a way to use the culturally familiar to scaffold his Black students' curricular encounters with new and unfamiliar texts. While this pedagogical practice is not necessarily limited to Black male teachers, Bill did go on to contrast his awareness of rap songs and other popular forms of Black music to the lack of such awareness among some of his White teacher colleagues. He also described employing song lyrics by the recording artist Jill Scott to achieve gender parity and appeal directly to Black female students. Together, Greg's provision of positive Black images and Bill's incorporation of popular song lyrics exemplified the adaptations of curriculum that emerged from their culturally responsive pedagogies.

A third study participant who described a culturally responsive negotiation of curriculum was Ira. Recounting a unit on the 1990s educational policy debates over Ebonics (see Perry & Delpit, 1998), Ira described how his students read texts that were sensitive to and critical of the Oakland, CA, school district's attempts to recognize Ebonics before engaging in their own passionate debates over the topic in class. Centering this debate in the curriculum served two prongs of Ira's pedagogical mission. As he explained in the following interview excerpt, the first prong of that mission was to affirm his Black Brewerton students' identities and ways of being:

Ira: What I try to do is I try to legitimize who they are. This whole idea of legitimacy. Kids come in thinking that they're not legit, they're illegit and incapable, they're written off. They're outcasts. They're this outlier from the norm, you know. What's normal? They're not normal because it seems throughout their lives and this whole academic sphere that they're being told to be something other than who they are. To speak outside of who you are, to behave outside of who you are, to dress outside of who you are. And I don't do that.

Ed: Outside of who they are as. . .

Ira: As urban African American children at risk, all of that. There's a whole bunch of stuff that comes with that psychologically.

Building upon this foundation, Ira used the Ebonics unit to reaffirm his Black Brewerton students' identities and cultures while also pursuing the second prong of his pedagogical mission: making sure his students acquired the necessary skills to participate in mainstream American culture. Reflecting on the Ebonics unit, Ira spoke to this second prong:

> No one speaks like a computer. There's a difference between written standard English and spoken English. There just is. And I let them know, when I'm up here speaking to you, I don't think I'm 100% standard. So the kids were just like, they were seeing it, but pushing them at the same time and saying listen, you have to learn this or know this in the best possible way that you can because our society is built on this particular norm. This is how we function. In order for you to function effectively, you have to be able to identify with it. Adapt to it. Participate in it and all of that good stuff.

Noting his own deviations from standard American English, Ira validated his students' deviations from it as well while simultaneously underscoring the need for them to adapt to and perform it. Mirroring other Black educators' efforts to prepare Black students to participate successfully in cultures of power (Delpit, 1995), Ira sought to equip his students with the requisite tools for navigating and excelling in multiple social worlds. The Ebonics unit was one example of Ira's culturally responsive efforts as a Black educator to empower Black students through the selection of curricular content.

In the examples cited thus far, Greg, Bill, and Ira described how their culturally responsive pedagogical sensibilities came to bear on their curricula. Other examples from study participants' narratives recalled discussions with students that did not stem from curricular content but nevertheless afforded culturally responsive teachable moments with Black students. For instance, during a focus group, Victor recalled his students' reactions to a recent rebroadcast of *Roots* (Wolper, 1977). While the miniseries had not been a part of his curriculum, students' reactions positioned Victor, as a Black teacher, to discuss race and racism with them. As he recalled, this was not the case for one of his White peers:

> Something interesting went on in my class more recently. *Roots* came out again, it was on TV. And so my kids were percolating, coming in and talking about it. So they went to the art room, and the art teacher is White, and they were like, "Oh, we're not going to do any work!" [*Others: laughter*]. You know, it was just this whole percolation around *Roots*.

Students' *Roots*-inspired defiance against the White art teacher contrasted with their engagement with Victor. As he noted, one Black male student was especially consumed by an animosity toward White people and White supremacy after seeing the miniseries. Despite efforts to counsel this student, Victor reported during a focus group that the boy's animosity surfaced one day at a chess tournament:

> So earlier, he would talk about how he just dislikes White people and he hates White people, and he's talking about hate. I'm like, "Why you wanna waste your energy hating?" "Because they hate . . ." You know, so we have this . . . And so he sits across from this little Caucasian boy [at the chess tournament], and he's like, "No offense, but I hate White people." [*Others: laughter.*] Yeah, like trying to start a racial war, a race riot. I had to pull him aside like "yo man, you tryin' to like . . . like, chill." But a part of it, because I did have after-school discourse with him about his feelings . . . I don't know. I don't think he would've had the same kind of conversation with a White teacher. We stayed after school and talked about his feelings and, you know, how he was feeling about hating White people. And I told him, you know, what you're feeling is not abnormal. I went through it. My son, he's like a revolution-will-not-be-televised type of kid, and so he's kinda going through that as well. And that was really interesting, and more recent.

Victor's *Roots* example revealed a culturally responsive capacity to address race-centered teachable moments with Black students that emerged beyond official curriculum content and lesson plans. His own experiences with anger toward Whites and White supremacy as a Black man, along with the experience of shepherding his son through that anger, enabled Victor to empathize with and counsel his Black male student. That Victor questioned whether his student would have discussed such matters with a White teacher further underscored the importance of Victor's lived experiences as a foundation for his culturally responsive insights into the lives and learning of his Black students.

Lived experiences as an anchor for culturally responsive discussions with students emerged in Quincy's narrative as well. In a one-on-one interview, Quincy discussed his role in mitigating tensions at his school between Black American and African students. Cross-cultural tensions between the two groups routinely flared up in the school's hallways, leading to fights and, in one case, a shooting right outside of the school. Given Quincy's Black American identity, some Black American students would seek his validation of their prejudices against Africans as "bad" and AIDS-infected, providing him with opportunities to intervene. As expressed in the following passage, Quincy saw himself as better-positioned than his White counterparts to attempt such interventions:

> When they talk to me, it's like, "*YOU* know what I'm talking about, Mr. Stinson." And I'm like, "I know where you're coming from, I know the mindset you're coming from. I understand that, but

I don't agree with it." So for them that's reasonable, but for a White teacher they [the students] wouldn't say it like that—"we just don't like these African kids"—and just point blank like that and have no explanation. For them there's some sort of "he's supposed to understand what I'm saying. And when he doesn't then let me think about it for a little bit." So it allows me a little more foot-in-the-door about some of these issues.

From Quincy's perspective, his Black American identity seemed to encourage Black American students to share their disdain toward African students with him, thus creating teachable moments around bias. His readiness to respond in those moments was informed by his prior exposure as a Black person to the tensions between Black Americans and Africans:

> Whereas they might try to explain themselves to a White teacher because there might not be that same understanding with them, with that person if they haven't had a lot of experience with this issue, I've seen this my whole life. It may not be as blatant as it is in the Brew, but when I was in college, "Oh, the Africans hate us." So that whole thing is always an undercurrent, so for me it's not brand new. It's not something that I'm just seeing for the first time. So because it's something that's in the Black community to begin with, there's that implicit thing that they feel more comfortable talking to me about, and the whole Black thing helps, too.

As Quincy noted in this excerpt, not only did his status as a Black American teacher seem to encourage Black American students to share their prejudices against their African classmates with him, but his own background as a member of the Black community—which he casually summed up as "the whole Black thing"—gave him insights that might have eluded cultural outsiders. Drawing upon the cultural responsiveness of Black educators as an analytic framework, Quincy's account revealed his understanding of how his insider status in Black culture uniquely positioned him to facilitate culturally resonant discussions with his Black students.

Together, the preceding examples point to curriculum content and discussions as productive sites of culturally responsive pedagogical engagements. The participants who were cited in this section drew upon their lived experiences as Black men to design and adapt curricula, and to facilitate race-related discussions, that addressed the salience of race in the lives of their Black students. Echoing previously reviewed scholarly literature on Black educators, the narrative passages cited thus far indicate how study participants' racialized identities and worldviews mediated their culturally responsive approaches to educating their Black

Brewerton students. This was also evident in participant accounts of other facets of their pedagogical work, as discussed in the sections that follow.

Discipline and Classroom Management

Discipline emerged as a prominent and complex issue for the participants in this study. As explored in depth in Chapter 4, some participants were critical of the discipline-related responsibilities that colleagues routinely doled to them as Black male teachers, and some also struggled to perform the authoritarian modes of Black masculinity that were expected of them as disciplinarians. Yet even amidst these critiques and complications, discipline and classroom management emerged in several participants' narratives as value-added aspects of their culturally responsive pedagogies. In what follows, accounts offered by five of the men in this study are used to illustrate their understanding of discipline and classroom management as facets of their culturally responsive pedagogical engagements with Black students.

Even before disciplinary or classroom management norms were fully established, the symbolic capital of being a Black male teacher proved advantageous for some of the men in this study. Two participants, Ira and Damon, described being a Black male teacher as an initial hook that secured temporary buy-in and compliance from Black students. Another participant, Solomon, went on to operationalize that symbolic capital in his management practices. With his own hair in an afro, and with a classroom poster of Tommie Smith and John Carlos' iconic Olympic Black power salute in the backdrop (Davis, 2008), Solomon used the Black power fist as a gesture to bring his class to order. In all three cases, the discipline-related symbolic capital associated with Black male teachers became evident in these early examples provided by Ira, Damon, and Solomon.

One participant who spoke at length about his approach to discipline and management was Mitch. While noting some exceptions, Mitch stated that he had "kind of become the teacher where you have problem kids that act up in other places but they don't act up with me." To illustrate this claim, Mitch noted how his special education students, along with other students in his class, might misbehave with other teachers but not with him:

> This year they gave me six special ed kids in my section. And they're crazy, they're wild. But they're not wild with me. If they're in my room, they're still special ed. You can look at them and tell that the things that they're doing, they do special ed things, and they require special attention. But they don't pull the kind of stuff they pull with their special ed teacher, and they kind of know not to even think

about it. And my kids [the nonspecial education students], if they're with another teacher, I've walked in on them acting wild and crazy, and then as soon as they see me, a hush falls over them. They sit down and act like that piece of paper in the air magically appeared.

The preceding excerpt included examples that Mitch provided of his students' responsiveness to his disciplinary authority. That responsiveness stemmed from what Mitch characterized as a no-nonsense, culturally rooted approach to management:

I think my approach to teaching, if you had to define it in any way, would first be like a Black approach, and then a male approach after that. Black because it's just kind of old-school Black. And the reason [is] because my philosophy in teaching is nearest to my lead teacher's philosophy, who's a Black woman. And it's like an old-school way of—and first I'll just talk about management—this old-school way of just approaching management. And that's like there's certain things you're supposed to be doing at all times, and there's really no gray area. I'm not gonna play with you about it. And if I told you to walk left and turn 90 degrees, if you do 89 degrees, I'm gonna be in your behind just like if you did 45 degrees.

Elaborating on the "old-school Black" philosophy of his lead teacher (a more experienced teacher who served as a leader and resource for other teachers on Mitch's floor), Mitch described her no-nonsense approach to running her classroom which had earned her a reputation as a strong and successful instructor. Mitch stressed that his lead teacher proceeded with lessons at a rigorous pace, and that students who could not keep up paid the consequences of being left behind. While not averse to having fun with students, she would still enact swift consequences when students did not abide by her rules or meet her stated expectations. Mitch's description of his lead teacher's classroom management style echoed scholarly accounts of the culturally rooted discipline styles of Black teachers (Ford & Sassi, 2014; Milner, 2012; Monroe, 2009) as well as descriptions of the traditional discipline styles of Black parents (Adkison-Bradley, Terpstra, & Dormitorio, 2014; Bradley, 1998). It was not surprising, therefore, that Mitch himself likened this old-school Black approach to the traditional Black parenting style that he had witnessed as a child:

I think it's Black, I think it's southern. I think the two of them kind of go together in a lot of ways, Black and southern, for a lot of other reasons. But the most typical thing, you can listen to the comedians talk about raising kids, and you see the White kid in the store who's like "Mommy, I want it!! Awww!!" And they throw a temper tantrum. And then, you know, Black parents, nowadays not so much, but especially 20 years ago when I was a kid—I think it was a little dying down when I was a kid, although my mother was part of the old school, so it didn't die on her—like you act up in public, it's like "are you serious? We can act up together. Let's make it a show. Let's make it a show." I mean seriously, growing up, I had a belt in my cubby-hole in pre-school. My mother put a belt in my cubby hole and told my teachers, "Don't have a problem using it."

This similarity that Mitch observed between traditional Black parenting styles and his Black female lead teacher's style of management helps to explain why he marked this approach as old-school Black. This approach consequently informed his own emphasis on order and self-reliance:

I'm supposed to let you know something, model it for you, work through it with you, and then at some point I shouldn't have to be there for you to be able to do it. I shouldn't have to stand over top of you for you to be able to convert a fraction to a decimal. In the same way, I shouldn't have to stand over top of you to make sure that you're staying in your seat, you're not yelling, you're concentrating on whatever it is you're supposed to be concentrating on. That's how I feel, that's how I do it. That's honestly how I treat them because I'm not a babysitter, and that's just how it is. I'm not a babysitter.

Just as his Black female lead teacher refused to pamper her students, Mitch refused to babysit his. The similarities that he saw between his approach to running the classroom and that of his lead teacher were in stark contrast to the approach of his partner teacher (a peer in a separate classroom who shared the same group of students). In Mitch's eyes, this teacher, a young White woman, treated her students like babies:

She's very big into systems. She has a token economy. She's very big into things that have buzzwords and things like that. So they do things that they're supposed to do, they get paychecks, all these things. They work fine for her, and her kids eat it up. But they're babies, and they really are babies. They live for just getting something, getting something for doing what it is that they're supposed to do.

His White female partner teacher's use of token economies conflicted with one of Mitch's pedagogical aims, which he attributed to his Blackness:

I guess this comes out of being Black: I don't want them to feel like they are supposed to get something just because they do something they're supposed to do. You're supposed to do it. You're not gonna get something every time you do something you're supposed to do.

What's the point? You're gonna get something if you don't do what you're supposed to do, definitely, but I'm not going to give you something. I'll let you know, I'll give you a shout out, but that's really the most you can expect in life, so get used to it.

Mitch's childhood experiences with his mother's "Black and southern" parenting style, his identification with his Black female lead teacher's approach to running her classroom, and his critique of his White female partner teacher's use of reward systems all brought into relief his own culturally responsive stance on discipline and management. For Mitch, a no-nonsense approach to establishing order drew upon Black parenting and teaching styles, and it reflected his racialized worldview that his students should not become accustomed to receiving rewards for the things that they were supposed to do. That this approach worked with his students was attributable, in Mitch's view, to their familiarity with Black cultural expectations around discipline:

> I definitely think it works because they're Black. I don't know if it works only because they're Black. I definitely think it works because they're Black though. Yeah, definitely, I think it works. I think there's a cultural thing that goes into it where even if you're the Black kid that gets away with stuff, whose parents just kind of just are like "whatever," you kind of have an idea . . . I think by sixth grade, you've been socialized to a point to where you kind of have an idea of, a Black idea as far as discipline and management and those types of things. So even if you aren't from that, you don't live that life, you react to it in a certain way.

The "cultural thing"—a shared cultural background as Black people— was cited by Mitch as the factor that enabled him to engage a culturally responsive pedagogical style to instill disciplined behavior and self-reliance in his Black Brewerton students.

Another participant who described a culturally responsive approach to discipline and management was Felix. His success with classroom management became especially evident to him when other teachers would cite discipline issues with students who were positively engaged in his class. At several points throughout his narrative, Felix explained how he drew upon Black cultural styles of discipline to successfully maintain order in his classroom. In the following exchange, Felix described his use of "the look," a technique that he ultimately attributed to Black parenting and teaching styles:

Felix: When I stare at a student and I give them direct eye contact, they know. They missed out what I'm doing. They know what that means for me. And I don't even have to tell, "When I stare at you that means be quiet." They just know. And maybe it's something they learned at home or it's been a disciplinary technique for them at home. But I sit down and stare at a student and if I'm looking at them. . .

Ed: You look at them like that [*Felix demonstrates look, Ed laughs*]. Pull out the grill [the tough look]!

Felix: Or, I love . . . I just give them direct eye contact. Since you want to talk in my class, my focus is on you. You have now disturbed my class. So when I hand them the demerit pink slip, they know exactly what it's for.

Ed: So you do or do not identify that or characterize that as a Black sort of cultural. . .

Felix: It probably is. I could identify that. I know my mom gave me a certain look, I'm like, "Ok, I need to chill out for a second! Something I'm doing is not right." So I guess . . . I'm trying to think, how did I start doing that? Where did that come from? That had to come from somewhere. And I guess it was from when I was at school, my teachers, I had Black teachers, so my teachers did it. My mom did it. So I guess that's something that I picked up on. Because it works! You put all eyes on a student, you let them know that (1) I know you're talking, (2) I know you're violating school policy, (3) you're about to get written up, and (4) Mr. Jones is about to kill you.

Ed: All in a look.

Felix: All in a look. Because a look says, "Say something, I dare you." Or, if I hear something, I'm like, "Oh, really?" And the class is like, "Kill her, Mr. J! Kill her!" That means, hit them with the sarcasm, say something to shut the whole situation down, which I will do. I'll say one thing and just shut the whole thing right down.

Just as Mitch compared his no-nonsense management approach to the discipline styles of his mother and his Black female lead teacher, Felix ultimately cited his mother and his former Black teachers as sources of the disciplinarian gaze that he strategically directed at his students. The responsiveness of Felix's students to this technique, as well as their validation of its disciplinary meaning through vernacular prompts like "Kill her, Mr. J!," underscored the culturally responsive nature of the look.

Like Mitch and Felix, another participant, Damon, offered insights into his culturally responsive approaches to discipline and classroom management. As noted in Chapter 4, Damon was one of the participants who critiqued his colleagues' reliance on him and other Black male teachers to serve as schoolwide disciplinarians. Nevertheless, Damon accepted that responsibility, stating in a one-on-one interview that "if my strength is the fact that I happen to be a Black male who has control over students, then I have to play that role, even if I don't want to." Reflecting further on that role, Damon explained his heavy management focus on routinizing students to the habits of schooling:

> A lot of my students last year had no teacher. Same thing this year. Or they had teachers who, like, they had four teachers in one year. There was never any routine set, there was never anything that they got into. They felt like it was okay to just walk out of class and run through the hallways. They need to have a structure to say, like, I know when I walk into this class, I sit down and do this, and I do that, and I do this. This is what is expected. That's how you learn to be a student. Especially as you get older and older and older, and things become more independent and more just you having to figure out and negotiate your own terms in terms of your education. It's important that students, especially in the middle grades, get that structure, especially if they didn't have it beforehand.

In this excerpt, echoing some of the earlier sentiments expressed by Mitch regarding the need for student discipline and independence, Damon felt that routinizing his middle grades students to the habits of schooling would help them to successfully navigate high school environments. He went on to explain that his emphasis on structure was in response not only to gaps in their prior schooling experiences, but also to the family and home life issues that made it difficult for some of his students to focus on school tasks. After describing the turbulent home life of one of his Black male students, Damon noted:

> So when he comes to school, he feels it's time to act out. And this guy's a bright guy, very articulate, but because of what's going on at home and this lack of love, structure, whatever you wanna say is going on at home, he comes to school and acts a fool sometimes. So for me, it's very important to say, like, "This is how you behave in school. This is how you behave in the classroom. These are the things you don't do in school. When you have this feeling or you come to school feeling bad, this is how you should address it. This is how you should approach certain things." That for me is an example of what I'm talking about. Again, they're coming, a lot of them, from places where it's already so chaotic or so you-never-know-what's-going-on that you have to come to school and give them that. These are certain things that you need to be doing. This is how this goes. Because then when you learn how to do those things in school, considering we're in school most of the time, you know when I go home if I have all this work to do, I can try to shut as much as I can of it out so I can use those same things to do homework. Or I can involve myself—these two kids have done that—in extracurriculars so I stay

at school longer on certain days. So school kind of becomes your way of organizing your life, that you can kind of get rid of some of those issues. I think that if they see the structure and the purpose in school and the things they can get out of it, then some of those home life issues can maybe be pushed to the side.

While many educators may attend to management-related routines and structure in their classrooms, Damon's focus on these issues was in direct response to the prior schooling experiences and challenging home life situations that made self-monitoring difficult for some of his Black Brewerton students. That he was more successful at attending to these issues than many of his colleagues was, for Damon, attributable to his disciplinary sway over Black students as a Black male teacher. These two factors—his attention to students' educational and familial contexts and the resonance of his positionality as a Black male teacher—index the cultural responsiveness of Damon's disciplinary and classroom management practices.

As previously noted, Damon was one of the study participants who critiqued the pervasive presumption in Brewerton schools of Black male teachers as ready-made disciplinarians. While the critiques offered by Damon and other men in that regard certainly warrant close consideration, they do not negate the significance of the accounts shared in this chapter. Working in schools where many teachers struggled to establish and maintain order, the participants referenced above revealed that their cultural responsiveness as Black male teachers could inform successful approaches to discipline and management in their predominantly Black classrooms. Their narratives echo both scholarly and popular media accounts of the disciplinary prowess of Black male teachers, and the value-added potential of that prowess for the education of Black students.

"EZ Pass Into Their World": Language, Culture, and Attire

Scholarship on Blacks in the American teaching profession has attributed Black teachers' culturally responsive pedagogies to, among other factors, the shared cultural backgrounds between Black teachers and Black students. To that end, narrative excerpts in the preceding sections of this chapter illustrated how Black cultural backgrounds informed study participants' approaches to curriculum and discussion, and to discipline and classroom management as well. Further analyses reveal how shared culture also facilitated participants' efforts to nurture and retain a culturally meaningful rapport with Black students—a rapport that could reinforce disciplinary authority or enhance instructional practices. Three strategies proved particularly useful to these ends: the use of Black vernacular language and communicative styles; the open identification with shared cultural backgrounds and experiences; and the donning of certain styles of dress. The first two of those strategies are evident in narrative accounts cited elsewhere in this chapter. What follows are a few additional examples from the narratives of five participants that illustrate how all three strategies could enhance their culturally responsive pedagogies.

The first strategy mentioned—the use of Black vernacular language and communicative styles—was apparent in participants' accounts of signifying with their students. Signifying refers to a style of verbal expression in Black culture that can take on several forms (Caponi, 1999). Here, it is being used to describe a stylized strategy for calling out others for their wrongdoings, often by combining chastisement with quick and sharp wit, Black vernacular expressions, and evocative vocal inflections. In some instances, participants used signifying not only to sustain their rapport with Black students but to also reinforce disciplinary authority. Mitch, for instance, characterized his use of signifying (which he referred to as "verbal play") as one of the traits that made his management style culturally Black in nature. He offered the following anecdote to illustrate his use of signifying in the classroom:

> So they'll just be like "blah blah blah blah." I'm like "stop talking." They're talking to me about something [and I'll say], "You're in my face right now and I don't know why. One thing about this picture right now is that you're here and you shouldn't be." And they're just, "Uuuuhhhh [*Mitch imitates student's groaning sound*], you're always just . . ." "All that noise, what is wrong with you? Do you have something in your throat? Then you need to go to the doctor. Do not come here tomorrow unless you've been to the doctor. If you come here tomorrow and you haven't been to the doctor, I'm gonna call your parents and let them know that you need to be at the doctor, not here." I just talk, and they just . . . the rest of the class know, whoever I'm not talking to, if they think it's funny, they'll laugh—unless I'm really being upset and getting into someone, then they just shut up and they're just like "damn." But otherwise, I play them. So they don't really do it like I guess they could sometimes. Because some of my kids could go back and forth with me. I have a couple who we could have a good time going back and forth. But they don't because they've gained the respect for me to not do that. And they know that if I do it, I'm not doing it just to let off steam. I'm doing it because you kind of deserve it at that point and you need to be checked.

In this example, Mitch's performative riff in response to his student's groan illustrated the combination of chastisement and quick wit that characterized his signifying. The suggestion that the student should go to the doctor poked fun at the student for groaning while also communicating Mitch's impatience with the student's behavior. Noting that this strategy conveyed to students that "you need to be checked" corroborated its disciplinary function for Mitch. Additionally, his sense that some of his students could respond to him with their own signifying—but that they also could discern when doing so would be inappropriate—suggested the cultural familiarity of signifying as a Black communicative practice between Mitch and his students.

Other examples of signifying emerged in Damon's narrative. As with Mitch, some of the examples illustrated Damon's use of signifying to reestablish his authority and reinforce proper student conduct. For instance, once when a student was not paying attention during class, Damon said to the student, "Excuse me, can you tell us what we're reading right now? Read the next sentence for us. Oh, caught out there like Kelis, ha? Pay attention!" The reference to the song "Caught Out There" by soul music artist Kelis (Williams & Hugo, 1998) drew upon a cultural reference that was meaningful to Damon's Black students. Furthermore, like Mitch's "go to the doctor" remark, Damon's Kelis-aided call-out was a creative and quick-witted use of signifying to carry out his classroom management.

Like the act of signifying, the use of Black vernacular English could also capitalize on a common cultural background between a Black teacher and his Black students. Felix provided examples of using vernacular expressions as he recounted his incorporation of certain terms and phrases into a math lesson:

Felix: I said, "What words associate with a positive integer?" And one student said, "Making a come up." Now, I knew instantly what he meant, every other student knew what he meant, so therefore I allowed it to be on the board. Maybe one person didn't know what it meant, but that was different. For the most part, they understand. If I put on paper "Tyree made a come up on five," they would know to put plus five, or five. They would know that. Or if I say, "Paula took an L and ten dollars." They know what I meant by minus ten.

Ed: The loss [*referring to "an L"*].

Felix: Right. I can make it formal. I can also use, I guess, Ebonics, or our vernacular. You know, suited to them, make them understand it better. I do believe I have an edge because I'm around it all day.

As he recalled in this excerpt, Felix's familiarity with local Black colloquialisms enabled him to incorporate them in his lesson on integers. Doing so, in Felix's eyes, enabled him to support student comprehension by engaging students in mutually understood Black vernacular terms.

Another strategy for drawing upon a shared cultural background was to openly identify with aspects of that shared culture that appealed to

Black students. For instance, Damon described how students' connectedness with him was positively influenced by his knowledge and demonstration of popular dances. Both Felix and Ira recalled how disclosing their own upbringings in Brewerton and their own attendance of Brewerton public schools had increased students' identification with them. Additionally, Felix noted that he allowed kids to make up nicknames for him like "J-Boogie" (based on his last name, Jones) and that he intentionally allowed his cell phone to ring in class at times so that kids would hear the popular songs that he used for his ringtones. On the benefits of a shared cultural background with students, Felix remarked, "I use it as my token. I use it as my EZ pass into their world. Because I know what they're thinking, I know how they think. Because I was one of them." As the "EZ pass" comment indicated, identifications of common cultural experiences enabled study participants like Felix to enhance their rapport with Black Brewerton students.

One last strategy for capitalizing on shared cultural backgrounds was the choice of attire. Participants' narratives revealed that their style of dress could garner the respect of and/or mark their similarities with their Black students. For instance, after asserting that a White male colleague routinely managed to get by with a more disheveled appearance than he, Solomon explained how his own appearance was influenced by student expectations:

> Students expect a certain level of style from Black teachers. And I don't know where that stems from. But I think to some degree, when I am looking more professional or, not even more professional, just more stylish, or my tie was a little more expensive, my kids are very, very well-aware of these things somehow. Like the better-quality ties, or the better-quality shirts that I wear, or the better-quality pants. They're very attuned to these things. They treat me better. They treat me with more respect.

Like Solomon, Felix and Mitch attested to the significance of attire as well. However, both men recounted the advantages gained by eschewing conventional teacher attire for the more casual sweaters, polo shirts, jeans, sneakers, and Timberland boots that were popular among their students. Felix described "dressing down" occasionally as a way to reinforce his common cultural experience with students. Mitch described a more permanent shift in attire that helped him to gain students' respect:

> [*Quoting his students:*] "Mr. Abrams got like a lot of shoes, his sneakers, blah blah blah. Mr. Abrams is always fresh." I see [students], they come and wanna talk. "Mr. Abrams, where you get your shoes from? Mr. Abrams, if I see you after school, I'm gonna get those shoes off you, rob you." "Really? Okay. I'll be outside at 4:15. So please, be out there so we can go at this." They're responding to me

in that way, as they kind of saw me as that type of person, as I kind of got put on that pedestal—it was a small pedestal for me to be put on—they kind of responded to me with a little more respect. So for the [students], I'm the cool guy. And this has to do implicitly because I'm Black. Because they're not really gonna look at the White guy too much as the cool guy, just because he's White and they're not. So Mr. Abrams is cool.

Like Solomon, Mitch contrasted the politics of style along racial lines to mark how his sense of fashion worked in his favor specifically as a Black male teacher. For all three men mentioned (Solomon, Mitch, and Felix), Black students' reactions to their wardrobes influenced how they dressed, as student approval of their fashion sense created culturally mediated opportunities for building rapport.

In all, the narrative passages referenced in this section point toward a wider range of factors that may come to bear on culturally responsive pedagogies. Vernacular language and communicative styles, personal identifications with shared cultural backgrounds, and attire may not appear in some literature on pedagogy as frequently as topics like cooperative learning and differentiated instruction, but these factors nonetheless influenced study participants' abilities to build rapport with Black students in Brewerton. Thus, it is important to recognize how a facility with these factors shaped study participants' culturally responsive pedagogical work with Black youth.

"A Different Kind of Pride": Connections With Black Boys

Given the centrality of Black boys in both scholarly and popular discourses on Black male teachers, participants' accounts of their relationships with Black male students were closely examined in this study. As discussed in Chapter 4, the father-like status of Black male teachers produced tensions between some study participants and the Black boys in their classrooms. There were, however, a number of accounts to the contrary. In total, six of the men in this study pointed to their connections with Black male students as productive, defining, and transformative aspects of their culturally responsive pedagogical work as Black male teachers. The salience of these connections emerged in participants' descriptions of Black boys' responsiveness to them as Black male educators, as well as in participants' accounts of their own unique investments in the fate of their Black male students.

Black boys' responsiveness to the men in this study emerged in some participants' accounts of their disciplinary sway over Black male students. Damon, for instance, recalled how he was quickly able to calm a Black male student one day after a White female colleague had yelled at him to no avail to sit down. In another account, after recalling his Black students' disregard for a White male colleague, Damon cited further evidence of his unique influence over young Black males:

Damon: This year, a Black female from [my alternative certification program] is in the classroom [across the hall]. Had some issues; I mean I'm not saying that they're resolved, but the major issues she was having when she first came to my school are much less than now. I pulled her homeroom aside, and I said, "Listen, someone has got to tell me why you come in here and you act fine, and then you go across the hall and you act a fool." And it was said that basically because I'm a man, they're gonna listen to me more than they listen to her.

Ed: Who said that?

Damon: Black men in the classroom. Several of them.

Ed: And they said explicitly, "We're gonna listen to you more because you're a man?"

Damon: Yes.

Ed: And how'd you respond to that?

Damon: I was trying to make it like that's not the issue here. She's still an authority figure, she's still a teacher. And their whole thing is that, I guess related to that is also that I kind of came into it very stern and very like "this is the deal." Yet I still have those connections and crack jokes with them. But first, I'm your teacher. They said maybe she came in more motherly, more "hey, here I am" and didn't give that. But the first thing they said before they even got to that was "it's because you're a man."

Like Damon, another participant, Ira, described having a special disciplinary influence over Black male students. As he stated during an interview:

Some of the boys, some of the males, they will approach me to talk about things they feel that I can identify with. Like if there's disciplinary issues that they're dealing with, "so-and-so teacher just doesn't understand." And they just want to talk it out because they feel like I understand, one Black male to the next.

When asked to recount a situation that illustrated this connection with Black male students around discipline issues, Ira described a conversation with a young Black male who sought him out after a contentious disciplinary encounter with a Black female teacher:

He can say things that come off as aggressive or disrespectful, even when he doesn't understand that they come off that way, because he's just being himself and he thinks it's okay. He needs to learn that it's not okay in certain situations. You cannot be who you want to be all the time in every single situation. Like your area, your space, you have to adapt. He needs to learn that. So he, I think he knows this, but he wanted to hear it from another African American male and try to figure out how I did it.

In this excerpt, Ira, sensing that this student "wanted to hear it from another African American male," wielded his influence as a Black male teacher to encourage the student to adapt his demeanor to the interactional norms of the school. That the student sought Ira's counsel for a disciplinary encounter with a Black female teacher underscored his special sway over this Black male student as a Black male teacher.

Echoing Damon and Ira, Karl cited his unique disciplinary influence over Black male students. As he recalled in the following excerpt, his influence over one student even surpassed the efforts of a special behavior modification program:

> I remember specifically we have a HELP [Helping Enlightened Learners Persist] program in my school, which is sort of a behavioral adjustment type thing where certain students go to. They really talk about problem solving and how to make better decisions, and not curse and yell and act like fools [*chuckle*]. There was one particular student, Sammy, who's MR [mentally retarded], ILP [individual learning program], HELP—like any other intervention in the book, every lingo, he's had it. He literally would, like, he'd have episodes where he'd cry. In seventh grade, someone would piss him off and he would start cursing and run out in the hallway and cry. So there would be times where even the people from HELP couldn't do anything. I'd come back from a meeting and he'd be in the hallway with the HELP people. And they're like, "He won't talk to anyone but you. Can you talk to him? He won't go back in the classroom." And I'd just be like, "Sammy, go in and have a seat," and he'll just walk in [*chuckle*]. I mean, it had just got to the point where it was just like that, and they were just like, "I don't get it." Like one of the women, the woman that works for HELP, she was like, "I don't know what you've done to him" [*chuckle*]. She was just like, "He really respects you, and he really listens to you."

Sammy's responsiveness to Karl in the example was not an isolated incident. Elsewhere in his narrative, Karl described how Sammy and two other former Black male students, Todd and Roger, had been the focus of his own in-class behavioral improvement efforts during the previous academic year. None of the boys were his students during the year of this study, yet according to Karl, all three would attempt to abscond to his classroom. Additionally, Karl recounted how Todd had managed one day to surreptitiously peek at his cell phone to retrieve his phone number. Karl reported that Todd would sometimes call him to talk: "He'll call me, like when he got his work accepted in one of those millions of poetry anthologies that they have to make money. He was just so excited, and he'd call me over the summer and we talked." Furthermore, when another of his Black male students, Simon, was experiencing home difficulties, Karl was able to call Todd and ask him to check up on Simon, since both boys lived in the same neighborhood. In all of these cases, Sammy, Todd, and Roger demonstrated a special responsiveness to Karl, their only Black male teacher, which Karl did not witness in their interactions with other teachers and staff.

The examples cited thus far have offered participants' accounts of Black male students' responsiveness to them as disciplinarians. Other narrative excerpts revealed how this responsiveness could extend to non-disciplinary matters as well. For instance, Quincy and Damon described being approached by Black male students with questions about sexual matters such as the effectiveness of condoms and the prevalence of sexually transmitted diseases. Both teachers described their willingness to clarify (mis)information on these matters for their Black male students. Additionally, as the faculty advisor to his school's dance teams, Damon recounted the increased willingness of Black male students to participate once the teams fell under his charge:

Damon: It's just really interesting. Because there are boys in the school who are just like, "Are you the dance person? I wanna join the boys' dance team." I think for some of them it's a really interesting thing because it's like, "This Black guy likes to dance." And a lot of the guys do dance, but they never saw that before. They never got that, like, it's okay. . .

Ed: To join the dance team.

Damon: . . . to join the dance group. And when I started it, a lot of them came. And again, some of the kids who I had in the dance group last year who I don't teach at all because they're in younger grades, one kid runs up to me and he gives me a hug every day. Every time I see him I'm like oh my god. He's like "Hubert!!!!!" [Damon's last name]. Runs up and gives me a hug, and I'm like, "Hello, Kadim, how are you?" In that sense, at least with the boys specifically, some of them who like to dance . . . and there are not even any, you know, you can see them like being a little bit flamboyant. They're just regular guys. The kid who I was saying . . . he's a boxer, but he just likes to dance. He likes to go to parties and dance.

Ed: So being a Black man doing it makes it okay for the. . .

Damon: Yeah.

As Damon recounted, coaching the dance teams not only made it more acceptable for his Black male students to join, but it also led to opportunities for Black male students like Kadim to connect with him as a Black male adult figure. Building on the dance teams anecdotes, Damon went on to describe Black male students' more intimate expressions of their connectedness to him. For instance, one afternoon, after the misbehavior of one class had reached a breaking point for him, Damon packed his belongings and sat quietly for the last ten minutes of class. Fearing he was ready to quit, two Black male students approached Damon at the end of the period:

Damon: As I'm walking them out, well one of my students—two guys—one of them first came over to me and was like, "I need you to calm down. I need you to relax."

Ed: He said that to you?

Damon: "This weekend, I want you to relax. Come on, Hubert. You gotta calm down." And the other one was like, "Are you really gonna leave?" And I was like, "I don't know." And he said to me, "You can't leave. People need you. I need you." So these are just some of the emerging things that I think . . . and that student also wrote a letter to me early on in the year that said he wishes that I was his father.

Ed: The one who said I need you?

Damon: Yeah. So I guess there's just certain things that at least with the guys in my classes that like . . . my first class I don't have too many Black men. Actually I have one in particular in that first class, him and I have a really good connection. But definitely in the other classes, there's definitely a . . . something comes out of the fact that I'm a Black man teaching them.

The letter to which Damon referred in this excerpt—the letter in which a Black male student revealed that he wished Damon were his father—was written under similar circumstances. In that instance, also in response to student misbehavior, Damon instructed his students to write letters explaining why they should be more respectful to their teachers. It was in one of those letters that the same Black male student who, in the passage above, told Damon that he needed him, also said that he wished that Damon could be his father. Both cases illustrated this student's deep responsiveness and connection to Damon as a Black male teacher.

Private, one-on-one interactions seemed particularly effective in surfacing Black male students' responsiveness to Damon. Elsewhere in his narrative, Damon noted:

One on one, they'll tell me like "my dad is in jail right now" or "this is what's going on." Or this one will cry in front of me, or this one will apologize for something he would not have apologized for in front of the whole group.

Similarly, Quincy described the willingness of a Black male student who regularly misbehaved during class to not only apologize for his actions in one-on-one encounters, but also reflect quite thoughtfully on the underlying issues of his misbehavior. Another participant, Bill, cited a Black male student who sought him out in private after being assaulted during a domestic abuse incident. In all of these cases, study participants cited personal interactions that conveyed Black male students' rapport with them as Black male teachers.

Thus far, this analysis has highlighted study participants' awareness of Black male students' responsiveness to them as Black male teachers. The converse—the significance of Black male students in the lives of the men in this study—provides another important perspective. Just as scholarly and popular discourses on Black male teachers presume a distinct commitment to reaching Black boys—a commitment that consequently situates Black male teachers as role models and father figures—several passages from study participants' narratives revealed their deep personal investments in inspiring and empowering young Black males.

One of the study participants who ascribed a special meaning to his relationships with Black male students was Bill. In the following passage, Bill explained how his strong investment in his own Black male identity fueled a palpable connectedness to Black male students:

Bill: I think that I'm always aware [of my Black maleness], and I think that I feel a really strong connection to Black maleness. So I think that even with my students and things like that, I feel very connected to Black males and Black male students and other Black males. I feel a relationship to them even if I don't feel like I can necessarily relate to certain aspects. So one of my students came in, he got a tattoo over the holidays. He got a tattoo here on his neck, which just irks me so bad, like the tattoos. And today he and I were talking about it. Because he went, "Yo, you like my tattoo?" And I was like, "I'm not big on the tattoo on the neck thing." And he was like, "Well, why? Why?" And I was like, "Well what happens when you wanna become a doctor, you know, and you have this big tattoo on your neck? Or what happens when you wanna become a stockbroker, who's gonna want to hire you with this big tattoo on your neck?" And he went into, "Well I'll just be a drug dealer." And I was like, "Yeah because that's probably all that you'll be able to do" [*chuckle*]. But even in my not feeling where he was coming from, I felt like I could talk to him in a way that I might not be able to talk to him if I was Miss Susie across the hallway. So. . .

Ed: That you could be frank?

Bill: Right, in a way that I don't know that others could be. So I think I'm always connected to my Black maleness. I'm always connected to my Blackness especially, but my Black maleness also. And at the same time, I do feel like it's a different kind of Black maleness that I am exuding.

In this account, Bill's disdain toward neck tattoos illuminated the contrasts between the brand of Black masculinity that he preferred and the brand to which his student aspired. Nonetheless, for Bill, their shared identity as Black males afforded genuine deliberations over the implications of various performances of Black masculinity. Unlike "Miss Susie across the hallway"—a colloquial reference to a White female teacher—Bill was a Black man who embraced his Black maleness and, thus, could capitalize on his special affinity with Black male students.

When Bill revisited this topic during a focus group, he and other participants wrestled with what it meant to have a special connection to Black male students versus Black female students. At one point, Bill stated, "I think I definitely feel a different kind of pride when I reach a Black male student than when I reach a Black female student." After sharing an anecdote about his success in reaching a young Black male in his class, Bill referred to his relationship with that student as he tried to tease out his explanation of a "different kind of pride":

Bill: Something about the interaction we had, it had a different kind of effect on me. I think I'm affected differently by the Black males. I think I seek to reach the Black females also, in a similar way. But there's something about when one of the guys can come around, and when one of the guys shows something, it means something different to me.

Ed: You say it means something different. Does it mean something more?

Bill: I don't know if it's more. I don't wanna say that it's more. I don't wanna say it's so much better when I reach one of the male students than when I reach one of the female students. But it definitely is different. I think there is a little more . . . I guess it's more. [*Others: chuckle.*] I don't know, it's a different kind of pride.

Solomon, another study participant who was in this focus group session with Bill, chimed in in agreement:

I think there's a moment when I see Black male students watching me. The girls don't . . . it's a different vibe that I feel when the girls are looking at me, you know. So it's like there is something about that that is . . . and that's partially me fitting that father role, like I wanna be that. I wanna fill some of that void.

By noting his desire to serve as a father figure, Solomon identified the symbolic weight attached to a Black male teacher's rapport with Black male students. Still, this did not fully account for why that rapport would stir a "different kind of pride" than the rapport felt with Black female students. When Felix, who was also in this focus group, noted the greater willingness of his Black female students to congregate around his desk and engage in class, he, Bill, and Solomon collectively unpacked the significance of their connectedness to young Black males:

Bill:	I think that's part of it, at least with me. I also probably have strong relationships with the Black females. Not strong, but they tend to. . .
Felix:	Gravitate.
Bill:	Yeah. They're talkative. They come and just kind of. . .
Felix:	That's true.
Bill:	So I think that there's something about when one of the guys does kind of let that guard down. . .
Felix:	Or more receptive to it. Because the last thing you expect any student to do is come to see a teacher after school on their time, just to kind of hang out.
Solomon:	You know what it is, it's because so many kids, I'm used to seeing them posture. This hard stance and posture. . .
Ed:	All kids?
Solomon:	No, no, males in particular. So they have to posture for a number of reasons. But then the issue is when they look at you in that certain way, there's a deference and a vulnerability that I've become very attuned to. That vulnerability means that they're trying to learn something about you. So I feel it, I feel that.

Building upon Bill's initial statement about the different kind of pride he derived from connecting with Black male students, he and other focus group participants contrasted the willing classroom engagement of Black female students with the masculine posturing of their male counterparts to explain the special value of reaching Black boys. Overcoming the guardedness of Black male students constituted a unique interpersonal and pedagogical success for these participants.

In this focus group exchange, Solomon noted that numerous reasons might account for the guarded postures assumed by some Black male students. This was a point to which Karl attested in a one-on-one interview while discussing his relationship with Simon, a Black male student in his class who, while not troublesome, was initially inattentive and withdrawn. After choosing Simon as the subject of a child study project for a graduate course, Karl learned about prior academic and ongoing home life issues that shed light on Simon's demeanor in class. With new information on Simon's school and home situations, Karl was able to nurture a connection with him that, echoing the sentiments expressed by others, held a very special meaning:

> I feel like because I was an African American male, we were able to forge this relationship. I feel like out of any student I've taught, this would probably be like one of them that I was the closest to. This summer, I would literally visit him at summer school to make sure he made it every day. I'd take him out for lunch, and we'd just talk. It was really important for him to just have a space where he had some-one that was stable in his life, someone that he knew cared about him, and that he knew was just there for him. That was just really important. I just remember one poignant moment when there was one time in the summer, we were leaving and I dropped him off at his house. I had talked to his mom. I looked out of the car and I was just like, I told him that I loved him. And it was just really weird because it was something that I didn't plan or anything that I thought I was going to say. But it was just like, I really realized at that point just the gravity of this work, especially in urban education. Like how it is so emotional and how you do get wrapped up in the lives of your students.

The emotional investment that Karl developed in Simon's welfare extended beyond the conventional confines of classroom learning. Not only would Karl keep tabs on Simon's home situation, but as mentioned earlier in this analysis, he would call upon another student, Todd, to check up on Simon when he could not. Karl's unique rapport with Simon was not lost on his coworkers, as he noted in the follow-ing passage:

> I feel like he saw me as more than a teacher. I mean it literally got to a point where it was like . . . I feel like towards the end of my first year it was like, we didn't even call his house. It was like, if any teacher had a problem with Simon, they had to come see me [*chuckle*]. And like, I fixed it. I worked on it with him. I mean, that was a good thing for him, just because as I said, there wasn't as much stability as he would've, I feel like, liked to have had at home, and there were other issues. I feel like for his parents, too, people go through things, and if there's a second line of defense or an ability to help your child, you know, why not? Obviously as parents ideally, you would want to be able to see and fill every need that their child has, but in reality that isn't the case for everyone. I feel like it was fortunate for him that I was able to kind of step in and assume, you know, maybe a role sort of like a second father or something like that for him because that was important for him at the time.

As these passages revealed, Karl drew upon his knowledge of Simon's home life, his rapport with Simon in the classroom, his deep sense of care for Simon, and the occasional assistance of one of Simon's Black male classmates to serve as both a supportive teacher and second father figure. His ability to play these dual roles, as Karl noted, grew out of his sense of purpose as a Black male teacher working with a Black male student in need.

In addition to his rapport with Simon, Karl also described a special connection, as mentioned earlier, with other Black male students. During a focus group, Karl expressed the importance of those connections to his work as a Black male teacher. When asked whether it was fair for Black male teachers to be expected to serve as role models, father figures, and disciplinarians, Karl replied:

> I think when I heard those three things that you listed, I feel like those are more expectations that I put on myself, and less of things that were created from an outside source. I feel like for me, I kind of wanted to fit those roles, especially for my seventh and eighth grade Black males, who I feel like a lot of them came to me very ill-prepared, less academically but more socially. And I really just kind of made it my business to make sure that when they left me this year, that socially they were able to interact, and they were able to do some of the things that I felt like, coming to me in seventh grade they should've been able to do.

Karl's response was particularly noteworthy given his frustrations with his role as a disciplinarian. As noted in Chapter 4, Karl was critical of how his classroom could become "the discipline stop," where other teachers would send students whom they could not control in their own classrooms. Yet when acting as a disciplinarian was combined with serving as a father figure and role model, Karl expressed his commitment to perform these roles for his Black male students. His efforts not only resulted in a unique connectedness with Black boys in his classroom, but, in the case of Simon, it extended into a relationship beyond school that positioned Karl as a (second) father figure for his Black male student.

In some cases, the special meaning of study participants' rapport with Black male students was specifically linked to their awareness of the potential risks facing Black boys in American society. Nurturing a connectedness with their Black male students, thus, enabled some participants to speak frankly with them about the choices they were making as young Black males. At least three previously cited examples illustrated this: Ira's discussion with a student about the need to more effectively adapt his behavior to the norms of spaces like school; Bill's discussion with a student about the potential drawbacks of a tattoo on his neck; and Quincy and Damon's willingness to clarify Black male students' misinformation on safer sex. Another example was offered by Solomon, who expressed his investment as a Black male teacher in Black male students several times throughout his narrative. In a one-on-one interview, Solomon recalled how that investment had informed a "tough love" moment with a Black male student whose poor decision-making was becoming an increasing concern for him and the student's parents:

> So with Jacob, I saw a lot of potential, a ninth grader, but I saw him teetering on the edge of could-go-to-jail or could-do-great-things, you know. So one day I called his parents up, basically ripped him up against the wall. We were like, "Listen, this is serious. This world is not going to give a young Black male chances and we've given you five chances already." And so we're saying, "I'll take you to the jail tomorrow." So the three of us said, "I'm going to take you to the jail tomorrow. And I have clearance in the Brewerton prison because I did some volunteer work there, but I can take you, we can show you. It's not a joke Jacob, it's not a joke!" And I just remember I was using a lot more vernacular when I was in his face, but I mean, yeah, I think I made it very clear to Jacob that to not see yourself and to not see my interaction with you as something that can redefine or expand your notions of Blackness, I think I made it very clear that there is, there is a need to deal with what it means for you to be growing up with this experience.

As Solomon's account made clear, his concern for Jacob was explicitly informed by the possible ramifications of Jacob's poor decision-making as a young Black male. Speaking in frank, vernacular terms with Jacob, and making direct references to his own access to the prison system where Jacob could end up, Solomon wielded his influence as a Black male teacher to intervene in the potentially ill-fated life path of a Black male student.

The moments referenced across preceding paragraphs—when participants invoked their connectedness to Black male students to steer them away from potentially poor and costly school and life choices—spoke to a deeper sense of purpose driving the men in this study. More than the typical, teacherly expressions of concern for students, these moments reflected participants' own awareness as adult Black men of the precarious circumstances of the Black male experience in America, and they exhibited participants' desires to disrupt academic underachievement and social and economic marginalization in the lives of their Black male students. Along with the narrative passages referenced, an excerpt from an interview with Damon poignantly captured this sense of purpose:

> I feel like a Black man every moment of my life right now. Because I'm standing in front of a lot of Black men who I know are smart but don't believe in themselves. So I feel like I have to assert me being

a Black man. I'm constantly reminding my students, especially my male students, like my Black male students, this is what they want for you and this is what you can be. So I feel like for me now, 7:45 to 3:30, and even sometimes when I come home from school and I'm thinking about my students, I'm just always reminded of it.

As a socially conscious Black man in the urban teaching profession, Damon looked at his Black male students and was reminded of society's narrow and minimal expectations for them. For Damon and other participants in this study, being Black male teachers forced them to face the precarious fates of Black male lives as they worked with Black boys in their classrooms. Being Black male teachers also presented them with unique opportunities to help their Black male students to defy the odds.

For all of the participants cited in this chapter, their connections with Black male students represented important dimensions of their work as Black male educators. Whether through Black boys' responsiveness to them, their own investments in their Black male students, or both, the teachers referenced in the preceding discussion attested to the rapport with Black male youth that is so often imagined in saviorist discourses on Black male teachers. As the accounts made clear, a connectedness to Black male students was a central and valued aspect of some study participants' culturally responsive pedagogies.

Toward More Balanced Portraits of Black Male Teachers

Previously published iterations of my work on Black male teachers have emphasized the dilemmas around Black masculinity and racial identity politics faced by the men in my study (Brockenbrough, 2012a, 2012b, 2012c, 2013, 2015). That emphasis was crucial given the limited perspectives on Black male teachers' experiences that dominated saviorist discourses across popular media and scholarly texts (as reviewed in detail in Chapter 2). While my prior publications made critical and justified interventions in the scholarship on Black men in teaching, they also left out vital portions of my study participants' stories: namely, their insights, strengths, and triumphs as culturally responsive pedagogues working with Black youth in Brewerton schools. This chapter acts as a corrective of sorts by presenting previously unpublished findings that highlight my study participants' pedagogical efforts to empower Black students. In doing so, this chapter helps to provide a more balanced portrait than in my previous works of the narratives of the men in my study.

In addition, this chapter situates my study participants' narratives within the culturally responsive pedagogical traditions of Black teachers in American K–12 schools. As discussed earlier, educational researchers have asserted that Black educators, through their own membership in Black communities and their insider perspectives on Black cultural experiences, are uniquely positioned to connect with and instruct Black students. The narrative accounts referenced throughout this chapter echo those claims, as participants repeatedly explained how their own lived experiences as Black men informed their insights into, and their strategies for addressing, the needs of Black youth. While some accounts described specific practices employed by the men in this study, this chapter overall speaks to culturally responsive pedagogy as a deeper set of beliefs about the intersections of culture and learning. As Howard (2010) cautions, attempts to package culturally responsive pedagogy as a toolkit of discrete instructional practices overlook the nuanced and complex nature of culture in the classroom. Rather than offering an enumerated how-to guide for working with Black students, this chapter provides further evidence that we may better understand how to educate Black youth by centering critical reflections on students' and teachers' cultural backgrounds as meditators of relationship building and classroom learning.

By focusing closely on the role of cultural background, this chapter illuminated study participants' perspectives on the pedagogical affordances of their shared cultural identities and experiences with Black students. Those affordances, while compelling, were also contingent. As I have discussed elsewhere (Brockenbrough, 2013), the men in this study described intraracial divides along factors like class status and regional background that confounded their culturally mediated rapport at times with Black Brewerton students. The significance of such divides has been echoed in other scholarly works on the potential tensions between teachers and students of color (Achinstein & Aquirre, 2008; Dingus, 2006; Fairclough, 2007). Additionally, that the only man in this study who did not describe a culturally responsive pedagogical stance was Oliver—who was also the only participant born outside of the United States—speaks further to the cultural disconnect that may emerge at times between Black male teachers and Black students. While educators of color may enjoy pedagogical advantages in their work with students from similar racial and ethnic backgrounds, they also may encounter intraracial fissures that challenge the solidarities and affinities traditionally associated with their culturally responsive pedagogies. Thus, it is crucial to appreciate my study participants' insights on their cultural responsiveness while concurrently considering how they and other Black male teachers may struggle on occasion to connect with culturally diverse populations of Black students.

Along with striking a balanced view of the affordances and challenges of Black male teachers' culturally responsive pedagogies, two other implications of this chapter's findings are worth raising. The first is thinking further about the status of White teachers in the mind's eye of Black men in urban teaching. Across multiple narrative accounts, the men in this study cited their White colleagues' shortfalls to underscore the significance of their own cultural responsiveness with Black students. Put differently, the value-added nature of the latter depended in part on the deficit status of the former. In that respect, participants' narratives mirrored saviorist discourses in the popular media which, as discussed in Chapter 2, have situated White women teachers as the less capable foil to Black male educators. While not discounting study participants' views on their White colleagues, it is worth noting that educational scholars have devoted serious attention to mapping White teachers' engagements in culturally responsive pedagogical work with Black students (Brockenbrough, 2014; Ford & Sassi, 2014; Ladson-Billings, 2009; Milner, 2011). Nonetheless, the repeated references in this chapter to White teachers' limitations suggest that critiques of and/or deficit lenses on White colleagues informed how study participants understood the significance of their presence in predominantly Black Brewerton schools.

Just as Chapter 5 highlighted the complexities and importance of study participants' perspectives on women, future inquiries might delve more deeply into Black male teachers' beliefs about and interactions with White educators. For teachers like the men in this study, how do they conceptualize and negotiate their relationships to White teachers as Black men working in a majority-White profession? More specifically, how do factors like White teachers' racial privilege, racial attitudes, and interactions with Black children inform how Black male teachers fashion their own identities and pedagogies? And what opportunities and challenges emerge as these men negotiate the racialized participatory politics and pedagogical tasks of the profession with White peers, especially in predominantly Black urban contexts that may strain conventional racial hierarchies? Both the frequency and tone of study participants' references to White colleagues suggest that the impact of White teachers on the lives and culturally responsive practices of Black men in urban teaching is worth unpacking.

One more theme from this chapter that begs for further consideration is the significance of Black male teachers' relationships with Black boys. As noted repeatedly throughout this book, the transformative pedagogical connection between Black male teachers and Black male students has been a central feature of saviorist discourses on Black men in teaching. The relative inattention in those discourses to the complexities of that connection has been a key concern of this book, and the findings shared in Chapter 4 directly addressed the psychological and emotional baggage that may burden encounters between Black male teachers and the young Black males in their classrooms. While it remains necessary to draw more attention to the possible tensions that can confound Black male teachers' relationships with Black boys, it is also crucial to recognize the potential upsides of those relationships. As captured in this chapter, several of the men in my study described deep commitments to serving young Black males. These commitments drove concerted efforts to prepare Black male students for academic success, and in some cases, they led study participants to play active and supportive roles in Black male students' out-of-school lives. Importantly, it was vis-à-vis their pedagogical and emotional investments in Black male students that study participants spoke most directly to their status as role models and father figures. The connectedness expressed by some of the men in this study to their Black male students raises a crucial question: How do we take a critical stance on Black masculinity politics in the lives of Black male teachers when certain aspects of those politics—for instance, modeling Black manhood for Black boys—are deeply valued by some Black male teachers? This question speaks to the very heart of this book project, and although it has been considered throughout this book, it takes center stage again in the concluding chapter.

Conclusion

Just as saviorist discourses that ignore the potential fall-out of dicey masculinity politics offer limited insights into the lives of Black men in teaching, so, too, do analyses that inadvertently define Black male teachers' experiences solely by their trials and tribulations. Drawing upon previously unpublished research findings, this chapter explored study participants' accounts of the affordances of their culturally responsive pedagogies. Across multiple participants' narratives, four themes conveyed these teachers' perspectives on the culturally mediated affordances of their pedagogies: their racially aware adaptation of curriculum content and facilitation of race-centered discussions; their facility with discipline and classroom management practices with Black students; their connection with Black students through certain language practices, shared cultural backgrounds, and choices of attire; and their special connectedness with Black boys. Echoing previously cited educational scholarship on Black teachers and Black male teachers, this chapter conveyed study participants' understandings of cultural connectedness as a crucial facet of their pedagogical work with Black youth. Moving forward, it is important to value study participants' insights on their culturally responsive pedagogies while also considering how they and other Black male teachers may struggle at times to connect with culturally diverse populations of Black students in American urban schools.

8 Conclusion
Doing Black Masculinity Work

By graciously and honestly sharing their stories through extensive life history narratives, the 11 men who participated in my study offered thoughtful and nuanced perspectives on their experiences as Black male teachers in Brewerton's predominantly Black middle and high schools. As noted before, prior iterations of my work have drawn upon some of those participant perspectives to raise questions about how we understand and address Black men's experiences in urban teaching. Since the questions posed in my earlier publications have not been routinely engaged in other scholarship and popular media discourses on Black male teachers, it seemed important to revisit them in a more extensive, and hopefully more accessible, book format. This book not only revisits previously published findings in Chapters 4 through 6, but it also introduces previously unpublished findings in Chapters 3 and 7 that trace a fuller portrait of my study participants' narratives. Additionally, the two analytical premises on Black masculinity and the review of saviorist discourses in Chapter 2 provide a richer framework than in my earlier works for considering what is at stake in how we talk about, perceive, and position Black male teachers in urban schools. Together, these factors reflect my rationales for writing this book.

While this book has the potential to make important contributions to ongoing deliberations over Black men's participation in urban teaching, it also, like any scholarly project, has its trade-offs. On the one hand, the combination of participants' rich life history narratives and my critical lens on saviorist Black masculinity afforded poignant insights on the dilemmas that complicated these teachers' experiences as Black men in Brewerton schools. On the other hand, the in-depth and nuanced analyses of participants' narratives were enabled by my focus on a numerically and geographically limited sample of teachers. The extensive literature reviews in Chapter 2 suggest the relevance of my analyses for understanding the experiences of other Black men in urban teaching, but they cannot replace additional research that actually chronicles those experiences. Thus, the findings presented in this book may not be generalizable, but when read alongside the scholarly and popular discourses reviewed in Chapter 2, they do indicate several concerns that deserve further consideration. Many of those concerns were raised in the closing sections of the preceding chapters. In this concluding chapter, I want to address three broader implications of the book as a whole.

The Contingency of Counterhegemonic Black Masculinities

Drawing upon the scholarly field of Black masculinity studies, I opened the second chapter of this book by establishing two analytic premises. The first premise was that a full grasp of Black masculinity's significance and effects demands a critical investigation of how individual Black men agentically negotiate prevailing constructions of Black male subjectivity, and the second premise asserted the need to disrupt patriarchal and heteronormative constructions of Black maleness to enable counterhegemonic Black masculinities. These two premises undergirded the book's subsequent analyses, starting with the identification of saviorist Black masculinity as a prevailing construction of Black male teachers' subjectivity that reproduces hegemonic modes of Black manhood in schools. The examination of study findings that followed traced the resonance and dilemmas of saviorist discourses that emerged in study participants' narratives, prompting considerations across chapter conclusions of counterhegemonic negotiations of Black masculinity politics for Black male teachers. Through these analytic maneuvers, I have tried to illuminate urban Black male teachers' location within a larger cultural and ideological project—one that reinforces the legitimacy of patriarchy and hegemonic masculinity and situates Black male teachers as patriarchal and masculinist agents over urban Black youth. By explicitly linking discourses on Black male teachers to the re-masculinization of schools (Martino, 2008), I hope to push various educational stakeholders to wrestle with the deeper impulses that may drive the desire to attract more Black men into urban classrooms.

Convincing advocates for Black male teacher recruitment and retention to question patriarchal and masculinist logics is no small feat. These logics, as noted by other scholars (S. Johnson, 2008; Martino, 2008; Weiler, 1989), have scripted the role of men in the American teaching profession for over a century. Additionally, as I argued in Chapter 2, saviorist discourses specifically on Black male teachers index the epistemological nature of recuperative Black masculinity politics in some strands of Black cultural and knowledge production. As consequences, being a male teacher is widely understood as an inherently patriarchal and masculinist calling, and fulfilling that calling is seen as a victory of sorts for Black men. The findings presented in Chapters 4 through 6 challenge these logics by charting my study participants' trying negotiations of saviorist Black masculinity politics, and by suggesting that men like the teachers in my study might benefit from alternatives to patriarchal and hypermasculine modes of participation in schools. In doing so, this book reinforces educational scholarship that troubles hegemonic masculinity politics in the experiences of male teachers in American schools (Allan, 1994; King, 1998; Martino, 2008; Sargent, 2001; Sternod, 2011; Weaver-Hightower, 2011) and problematizes American popular discourses on Black male teachers as hypermasculine enforcers over and patriarchal saviors for Black youth (Brown, 2011, 2012; Jackson et al., 2013; A. Pabon, 2016; A. J-M. Pabon et al., 2011; Woodson & Pabon, 2016). Working in concert with these literatures, this book offers further cause for exploring new ways of imagining and positioning Black men in urban classrooms.

While the reasons for reimagining the participation of Black men in urban teaching should be evident at this point, the end goal of that process—the counterhegemonic masculinities of Black male teachers in urban schools—is still difficult to articulate. Despite my consistent critiques of saviorist discourses on Black masculinity, I hesitate to prescribe specific resolutions to the quandaries chronicled throughout this text, primarily for three reasons. First, as discussed in Chapter 3, many of the men in my study cited the resonance of saviorist discourses while describing their motivations for becoming urban teachers. Regardless of whatever predicaments these men subsequently faced, saviorist discourses drew some study participants into the classroom as urban educators, and the value of that cannot be easily dismissed. Second, as discussed in Chapter 7, the special rapport that some participants experienced with Black male students—a central trope in saviorist discourses—not only imbued their work with a deeper sense of purpose as Black male teachers, but it also facilitated some compassionate and care-centered moments with Black boys that arguably disrupted hegemonic masculinity politics. And third, as captured in Chapters 4 through 6, the performance of patriarchal and masculinist personas was an effective, albeit problematic, survival strategy for many of these teachers. Working in settings riddled with contentious power dynamics, study participants could wield hegemonic masculinity to sustain or regain their credibility, even if doing so ultimately had deleterious ripple effects. It would be naïve to expect them to not seek protective measures for navigating confrontational work spaces. It would also be naïve to expect these protective measures to not have some drawbacks.

Together, these three themes reveal the affordances and salience of saviorist Black masculinity politics for the men in my study. As with depictions of Black male teachers elsewhere, performing patriarchal and masculinist personas as Black men in urban classrooms was, on certain occasions, a strategic and valued act for many of my study participants. Respecting their voices means being sensitive to their selective embrace of the Black masculinity politics associated with saviorist discourses, even while raising legitimate critiques of those very politics. Consequently,

I arrive at this conclusion chapter with both a critique of and an appreciation for the effects of saviorist discourses in the narratives of my study participants and other Black male teachers who, as depicted in popular media and scholarly publications, derive meaning and purpose for their work from saviorist constructions of Black men in urban teaching. Being simultaneously critical of and sensitive to the lure of saviorist discourses rightfully honors the contradictions of Black male teachers' positionalities—contradictions like occupying the margins of female-dominated spaces while accessing the spoils of male domination; like working under the White supremacist devaluation of Black teachers while capitalizing on culturally responsive pedagogical connections with urban Black youth; or like enforcing violent disciplinary authority over young Black male bodies while nurturing caring relationships with Black male students. As long as these contradictory realities continue to push and pull upon Black male teachers, patriarchal and masculinist modes of participation in urban teaching will remain attractive, even as they alternately enable the survival and reproduce the surveillance of these teachers.

Acknowledging the contradictions of Black male teachers' positionalities, as well as being both critical of and sensitive to their performances of hegemonic masculinity, sets the stage for considering an important implication of this book: the contingent deployment of counterhegemonic Black masculinities for Black men in urban teaching. Given the enduring appeal of saviorist discourses, it is likely that many Black male urban teachers will be expected for the foreseeable future to perform authoritative and indomitable modes of manhood. If so, their opportunities to engage a wider range of personas will be contingent on a host of factors like school and classroom disciplinary cultures and community norms, student and colleague expectations of Black male teachers, and Black male teachers' own flexibilities when performing their in-school identities. Considering this contingency is crucial for two reasons. First, it acknowledges the potentially high stakes of deviating from what is often expected of Black male teachers in urban schools. As suggested by a number of my study participants' narrative accounts, Black men can pay a heavy price for not successfully conforming to the culture of hegemonic masculinity for male teachers. These men should not be pathologized for adapting to pre-existing norms that are used by multiple stakeholder groups to determine their fit and success. Second, framing these educators' deployments of counterhegemonic Black masculinities as contingent can invite strategic deliberations over how to identify and capitalize on that contingency. For instance, it may make sense for a Black male teacher to perform an authoritarian, discipline-minded masculinity at the beginning of an academic year if he finds himself employed in a school where such personas are typical among Black male teachers, as was the case for many of the men in my study. Ensuring his successful participation in such a school may require a Black male teacher to juggle a patriarchal and masculinist persona with strategically timed engagements of alternative pedagogical demeanors. Marking such engagements as contingent in nature can facilitate Black male teachers' thinking about when and how to pursue them.

Strategic deliberations over when and how Black male teachers contingently engage counterhegemonic Black masculinities could also afford deeper explorations of what actually constitutes these masculinities. Robust critiques like the ones offered in this text can surely make the case for disrupting hegemonic masculinity, but they still leave a number of unanswered questions regarding Black male urban teachers' intentional enactments of counterhegemonic masculinities. For instance, how can Black male teachers create safe and orderly classroom environments in discipline-intensive urban schools without performing the authoritarian personas associated with patriarchy and hegemonic masculinity? Given what several scholars have characterized as the traditionally authoritative, no-nonsense disciplinary styles of Black educators (Ford & Sassi, 2014; Foster, 1994; Howard, 2001; C. Monroe & Obidah, 2004), how should Black male teachers resolve critiques of patriarchal modes of authority with the potential cultural resonance of strong authority figures, including patriarchal adult men, with Black students? Likewise, when considering the pressures to be role models and father figures, how should these teachers resolve critiques of patriarchy and hegemonic masculinity with the potential cultural resonance of patriarchal and masculinist adult Black men? Given what some have described as the surveillance of male teachers' sexualities during their interactions with youth (King, 2004; Sargent, 2001; Weaver-Hightower, 2011), how can Black male teachers challenge hegemonic masculinity with expressions of affection and compassion for students while not being cast as pedophilic? And shifting to workplace gender politics, how can Black male teachers working under female leadership assert their voices, especially in schools riddled with discord between teachers and administration, without relying on masculinist and anti-feminist tactics?

All of the preceding questions suggest that defining and operationalizing counterhegemonic masculinities may not be a straightforward process for Black male urban teachers. That process becomes further complicated when considering the diversity of Black men in urban teaching. Age, physical stature, marital status, sexual orientation, years of teaching experience, job security, and familiarity with local neighborhoods and communities are among the myriad factors that can mediate Black male teachers' negotiations of masculinity politics, once again underscoring the contingent nature of these enactments. Thus, rather than imposing my own grand vision of these masculinities, complete with an enumerated set of characteristics and a five-step plan for obtaining them, I am using this conclusion chapter to frame the contingency of Black male teachers' deployments of counterhegemonic Black masculinities, and to encourage inquiry-based deliberations with and by Black male teachers over how to manage that contingency. In doing so, this conclusion offers a heuristic for analyzing and addressing Black male teachers' masculinity-related work in urban schools while also positioning those teachers and their allies as the ones to shape the outcomes. By highlighting the contingent nature of enacting counterhegemonic Black masculinities, my hope is to make explorations of Black masculinity politics more palpable and manageable for Black male teachers in their particular school contexts. Those teachers are the ones who are living these experiences on a daily basis. They deserve to play a central role in determining what those experiences will be.

Black Male Teacher Initiatives

Both popular and scholarly discourses on Black male teachers ultimately strive to increase the number of Black men in the teaching profession. As discussed in Chapter 2, popular media outlets have described a number of initiatives sponsored by universities and school districts to recruit, train, and retain Black male teachers, and a strand of educational studies on Black male teachers has brought scholarly lenses to bear on recruitment and retention strategies. While my study dabbled into participants' perspectives on recruitment efforts, its major contributions emerged in my analyses of the dilemmas that Black male teachers may encounter after they have already entered the profession. That said, one possible implication for retaining men like my study participants in urban schools is to respond to their desire for male-centered interactions and spaces. That desire surfaced in study participants' focus group exchanges with each other about male spaces and professional mentorship, as well as in individual participants' enthusiastic reflections on experiencing—often for the first time—a collective, deliberative space for Black male teachers like the focus groups. Given several participants' accounts of the contentious gender politics they encountered with women colleagues and administrators, the desire for more opportunities to interact with, learn from, and support other male teachers was not surprising. However, as I noted in Chapter 5, one of my study's focus groups featured a conversation about masculinist posturing as a strategy for curtailing female administrative power, raising concerns for me about the capacity of such a space to reproduce hegemonic masculinity politics. Thus, while male-centered spaces and interactions may potentially enhance retention efforts, their affordances and constraints for facilitating anti-patriarchal consciousness building among Black male teachers deserve careful consideration.

To that end, a logical focus for future research is the burgeoning field of recruitment, training, and retention initiatives targeted toward Black male teachers. This field, as noted in Chapter 2, has received a lot of coverage in popular media outlets. That coverage, however, has tended toward laudatory profiles of Black male teacher initiatives with little-to-no specifics on the counterhegemonic Black masculinity work that may or may not occur within particular programs. Also cited in Chapter 2 was the emergent strand of educational scholarship on recruitment, preparation, and retention initiatives for Black male teachers. While providing more depth than popular media coverage, this scholarship has not centered the considerations of anti-patriarchal consciousness building and counterhegemonic masculinity work advanced in this book. As these initiatives grow in number and reach, close analyses of their missions and operations by program stakeholders and/or scholars who nurture research relationships with these programs could generate unique insights into how to train and support Black male teachers. For instance, what deeper conceptualizations of Black masculinity as a cultural, political, and pedagogical phenomenon drive these efforts? How is the purpose of being a Black male teacher defined and/or contested within these programs? What kinds of curricula, pre-service or in-service learning experiences, mentorship, and networking opportunities are provided in these programs, and how do they differ from teacher preparation and professional development programs that do not specifically target Black men? How do these Black male-centered spaces enable and/or impede critical interrogations of Black masculinity politics? And given the diversity that exists among Black male teachers, what kinds of Black men either flourish or founder in Black male teacher initiatives, and why? These are just some of the questions that could inform a more robust research agenda on the insights, dilemmas, and impact of recruitment, preparation, and retention efforts targeting Black men in teaching. Delving deeply into the affordances and challenges experienced in these unique pedagogical spaces could enrich our considerations of how to effectively prepare Black male teachers for the complicated tasks that await them.

A Collective—and Contested—Reimagining

On a final note, it is crucial to underscore a theme that has recurred numerous times in this text: The lives and work of Black male teachers are not shaped by these teachers alone. The scholarly and popular discourses revisited throughout this book have indicated the investments of Black students, Black parents and community members, school districts, teacher education programs, and policy-makers in attracting Black men to urban classrooms. Building on those discourses in their own narratives, the men in my study revealed the critical roles played by various stakeholder groups during their professional, pedagogical, and emotional journeys as Black male teachers. This book calls for a reimagining of Black male teachers' presence in urban schools, and that will not happen effectively without the involvement of the multiple stakeholder groups that shape the contexts and conditions of Black men's participation in urban teaching.

One strategy for this collective reimagining is to take advantage of academic settings that already afford critical inquiries in educational studies. As a university-based education faculty member, I have included earlier iterations of my work and the works of other scholars who study Black male teachers in a number of my courses. Those courses have allowed me to introduce a range of current and future educational professionals to critical perspectives on the experiences of Black men in teaching. I have also presented my work at academic conferences, sometimes alongside brilliant scholars like Thurman Bridges, Travis Bristol, Anthony L. Brown, Marvin Lynn, H. Rich Milner, Amber Pabon, Ashley Woodson, and others who examine the experiences of Black male teachers in American K–12 classrooms. While such spaces can be relatively insulated from the public at large, they do provide opportunities to pose critical perspectives on the lives of Black male teachers to fellow university-based teacher educators and educational researchers who, in turn, can share those perspectives with their students and colleagues. Relying solely on college- and university-based educational studies programs and academic research conferences would obviously be shortsighted, but those spaces do provide important opportunities to engage a range of educational professionals who train, work with, and support Black male urban teachers.

Numerous possibilities exist for engaging stakeholder groups located beyond the academy as well. Here, I want to emphasize two. First, scholars who study Black men's participation in the American teaching profession can present our research findings through venues and in spaces that are accessible to various publics. Travis Bristol (2013, 2015) and Ivory Toldson (2013a) are two scholars who have modeled strategic distributions of their work on Black male teachers to audiences outside of the academy. Using the publication of this book as a springboard, I hope to follow in their footsteps. Widely disseminating scholarly insights on Black men's teaching experiences can be difficult for scholars whose job security depends on traditional measures of productivity and impact within academia. Nevertheless, a collective reimagining of Black men's participation in urban teaching demands that we find ways to engage stakeholder groups who bear a heavy influence on Black male teachers' lives, even if those groups do not read peer-reviewed academic journals.

Those stakeholder groups could also be engaged through a second strategy: the creation of publicly accessible, deliberative spaces that are led by Black male teachers themselves. Since some Black male teacher initiatives have already convened meetings for current and prospective Black male teachers (Graham, 2017; Pitkin, n.d.), members of those sponsoring organizations might be ideal candidates for hosting or co-facilitating forums that help multiple stakeholder groups—from other educators and policymakers to parents and students—understand and reflect on the triumphs and trials that Black male teachers experience in urban schools. This second strategy could facilitate public conversations on the expectations facing Black male urban teachers while also centering those teachers' voices in deliberations over their work.

Again, the suggestions above are just a few possibilities for generating collective reimaginings of Black men's participation in urban teaching. I emphasized the potential contributions of two groups—scholars who study Black male teachers and Black male teacher initiatives—because of evidence that already indicates their interest in and capacity for this work, but other stakeholder groups can and should make significant contributions as well. Regardless of who leads such efforts, collectively reimagining the presence and purpose of Black male urban teachers will entail a reckoning with saviorist discourses that have cemented particular perceptions of and expectations for Black male teachers in the public imagination. Given the resonance of saviorist discourses among multiple stakeholder groups, including Black male teachers themselves, any attempts to redefine what we expect of Black men in urban classrooms is bound to be a contested process. The success of such an undertaking should be gauged not by widespread departures from entrenched beliefs about Black male teachers' roles in schools, but by signs that such departures are being considered by multiple stakeholder groups, even if tentatively, as possible.

Appendix
Data Collection Protocols

First in-depth interview protocol

I. Background and entry into teaching

1) Please provide your name and contact information.
2) How old are you? Where are you from?
3) What was your undergraduate institution(s) and major(s)? What was your graduate institution(s) and field(s)? What type of teacher certification do you have?
4) Have you pursued any other careers besides teaching? If so, what careers, and when?
5) How long have you been teaching? What grades and subjects have you taught? In what geographic locations and at what schools have you taught? Have you assumed responsibility for any extracurricular activities? Do you have, or have you had, any administrative experiences or responsibilities?
6) When did you first consider teaching as a career? At that time, what messages had you received about teaching as a profession, and how did those messages affect you?
7) Why did you ultimately decide to become a teacher? What responses did you receive from others when you decided to become a teacher?
8) What do you enjoy about teaching, and what do you not enjoy?
9) How would you describe your current school and students to an outsider?

II. Identities (Probe for stories, situations, etc. to illustrate themes.)

10) While this study is focusing on the experiences of Black male teachers, I do not want to assume that all participants identify themselves with labels like "Black" and "male." How do you identify yourself racially? Do you also claim an ethnic identity that is different from or more specific than your racial identity?

11) How do you identify in terms of gender?

12) How would you describe the relationship between these identities for you personally? Are they intertwined, or do you ever "experience" each identity separately? Is one more important to you than the other?

13) What messages did you receive as a child about what it meant to be [race/ethnicity] and [gender]? As a teenager? As a young adult? Where did those messages come from?

14) How has being [race/ethnicity] and [gender] shaped you as a person? Do these identities shape your view of the world? Your relationships with other people? Your daily life? Your self-image?

15) So far I have focused on race and gender. Are there other identity categories that play a major role in how you define yourself and/or how you see and experience the world? (Use #13 and #14 to tease out responses to this.)

16) Is there anything I didn't ask you about the topics of this interview that you think I should consider?

Second in-depth interview protocol

Probe for stories, situations, etc. to illustrate themes.

1) In what ways, if any, did being [race/ethnicity] and [gender] influence your decision to become a teacher?

2) How, if at all, has being [race/ethnicity] and [gender] influenced your:

- teaching practices (pedagogical stance, curriculum design, classroom management, instructional techniques, etc.)
- relationships & interactions with students (by gender, by race, by grade, etc.)
- relationships & interactions with colleagues
- relationships & interactions with parents

3) Do you consider yourself a role model as a [race/ethnicity] and [gender] teacher? If so, for whom and in what ways? If not, why? Do you consider yourself a father figure? Explain.

4) Are there other ways in which being [race/ethnicity] and [gender] has shaped your experiences as a teacher? Are there other moments when you feel the impact of being a [race/ethnicity] and [gender] teacher? Does being a [race/ethnicity] and [gender] teacher ever work in your favor? Does it ever work to your disadvantage?

5) What types of support networks did you have access to as a teacher-in-training, and were they able to provide support that addressed your needs as a [race/ethnicity] and [gender] teacher? Explain.

6) What types of support networks do you presently have access to as a teacher, and are they able to provide support that addresses your needs as a [race/ethnicity] and [gender] teacher? Explain.

7) Are there support networks or structures not currently in place that you would like to see established for [race/ethnicity] and [gender] teachers? Explain.

8) Is there anything I didn't ask you about the topics of this interview that you think I should consider?

Third in-depth interview protocol

1) What stands out for you in your teaching experience as the school year comes to a close? Can you offer anecdotes to illustrate those issues?

2) What plans do you have for the summer?

3) Why did you agree to participate in this study? What led you to volunteer your participation?

4) Which aspects of this study did you find most engaging, thought-provoking, and/or enjoyable? Why?

5) Which aspects of this study could have been conducted differently? What suggestions do you have for how follow-up studies on this topic should be pursued?

6) What do you hope will come of this study? Who should be the audience for this study, and what do you hope that audience will gain?

Focus group protocol

1) Context: I'm going to raise some of themes that have emerged during the one-on-one interviews that I've conducted for this study. These themes revolve around the significance of being a Black male teacher. Not only will this focus group give you a chance to revisit some of the issues from the earlier interviews, but it will also give you an opportunity to listen and respond to each other. In fact, the main goals of this focus group are to allow all of you to discuss the importance of being a Black male teacher with other Black male teachers, and to see what insights are generated when Black male teachers collectively examine their experiences.

2) Introductions: Please state your name and describe something you plan to do this summer.

3) Describe one incident from the past year that speaks to the significance and/or impact of your presence as a Black male teacher. This can involve students, colleagues, parents, etc., and it can be something that took place in school or outside of school.

4) How would you compare or contrast the relationships you have with Black male students to the relationships you have with other students?

- Do you feel pressure and/or a responsibility to pay particular attention to Black boys? If so, where does this pressure and/or sense of responsibility come from? Do you think this is fair?
- How much time and energy are devoted to Black boys versus other groups?
- Are interactions with Black male students a source of fulfillment? A source of stress? Is there some other way to characterize these interactions?

5) To what extent do you feel like you are expected as a Black male teacher to be a father figure and/or a disciplinarian?
- Is this expectation higher of Black male teachers than of other teachers in the schools in which you teach? If so, is this fair?
- How do you deal with discipline? What are your strategies?
- How (if at all) do you approach being a father figure?
- Are these roles sources of fulfillment? Sources of stress? Is there some other way to characterize these roles?

6) What are your relationships like with other adults at your school? Are there any trends that stand out based on race, gender, subject matter, level of authority, etc.?

7) How can urban schools recruit, retain, and support Black male teachers?

- Can you remember any recruitment strategies that appealed to you? Can you think of any strategies that might appeal to Black men at various career stages?
- When/Where should recruitment begin? Who should do it?
- What types of supports are in place now? What supports work? What supports don't work? What new supports can you imagine?

References

27 x 40 Lean on Me Movie Poster. (n.d.). Retrieved from www.amazon. com/27-40-Lean- Movie-Poster/dp/B001JKF85C

Abdul-Alim, J. (2004, September 19). A small class: Male kindergarten teachers are a rare sight in classrooms. *Milwaukee Journal Sentinel.* Retrieved from www.jsonline.com/news/metro/sep04/260294.asp

Achinstein, B., & Aquirre, J. (2008). Cultural match or culturally suspect: How new teachers of color negotiate sociocultural challenges in the classroom. *Teachers College Record, 110*(8), 1505–1540.

Adams, R., & Savran, D. (Eds.). (2002). *The masculinity studies reader.* Malden, MA: Blackwell.

Adejumo, V. (2015). *Black masculinity* [course syllabus]. Retrieved April 16, 2017, from http://afam.clas.ufl.edu/files/BlackMasculinityFall20152.pdf

Adkison-Bradley, C., Terpstra, J., & Dormitorio, B. P. (2014). Child discipline in African American families. *Family Journal, 22*(2), 198–205.

Adney, K. (2005). Savior, slayer, travailer: The Image of the knight in English Renaissance religious verse. *Interactions: Aegean Journal of English and American Studies, 14*(1), 1–12.

Akbar, N. (1991). *Visions for Black men.* Nashville, TN: Winston-Derek Publishers, Inc.

Alexander, B. K. (2006). *Performing Black masculinity: Race, culture, and queer identity.* New York, NY: AltaMira Press.

Alexander, M. (2012). *The new Jim Crow: Mass incarceration in the age of colorblindness* (revised ed.). New York, NY: New Press.

Alhassan, J. (2013). Opportunities to die for. In C. W. Lewis & I. A. Toldson (Eds.), *Black male teachers: Diversifying the United States' teacher workforce.* Bingley, UK: Emerald Publishing.

Allan, J. (1994). *Anomaly as exemplar: The meanings of role-modeling for men elementary teachers.* Dubuque, IA: Tri-College Department of Education. (Eric Document Reproduction Service No. ED 378 190). Retrieved from https://eric. ed.gov/?id=ED378190

Allen, D. (2015, June 9). The urgent need to have African American male teachers in elementary schools in the United States. *Our Black News.* Retrieved January 4, 2016, from http://ourblacknews.com/2015/06/09/ urgent-african-american-male-teachers-elementaryschools-united-states/

Allen, J. S. (2011). *Venceremos? The erotics of Black self-making in Cuba.* Durham, NC: Duke University Press.

Alsup, J. (2006). *Teacher identity discourses: Negotiating personal and professional spaces.* Mahwah, NJ: L. Erlbaum Associates.

Anderson, E. (1999). *Code of the street: Decency, violence, and the moral life of the inner city.* New York, NY: W.W. Norton.

Anderson, E. (2008). Against the wall: Poor, young, Black, and Male. In E. Anderson (Ed.), *Against the wall: Poor, young, Black, and male* (pp. 3–27). Philadelphia, PA: University of Pennsylvania Press.

Apple, M. W. (1986). *Teachers and text: A political economy of class and gender relations in education.* New York, NY: Routledge & Kegan Paul.

Armah, E. (2016, August 12). Toxic masculinity matters. *Ebony.* Retrieved April 17, 2017, from www.ebony.com/news-views/toxic-masculinity

Asadulla, K. M. (2016, December 29). Confessions of a misogynist Black male. *Rap Rehab.* Retrieved April 17, 2017, from http://raprehab.com/confessions-misogynist-fuck-boy/

Awkward, M. (1999). A Black man's place in Black feminist criticism. In D. W. Carbado (Ed.), *Black men on race, gender, and sexuality: A critical reader* (pp. 362–382). New York, NY: New York University Press.

Bailey, M. (2013, November 29). Out of 1,883 teachers, 56 Black males. *New Haven Independent.* Retrieved April 9, 2017, from www.newhavenindependent.org/index.php/archives/entry/new_haven_black_male_ teachers/

Baker, S. (2011). Pedagogies of protest: African American teachers and the history of the civil rights movement, 1940–1963. *Teachers College Record, 113*(12), 2777–2803.

Baldridge, B. J. (2014). Relocating the deficit: Reimagining Black youth in neoliberal times. *American Educational Research Journal, 51*(3), 440–472.

Barbini, E., & Kuntz, J. (Producers). (2013). *Blackboard wars* [Television series]. Los Angeles, CA: Discovery Studios.

Barris, K. (Writer), Patel, V. (Writer), Brown, N. (Writer), Patel, D. (Writer), & Asher, R. (Director). (2014). The talk [Television series episode]. In [Producer], *Black-ish.* Burbank, CA: American Broadcasting Company.

Basinger, J. (1999). 2 colleges train Black men to work in special education. *Chronicle of Higher Education,* A12–A13.

Beatty, R. (2013, February 14). Kunjufu: Hire more Black male teachers. *South Florida Times.* Retrieved May 29, 2016, from www.sfltimes.com/uncategorized/kunjufu-hiremore-black-male-teachers

Beauboeuf-Lafontant, T. (1999). A movement against and beyond boundaries: "Politically relevant teaching" among African American teachers. *Teachers College Record, 100*(4), 702–723.

Beauboeuf-Lafontant, T. (2002). A womanist experience of caring: Understanding the pedagogy of exemplary Black women teachers. *Urban Review, 34*(1), 71–86.

Bianco, M., Leech, N. L., & Mitchell, K. (2011). Pathways to teaching: African American male teens explore teaching as a career. *The Journal of Negro Education, 80*(3), 368–383.

Black, D. L. (Writer) (Director), Sant, G. V. (Director), Rees, D. (Director), Schlamme, T. (Director). (2017). *When we rise* [Television series]. Los Angeles, CA: ABC Studios.

Blake, J. J., Butler, B. R., Lewis, C. W., & Darensbourg, A. (2011). Unmasking the inequitable discipline experiences of urban Black girls: Implications for urban educational stakeholders. *Urban Review, 43,* 90–106.

Blount, J. M. (2005). *Fit to teach: Same-sex desire, gender, and school work in the twentieth century.* Albany, NY: State University of New York Press.

Bobic, I. (2016, March 16). Marco Rubio, once the "Republican Savior," bows out of GOP presidential race. *Huffington Post.* Retrieved June 5, 2017, from www.huffingtonpost.com/entry/marco-rubio-ends-2016campaign_us_56143762e4b0b134ad66b478

Bolch, M. (2006, March). Teacher man. *Scholastic.* Retrieved from www.scholastic.com/administrator/mar06/articles.asp?article=MaleTeachers

Boyd-Franklin, N., & Franklin, A. J. (2000). *Boys into men: Raising our African American teenage sons.* New York, NY: Dutton.

Bradley, C. R. (1998). Child rearing in African American families: A study of the disciplinary practices of African American parents. *Journal of Multicultural Counseling and Development, 26*(4), 273–281.

Brett, J. (2015, December 9). Uplifting father-son "daily pledge" video goes viral. *AJC.com.* Retrieved June 1, 2017, from http://buzz.blog.ajc.com/2015/12/09/uplifting-father-sondaily-pledge-video-goes-viral/

Brewster, J., & Stephenson, M. (2013). *Promises kept: Raising Black boys to succeed in school and in life.* New York, NY: Spiegel & Grau Trade Paperbacks.

Bridges, T. (2011). Towards a pedagogy of hip hop in urban teacher education. *Journal of Negro Education, 80*(3), 325–338.

Bristol, T. (2013, September 4). *Calling Black men to the blackboard.* Albert Shanker Institute. Retrieved June 13, 2016, from www.shankerinstitute.org/blog/calling-black-menblackboard

Bristol, T. (2015). Black male teachers: There aren't enough of them. *The Washington Post.* Retrieved October 10, 2017, from www.washingtonpost.com/news/answersheet/wp/2015/04/28/black-male-teachers-there-arent-enough-ofthem/?utm_term=.b263dec47529

Brockenbrough, E. (2006). *Black man teaching: Connections between identity, pedagogy, and practice among Black male teachers.* Presented at the American Educational Research Association Annual Meeting, San Francisco, CA.

Brockenbrough, E. (2012a). Agency and abjection in the closet: The voices (and silences) of Black queer male teachers. *International Journal of Qualitative Studies in Education, 25*(6), 723–739.

Brockenbrough, E. (2012b). Emasculation blues: Black male teachers' perspectives on gender and power in the teaching profession. *Teachers College Record, 114*(5), 1–43.

Brockenbrough, E. (2012c). "You ain't my daddy!": Black male teachers and the politics of surrogate fatherhood. *International Journal of Inclusive Education, 16*(4), 357–372.

Brockenbrough, E. (2013). Educating the race in postmodern times: The intraracial border crossings of Black male teachers. In C. W. Lewis & I. A. Toldson (Eds.), *Black male teachers: Diversifying the United States' teacher workforce* (pp. 25–42). Bingley, UK: Emerald Publishing.

Brockenbrough, E. (2014). Further mothering: Reconceptualizing White women educators' work with Black youth. *Equity & Excellence in Education, 47*(3), 253–272.

Brockenbrough, E. (2015). "The discipline stop": The contested role of Black male teachers in urban school discipline. *Education and Urban Society, 47*(5), 499–522.

Brooks, M. (2016, February 25). Where are all the male African-American teachers? *Fox 25 News*. Retrieved April 8, 2017, from http://okcfox.com/news/top-slideshows/where-arethe-male-african-american-teachers

Brown, A. L. (2009). "Brothers gonna work it out:" Understanding the pedagogic performance of African American male teachers working with African American male students. *The Urban Review, 41*(5), 416–435.

Brown, A. L. (2011). Pedagogies of experience: A case of the African American male teacher. *Teaching Education, 22*(4), 363–376.

Brown, A. L. (2012). On human kinds and role models: A critical discussion about the African American male teacher. *Educational Studies, 48*(3), 296–315.

Brown, A. L. (2013). Waiting for superwoman: White female teachers and the construction of the "neoliberal savior" in a New York City public school. *Journal for Critical Education Policy Studies, 11*(2), 123–164.

Brown, E. R. (2003). Freedom for some, discipline for "others": The structure of inequity in education. In K. J. Saltman & D. Gabbard (Eds.), *Education as enforcement: The militarization and corporatization of schools* (pp. 127–152). New York, NY: RoutledgeFalmer.

Brown, J. W., & Butty, J-A. M. (1999). Factors that influence African American male teachers' educational and career aspirations: Implications for school district recruitment and retention efforts. *The Journal of Negro Education, 68*(3), 280–292.

Brown, M. P. (2000). *Closet space: Geographies of metaphor from the body to the globe*. New York, NY: Routledge.

Brown, R., & Armstead, S. (Producers). (2012). *Save my son* [Television series]. Orange, NJ: TV ONE.

Bryant, J. H. (2013, May 29). Obama speaks as father-in-chief at Morehouse College commencement. *Huffington Post*. Retrieved February 21, 2014, from www.huffingtonpost.com/john-hope-bryant/obama-speaks-as-father-inchief_b_3352977.html

Byrd, R. P. (2001). Prologue: The tradition of John: A mode of Black masculinity. In R. P. Byrd & B. Guy-Sheftall (Eds.), *Traps: African American men on gender and sexuality* (pp. 1–26). Bloomington, IN: Indiana University Press.

Byrd, R. P., & Guy-Sheftall, B. (Eds.). (2001). *Traps: African American men on gender and sexuality*. Bloomington, IN: Indiana University Press.

Byrd, S. (2014, March 10). JSU program to increase number of Black, male teachers in elementary schools. *Jackson State Newsroom*. Retrieved April 9, 2017, from www.jsumsnews.com/?p=11738

Campbell, E. (2011, December 14). The importance of the Black father and son relationship. *ThyBlackMan.com*. Retrieved June 1, 2017, from http://thyblackman.com/2011/12/14/the-importance-of-the-black-father-and-sonrelationship/

Caponi, G. D. (Ed.). (1999). *Signifyin(g), sanctifyin', & slam dunking: A reader in African American expressive culture*. Amherst, MA: University of Massachusetts Press.

Carbado, D. W. (Ed.). (1999a). *Black men on race. gender, and sexuality*. New York, NY: New York University Press.

Carbado, D. W. (1999b). Introduction: Where and when Black men enter. In D. W. Carbado (Ed.), *Black men on race, gender, and sexuality: A critical reader* (pp. 1–17). New York, NY: New York University Press.

Carlton-LaNey, I., & Burwell, N. Y. (Eds.). (1996). *African American community practice models: Historical and contemporary responses*. New York, NY: Routledge.

Carrington, B., Francis, B., Hutchings, M., Skelton, C., Read, B., & Hall, I. (2007). Does the gender of the teacher really matter? Seven- to eight-year-olds' accounts of their interactions with their teachers. *Educational Studies, 33*(4), 397–413.

Carrington, B., Tymms, P., & Merrell, C. (2008). Role models, school improvement and the "gender gap"—Do men bring out the best in boys and women the best in girls? *British Educational Research Journal, 34*(3), 315–327.

Case, K. I. (1997). African American othermothering in the urban elementary school. *Urban Review, 29*(1), 25–39.

Causey, J. E. (n.d.). The reason we need Black male teachers. *JSOnline.com*. Retrieved January 4, 2016, from www.jsonline.com/blogs/news/339557631. html

Celeski, D. S. (1994). *Along freedom road: Hyde County, North Carolina, and the fate of Black schools in the South*. Chapel Hill, NC: University of North Carolina Press.

Centers for Disease Control and Prevention. (2016, February 23). *Half of Black gay men and a quarter of Latino gay men projected to be diagnosed within their lifetime*. Retrieved October 26, 2016, from www.cdc.gov/nchhstp/newsroom/2016/croi-press-releaserisk.html

Chandler, D. L. (2013, April 3). Dad hands out fade to teenage daughters over twerk video. *Hip Hop Wired*. Retrieved from http://hiphopwired.com/2013/04/03/dad- hands-out-fade-toteenage-daughters-over-twerk-video-video/

Chapman, B., & Colangelo, L. L. (2015, November 24). New York City seeks more male Black, Latino, Asian men to teach in public schools. *NY Daily News*. Retrieved January 4, 2016, from www.nydailynews.com/new-york/nyc-schools-seek-male-black-latino-asianteachers-article-1.2445149

Chideya, F. (2007, July 2). Putting men in the classroom. *NPR.org*. Retrieved April 6, 2017, from www.npr.org/templates/story/story.php?storyId=11658405

Chmelynski, C. (2006). Getting more men and Blacks into teaching. *The Education Digest, 71*(5), 40–42.

Connell, C. (2014). *School's out: Gay and lesbian teachers in the classroom*. Berkeley, CA: University of California Press.

Connell, R. W. (1995). *Masculinities*. Berkeley, CA: University of California Press.

Connell, R. W. (2000). *The men and the boys*. Berkeley, CA: University of California Press. Connell, R. W. (2002). On hegemonic masculinity and violence: Response to Jefferson and Hall. *Theoretical Criminology, 6*(1), 89–99.

Cook, D. A., & Dixson, A. D. (2013). Writing critical race theory and method: A composite counterstory on the experiences of Black teachers in New Orleans post-Katrina. *International Journal of Qualitative Studies in Education, 26*(10), 1238–1258.

Cosby, B., & Poussaint, A. F. (2007). *Come on, people: On the path from victims to victors*. Nashville, TN: Thomas Nelson.

Crenshaw, K. W., Ocen, P., & Nanda, J. (2015). *Black girls matter: Pushed out, overpoliced and underprotected*. Retrieved from https://static1.squarespace.com/static/53f20d90e4b0b80451158d8c/t/54dcc1ece4b001c03e323448/1423753708557/AAPF_BlackGirlsMatterReport.pdf

Crenshaw, Z. (2015, February 18). IU South Bend recruiting minority, male teachers. *WSBT.com*. Retrieved January 4, 2016, from http://wsbt.com/news/local/iu-south-bendrecruiting-minority-male-teachers

Crisp, T., & King, J. (2016). I Just love kids . . . is that a problem? *Taboo: The Journal of Culture & Education, 15*(1), 41–60.

Cuffee, S. M. (2008). *Manchild dying in the promised land: Strategies to save Black males.* Chicago, IL: African American Images.

Dancy, T. E. (2012). *The brother code: Manhood and masculinity among African American males in college.* Charlotte, NC: Information Age Publishing.

Davis, D. (2008). Olympic athletes who took a stand. *Smithsonian.com*. Retrieved September 16, 2017, from www.smithsonianmag.com/articles/olympic-athletes-who-took-a-stand- 593920/

Davis, J. E. (2001). Transgressing the masculine: African American boys and the failure of schools. In W. Martino & B. Meyenn (Eds.), *What about the boys? Issues of masculinity in schools* (pp. 140–153). Buckingham, UK: Open University Press.

Davis, J. E. (2005). Early schooling and academic achievement of African American males. In O. S. Fashola (Ed.), *Educating African American males: Voices from the field* (pp. 129–150). Thousand Oaks, CA: Corwin Press.

Davis, J. E., Frank, T. J., & Clark, L. M. (2013). The case of a Black male mathematics teacher teaching in a unique urban context: Implications for recruiting Black male mathematics teachers. In C. W. Lewis & I. A. Toldson (Eds.), *Black male teachers: Diversifying the United States' teacher workforce* (pp. 77–92). Bingley, UK: Emerald Publishing.

Davis, J. E., Parker, W., & Long, L. (2015, September 15). Black male teachers: Why do we need them and how do we recruit and retain them in classroom? *Afrikan Amerikan Journal.* Retrieved January 4, 2016, from http://afrikan-amerikanjournal.com/black-male-teacherswhy-do-we-need-them-and-how-do-we-recruit-and-retain-them-in-classroom/

Davis, S. (Producer). (1961). *Boys beware* [Motion picture]. Sidney Davis Productions.

DeJean, W. (2008). Out gay and lesbian K-12 educators: A study in radical honesty. *Journal of Gay & Lesbian Issues in Education, 4*(4), 59–72.

Delpit, L. D. (1995). *Other people's children: Cultural conflict in the classroom.* New York, NY: New Press: Distributed by W.W. Norton.

Delpit, L. D. (1997). Foreword. In M. Foster (Ed.), *Black teachers on teaching.* New York, NY: The New Press.

Dempsey, V., & Noblit, G. (1993). The demise of caring in an African-American community: One consequence of school desegregation. *Urban Review, 25*(1), 47–61.

Denzin, N. K. (1989). *Interpretive biography.* Newbury Park, CA: Sage.

Deruy, E. (n.d.). Student diversity is up but teachers are mostly White. *ABC News*. Retrieved November 27, 2016, from http://abcnews.go.com/ABC_Univision/News/studentdiversity-teachers-white/story?id=18782102

Dingus, J. E. (2006). "Doing the best we could": African American teachers' counterstory on school desegregation. *The Urban Review, 38*(3), 211–233.

Dixson, A. D. (2003). "Let's do this!": Black women teachers' politics and pedagogy. *Urban Education, 38*(2), 217–235.

Dixson, A. D., Buras, K. L., & Jeffers, E. K. (2015). The color of reform: Race, education reform, and charter schools in post-Katrina New Orleans. *Qualitative Inquiry*, 21(3), 288–299.

Dixson, A. D., & Dingus, J. E. (2008). In search of our mothers' gardens: Black women teachers and professional socialization. *Teachers College Record*, 110(4), 805–837.

djvlad. (2016, September 23). Dr. Umar Johnson: No African community ever legitimized being gay. *Youtube*. Retrieved April 21, 2017, from www.youtube.com/watch?v=IEJ3h- RUjGk

Drake, S. C. (2016). *When we imagine grace: Black men and subject making*. Chicago, IL: University of Chicago Press.

Dumas, M. J., & Nelson, J. D. (2016). (Re)Imagining Black boyhood: Toward a critical framework for educational research. *Harvard Educational Review*, 86(1), 27–47.

Dunu, C. (2016, June 28). Black male teachers critical, but a rare find in classrooms. *The Epoch Times*. Retrieved April 8, 2017, from www.theepochtimes.com/n3/2098857-blackmale-teachers-critical-but-a-rare-find-in-classrooms/

Dyson, M. E. (2005). *Is Bill Cosby right? Or has the Black middle class lost its mind?* New York, NY: Basic Civitas Books.

Dyson, M. E. (2008, July 19). Obama's rebuke of absentee Black fathers. *Time*. Retrieved from www.time.com/time/magazine/article/0,9171,1816485,00.html

Endo, H., Reece-Miller, P. C., & Santavicca, N. (2010). Surviving in the trenches: A narrative inquiry into queer teachers' experiences and identity. *Teaching and Teacher Education*, 26(4), 1023–1030.

Evans, D. (2016, May 17). Presence, consistency and love: A thank you to Black male teachers. *Educators for Excellence*. Retrieved April 8, 2017, from https://e4e.org/blognews/blog/presence-consistency-and-love-thank-you-black-male-teachers

Evans, K. (2002). *Negotiating the self: Identity, sexuality, and emotion in learning to teach*. New York, NY: RoutledgeFalmer.

Facey, S. (2012, April 10). The need for more Black male teachers. *Examiner.com*. Retrieved May 29, 2016, from www.examiner.com/article/the-need-for-more-black-maleteachers

Fairclough, A. (2007). *A class of their own: Black teachers in the segregated South*. Cambridge, MA: Belknap Press of Harvard University Press.

Farinde, A. A., Allen, A., & Lewis, C. W. (2016). Retaining Black teachers: An examination of Black female teachers' intentions to remain in K-12 classrooms. *Equity & Excellence in Education*, 49(1), 115–127.

Fashola, O. S. (2005). Developing the talents of African American male students during the nonschool hours. In O. S. Fashola (Ed.), *Educating African American males: Voices from the field* (pp. 19–49). Thousand Oaks, CA: Corwin Press.

Feierman, L. (2014, April 10). Troubling statistics for African-American males in the classroom. *CBS San Francisco Bay Area*. Retrieved June 14, 2017, from http://sanfrancisco.cbslocal.com/2014/04/10/troubling-statistics-for-african-americanmales-in-the-classroom/

Fenwick, L. T. (2010, September 29). Where did all the Black male teachers go? *ThyBlackMan.com*. Retrieved May 29, 2016, from http://thyblackman.com/2010/09/29/where-did-all-the-black-male-teachers-go/

Ferguson, A. A. (2000). *Bad boys: Public schools in the making of Black masculinity*. Ann Arbor, MI: University of Michigan Press.

Ford, A. C., & Sassi, K. (2014). Authority in cross-racial teaching and learning: (Re)considering the transferability of warm demander approaches. *Urban Education, 49*(1), 39–74.

Ford, J. C. (2016). "Very simple. I just don't lie": The role of honesty in Black lesbian K-12 teachers' experiences in the U.S. Southeast. *Journal of Lesbian Studies, 21*(4), 391–406.

Foster, M. (1990). The politics of race: Through the eyes of African-American teachers. *Journal of Education, 172*(3), 123–141.

Foster, M. (1991). "Just got to find a way": Case studies of the lives and practice of exemplary Black high school teachers. In M. Foster (Ed.), *Readings on equal education, volume 11: Qualitative investigations into schools and schooling* (pp. 273–309). New York, NY: AMS Press.

Foster, M. (1993). Othermothers: Exploring the educational philosophy of Black American women teachers. In M. Arnot & K. Weiler (Eds.), *Feminism and social justice in education: International perspectives* (pp. 101–123). London, UK: The Falmer Press.

Foster, M. (1994). Effective Black teachers: A literature review. In E. Hollins, J. King, & W. Hayman (Eds.), *Teaching diverse populations: Formulating a knowledge base* (pp. 225–242). Albany, NY: State University of New York Press.

Foster, M. (1997). *Black teachers on teaching*. New York, NY: New Press.

Foucault, M. (1995). *Discipline and punish: The birth of the prison* (2nd Vintage Books ed.). New York, NY: Vintage Books.

Francis, B., & Skelton, C. (2001). Men teachers and the construction of heterosexual masculinity in the classroom. *Sex Education, 1*(1), 9–21.

Francis, B., Skelton, C., Carrington, B., Hutchings, M., Read, B., & Hall, I. (2008). A perfect match? Pupils' and teachers' views of the impact of matching educators and learners by gender. *Research Papers in Education, 23*(1), 21–36.

Franklin, V. P. (1990). "They rose and fell together": African American educators and community leadership, 1795–1954. *Journal of Education, 172*(3), 39–64.

Fuss, D. (Ed.). (1991). *Inside/out: Lesbian theories, gay theories*. New York, NY: Routledge.

Gates, H. L. (1997). *Thirteen ways of looking at a Black man* (1st ed.). New York, NY: Random House.

Gatling, R. P., Gatling, V. S., & Hamilton, L. H. (2014). *An inexcusable absence: The shortage of Black male teachers*. Bloomington, IN: AuthorHouse.

Gay, G. (2010). *Culturally responsive teaching: Theory, research, and practice* (2nd ed.). New York, NY: Teachers College.

Gerson, M. (2016, September 12). The self-refuting idea that America needs Donald Trump as a savior. *Washington Post*. Retrieved June 6, 2017, from www.washingtonpost.com/opinions/the-self-refuting-idea-that-america-needsdonald-trump-as-a-savior/2016/09/12/d89a26ae-790b-11e6-beac-57a4a412e93a_story.html?utm_term=.738a2790bfe5

Ginwright, S. A. (2010). *Black youth rising: Activism and radical healing in urban America*. New York, NY: Teachers College Press.

Ginwright, S. A., Cammarota, J., & Noguera, P. (Eds.). (2006). *Beyond Resistance! Youth activism and community change: New democratic possibilities for practice and policy for America's youth*. New York, NY: Routledge.

Giroux, H. A. (2001). Mis/education and zero tolerance: Disposable youth and the politics of domestic militarization. *Boundary 2, 28*(3), 61–94.

Glaude, E. S. (2000). *Exodus! Religion, race, and nation in early nineteenth-century Black America.* Chicago, IL: University of Chicago Press.

Glaude, E. S., & Glaude, L. (2016, July 8). Read: Letters between a Black father and his son. *Time.* Retrieved June 1, 2017, from http://time.com/4398617/parents-police-shootings/

Goodson, I., & Sikes, P. J. (2001). *Life history research in educational settings: Learning from lives.* Phildelphia, PA: Open University.

Gormley, W. (2012, August 13). Column: What our schools need? A few good men. *USA Today.* Retrieved February 6, 2017, from www.usatoday.com/news/opinion/forum/story/2012-08-13/male-teacherseducation-reform/57039176/1

Graham, G., & Gracia, J. N. (2012). Health disparities in boys and men. *American Journal of Public Health, 102*(Suppl 2), S167.

Graham, J. (2011, February 1). Secretary calls Black men to the blackboard. *Homeroom.* Retrieved June 13, 2016, from http://blog.ed.gov/2011/02/secretary-calls-black-men-tothe-blackboard/

Graham, K. A. (2017, October 12). Why having more Black male teachers matters. *Philly.com.* Retrieved October 17, 2017, from www.philly.com/philly/education/philly-and-u-steaching-force-doesnt-match-its-student-population-how-do-you-fix-that-and-why-doesit-matter-black-teachers-philadelphia-diversity-20171012.html

Graves, K. (2009). *And they were wonderful teachers: Florida's purge of gay and lesbian teachers.* Urbana, IL: University of Illinois Press.

Graves, K. (2015). LGBTQ education research in historical context. In G. L. Wimberly (Ed.), *LGBTQ issues in education: Advancing a research agenda* (pp. 23–42). Washington, DC: American Educational Research Association.

Green, T. T. (2009). *A fatherless child: Autobiographical perspectives on African American men.* Columbia, MO: University of Missouri Press.

Gregory, T. (2016, February 15). African-American fathers, sons to strengthen bonds in Washington Park project. *Chicago Tribune.* Retrieved June 1, 2017, from www.chicagotribune.com/news/ct-african-american-fathers-sons-program-met-20160215-story.html

Grey III, S. (n.d.). Why African-American male teachers are needed in small rural areas. *Your Black World.* Retrieved January 4, 2016, from http://yourblackworld.net/2015/10/22/drsinclair-grey-iii-why-african-american-male-teachers-are-needed-in-small-rural-areas-2/

Griffin, P. (1991). Identity management strategies among lesbian and gay educators. *International Journal of Qualitative Studies in Education, 4*(3), 189–202.

Griffin, P., & Ouellett, M. (2003). From silence to safety and beyond: Historical trends in addressing lesbian, gay, bisexual, transgender issues in K-12 schools. *Equity & Excellence in Education, 36*(2), 106–114.

Guy-Sheftall, B. (2006). Remembering our feminist forefathers. In A. D. Mutua (Ed.), *Progressive Black masculinities* (pp. 43–53). New York, NY: Routledge.

Hamblin, J. (2016, June 16). Toxic masculinity and murder: Can we talk about men? *The Atlantic.* Retrieved from www.theatlantic.com/health/archive/2016/06/toxicmasculinity-and-mass-murder/486983/

Harbeck, K. M. (1997). *Gay and lesbian educators: Personal freedoms, public constraints.* Malden, MA: Amethyst.

Hare, N., & Hare, J. (1984). *The endangered Black family: Coping with the unisexualization and coming extinction of the Black race.* San Francisco, CA: Black Think Tank.

Hare, N., & Hare, J. (1985). *Bringing the Black boy to manhood: The passage.* San Francisco, CA: Black Think Tank.

Harper, H. (2006). *Letters to a young brother: manifest your destiny.* New York, NY: Gotham Books.

Harper, P. B. (1996). *Are we not men? Masculine anxiety and the problem of African-American identity.* New York, NY: Oxford University Press.

Harris, T. L., & Taylor, G. (2012). *Raising African American males: Strategies and interventions for successful outcomes.* Lanham, MD: Rowman & Littlefield Education.

Harris, T. W. (2017, March 9). Shedding (moon)light on toxic masculinity. *Bitch Media.* Retrieved April 17, 2017, from www.bitchmedia.org/article/shedding-moonlighttoxic-masculinity/problem-homophobia-not-gay-characters

Hawkins, D. (2015, September 22). Where are all the Black male teachers? *NEA Today.* Retrieved January 4, 2016, from http://neatoday.org/2015/09/22/where-are-all-the-blackmale-teachers/

Hayes, C. (2014). We teach too: What are the lived experiences and pedagogical practices of gay men of color teachers. *MSC—Masculinities & Social Change, 3*(2), 148–172.

Hayes, C., Juarez, B., & Escoffery-Runnels, V. (2014). We were there too: Learning from Black male teachers in Mississippi about successful teaching of Black students. *Democracy and Education, 22*(1), 1–11.

Healey, C. (2012, July 16). Video: Dad yells at son for wearing skinny jeans. *The Grio.* Retrieved from http://thegrio.com/2012/07/16/video-dad-yells-at-son.-for- wearingskinny-jeans/

Henry, C. (2014, April 17). Grants seek Black males to teach in elementary schools. *Westside Gazette.* Retrieved April 8, 2017, from http://thewestsidegazette.com/grants-seek-blackmales-to-teach-in-elementary-schools/

Hermida, A. (2012). Social journalism: Exploring how social media is shaping journalism. In E. Siapera & A. Veglis (Eds.), *The handbook of global online journalism* (pp. 309–328). Malden, MA: Wiley-Blackwell.

Hill Collins, P. (2000). *Black feminist thought: Knowledge, consciousness, and the politics of empowerment* (2nd ed.). New York, NY: Routledge.

Hill Collins, P. (2005). *Black sexual politics: African Americans, gender, and the new racism.* New York, NY: Routledge.

Hoffman, N. (1981). *Woman's "true" profession: Voices from the history of teaching.* New York, NY: McGraw-Hill Book Company.

Holderness, G. (2015). *Re-writing Jesus: Christ in 20th century fiction and film.* New York, NY: Bloomsbury Academic.

Holloway, K. (2015, June 12). Toxic masculinity is killing men: The roots of male trauma. *Salon.com.* Retrieved April 17, 2017, from www.salon.com/2015/06/12/toxic_masculinity_is_killing_men_the_roots_of_male_trauma_partner/

hooks, bell. (1981). *Ain't I a woman: Black women and feminism.* Boston, MA: South End Press.

Horan, M. (2015, September 11). In defense of the magical teacher movie. *Refinery29.* Retrieved June 6, 2017, from www.refinery29.com/2015/09/93826/movies-about-teachers

House, R. (2017, February 9). Column: How I learned my own value as a Black male teacher. *PBS.org*. Retrieved April 4, 2017, from www.pbs.org/newshour/updates/columnlearned-my-own-value-as-a-black-male-teacher/

Howard, T. C. (2001). Powerful pedagogy for African American students: A case of four teachers. *Urban Education, 36*(2), 179–202.

Howard, T. C. (2008). Who really cares? The disenfranchisement of African American males in prek-12 schools: A critical race theory perspective. *Teachers College Record, 110*(5), 954–985.

Howard, T. C. (2010). *Why race and culture matter in schools: Closing the achievement gap in America's classrooms*. New York, NY: Teachers College Press.

Howard, T. C. (2014). *Black male(d): Peril and promise in the education of African American males*. New York, NY: Teachers College Press.

Howard, T. C., Flennaugh, T. K., & Terry Sr., C. L. (2012). Black males, social imagery, and the disruption of pathological identities: Implications for research and teaching. *Educational Foundations, 26*(1/2), 85–102.

Hughey, M. W. (2014). *The White savior film: Content, critics, and consumption*. Philadelphia, PA: Temple University Press.

Humphries-Brooks, S. (2006). *Cinematic savior: Hollywood's making of the American Christ*. Westport, CT: Praeger Publishers.

Ingersoll, R. M., & May, H. (2011). The minority teacher shortage: Fact or Fable? *Phi Delta Kappan, 93*(1), 62–65.

Irvin, L. (2015, July 2). Why we need more teachers of color, especially men. *The Second Line Education Blog*. Retrieved January 4, 2016, from http://secondlineblog.org/2015/07/need-teachers-color-especially-men/

Irvine, J. J. (1990). *Black students and school failure: Policies, practices, and prescriptions*. New York, NY: Greenwood Press.

Irvine, J. J. (2002). African American teachers' culturally specific pedagogy: The collective stories. In J. J. Irvine (Ed.), *In search of wholeness: African American teachers and their culturally specific classroom practices* (pp. 139–146). New York, NY: Palgrave Macmillan.

Jackson, I., Sealey-Ruiz, Y., & Watson, W. (2014). Reciprocal love: Mentoring Black and Latino males through an ethos of care. *Urban Education, 49*(4), 394–417.

Jackson, J. M. (2007). *Unmasking identities: An exploration of the lives of gay and lesbian teachers*. Lanham, MD: Lexington Books.

Jackson, R. L. (2006). *Scripting the Black masculine body: Identity, discourse, and racial politics in popular media*. Albany, NY: State University of New York Press.

Jackson, R. L., & Hopson, M. C. (Eds.). (2011). *Masculinity in the Black imagination: Politics of communicating race and manhood*. New York, NY: Peter Lang.

Jackson, T. O., Boutte, G. S., & Wilson, B. S. (2013). Double-talking: The complexities surrounding Black male teachers as both problems and solutions. In C. W. Lewis & I. A. Toldson (Eds.), *Black male teachers: Diversifying the United States' teacher workforce* (pp. 117–131). Bingley, UK: Emerald Publishing.

Jackson, W. D. (2015, November 14). Black males in education. *A Titus Man*. Retrieved April 8, 2017, from www.atitusman.org/black-males-in-education

James, C. E. (2012). Troubling role models: Seeing racialization in the discourse relating to "corrective agents" for Black males. In K. Moffatt (Ed.), *Troubled masculinities: Reimagining urban men* (pp. 77–92). Toronto, ON: University of Toronto Press.

James, S. D. (2013, March 25). Why men don't teach primary school. *ABC News*. Retrieved February 5, 2017, from http://abcnews.go.com/Health/men-teach-elementaryschool/story?id=18784172

Jarrett, T. (2015, January 21). Diversity in the classroom: How to solve the Black male teacher shortage. *NBC News*. Retrieved January 4, 2016, from www.nbcnews.com/news/education/diversity-classroom-how-solve-black-maleteacher-shortage-n199471

Jenkins, E., & Hine, D. C. (Eds.). (2001). *A question of manhood: A reader in U.S. Black men's history and masculinity, Volume 2: The 19th century: From emancipation to Jim Crow.* Bloomington, IN: Indiana University Press.

Jennings, K. (Ed.). (1994). *One teacher in 10: Gay and lesbian educators tell their stories* (1st ed.). Boston, MA: Alyson Publications.

Jennings, K. (Ed.). (2005). *One teacher in 10: LGBT educators share their stories* (2nd ed.). Los Angeles, CA: Alyson Books.

Johns, D. J. (2016). Expanding high-quality early care and education for Black boys. In S. R. Harper & J. L. Wood (Eds.), *Advancing Black male student success from preschool through Ph.D* (pp. 1–19). Sterling, VA: Stylus Publishing.

Johnson, A. (2007, August 22). Wanted: A few good (Black and Latino) male teachers. *Austin Weekly News*. Retrieved May 29, 2016, from www.austinweeklynews.com/News/Articles/8-22-2007/Wanted:-A-few-good (black-and-Latino)-male-teachers/

Johnson, E. P. (2005). "Quare" studies, or (almost) everything I know about queer studies I learned from my grandmother. In E. P. Johnson & M. G. Henderson (Eds.), *Black queer studies: A critical anthology* (pp. 124–157). Durham, NC: Duke University Press.

Johnson, E. P. (2006). All in the family: Queering the projects. In F. L. Roberts & M. K. White (Eds.), *If we have to take tomorrow* (pp. 41–46). New York, NY: The Institute for Gay Men's Health.

Johnson, E. P. (2008). *Sweet tea: Black gay men of the South.* Chapel Hill, NC: University of North Carolina Press.

Johnson, K. A., Pitre, A., & Johnson, K. L. (Eds.). (2014). *African American women educators: A critical examination of their pedagogies, educational ideas, and activism from the nineteenth to the mid-twentieth century.* Lanham, MD: Rowman & Littlefield Education.

Johnson, S. (2008). The woman peril and male teachers in the early twentieth century. *American Educational History Journal, 35*(1), 149–167.

Johnson, W., Nyamekye, F., Chazan, D., & Rosenthal, B. (2013). Teaching with speeches: A Black teacher who uses the mathematics classroom to prepare students for life. *Teachers College Record, 115*(7), 1–26.

Jones, R. (2005, March 3). University program courts Black male teaching students. *NPR.org*. Retrieved March 28, 2017, from www.npr.org/templates/story/story.php?storyId=4521774

Judge, M. (2017, March 21). *Viral twitter video shows Black man stepping up to stop teens from fighting, educate them on doing better.* Retrieved June 1, 2017, from http://thegrapevine.theroot.com/viral-twitter-video-shows-black-man-stepping-up-tostop-1793503875

Kehler, M. (2009). Boys, friendships, and knowing "it wouldn't be unreasonable to assume I am gay." In W. Martino, M. Kehler, & M. B. Weaver-Hightower (Eds.), *The problem with boys' education: Beyond the backlash* (pp. 198–223). New York, NY: Routledge.

Kelly, H. (2010). *Race, remembering, and jim crow's teachers.* New York, NY: Routledge.

Kimmel, M. S. (1987). The contemporary "crisis" of masculinity in historical perspective. In H. Brod (Ed.), *The making of masculinities: The new men's studies* (pp. 121–153). Boston, MA: Allen & Unwin.

Kimmel, M. S. (2012). *Manhood in America: a cultural history* (3rd ed.). New York, NY: Oxford University Press.

Kimmel, M. S. (2013). *Angry White men: American masculinity at the end of an era.* New York, NY: Nation Books.

King, J. R. (1998). *Uncommon caring: Learning from men who teach young children.* New York, NY: Teachers College Press.

King, J. R. (2004). The (im)possibility of gay teachers for young children. *Theory into Practice, 43*(2), 122–127.

Kissen, R. M. (1996). *The last closet: The real lives of lesbian and gay teachers.* Portsmouth, NH: Heinemann.

Klein, T. (2012, June 4). *The messiah from Krypton: Superman's place in U.S. culture.* Retrieved June 1, 2017, from www.americamagazine.org/issue/5143/ideas/messiah-krypton

Kohn, A. (1993). *Punished by rewards: The trouble with gold stars, incentive plans, A's, praise, and other bribes.* New York, NY: Houghton Mifflin.

Kosciw, J. G., Greytak, E. A., Giga, N. M., Villenas, C., & Danischewski, D. J. (2016). *The 2015 National School Climate Survey: The experiences of lesbian, gay, bisexual, transgender, and queer youth in our nation's schools.* New York, NY: GLSEN.

Kunjufu, J. (1985a). *Countering the conspiracy to destroy Black boys, Vol. I* (Rev. ed.). Chicago, IL: African American Images.

Kunjufu, J. (1985b). *Countering the conspiracy to destroy Black boys, Vol. III* (1st ed.). Chicago, IL: African American Images.

Kunjufu, J. (2005). *Keeping Black boys out of special education* (1st ed.). Chicago, IL: African American Images.

Kunkle, F. (2015, April 9). *Black immigration is remaking U.S. Black population, report says.* Retrieved February 4, 2017, from www.washingtonpost.com/local/blackimmigration-is-remaking-us-black-population-report-says/2015/04/09/ded49c58-de29-11e4-a1b8-2ed88bc190d2_story.html

Ladson-Billings, G. (1995). Toward a theory of culturally relevant pedagogy. *American Educational Research Journal, 32*(3), 465–491.

Ladson-Billings, G. (2009). *The dreamkeepers: Successful teachers of African American children* (2nd ed.). San Francisco, CA: Jossey-Bass Publishers.

Landsman, J., & Lewis, C. W. (Eds.). (2011). *White teachers/diverse classrooms: Creating inclusive schools, building on students' diversity, and providing true educational equity* (2nd ed.). Sterling, VA: Stylus Publishing.

Lattimore, K. (2014, June 15). Honoring Black male teachers on Father's day. *The Good Men Project.* Retrieved April 8, 2017, from https://goodmenproject.com/featuredcontent/honoring-black-male-teachers-on-fathers-day-hesaid/

Lee, E. A. (1938). *Teaching as a man's job*. Homewood, IL: Phi Delta Kappa.

Lee, S. (1996). *Get on the bus*. Culver City, CA: Columbia Pictures.

Lemelle, A. J. (2010). *Black masculinity and sexual politics*. New York, NY: Routledge.

Lemons, G. L. (2001). "When and where [we] enter": In search of a feminist forefather-Reclaiming the womanist legacy of W.E.B. DuBois. In *Traps: African American men on gender and sexuality* (pp. 71–91). Bloomington, IN: Indiana University Press.

Lentz, P. (1989, March 26). Joe Clark's fame marred by squabbling, less-supportive figures. *Chicago Tribune*. Retrieved June 27, 2017, from http://articles.chicagotribune.com/1989-03-26/news/8903290854_1_mayor-frank-x-graves-joe-clark-clark-supporter

Lewis, C. W. (2006). African American male teachers in public schools: An examination of three urban school districts. *Teachers College Record, 108*(2), 224–245.

Lewis, C. W. (2013). Black male teachers' path to U.S. K-12 classrooms: Framing the national discussion. In C. W. Lewis & I. A. Toldson (Eds.), *Black male teachers: Diversifying the United States' teacher workforce* (pp. 3–14). Bingley, UK: Emerald Publishing.

Lewis, C. W., Butler, B. R., Bonner III, F. A., & Joubert, M. (2010). African American male discipline patterns and school district responses resulting impact on academic achievement: Implications for urban educators and policy makers. *Journal of African American Males in Education, 1*(1), 7–25.

Lewis, F. D. D. (2010). *Single mother's guide to raising Black boys*. Bloomington, IN: Franklin Donny D. Lewis, Xlibris.

Lewis, M. M. (2012). Pedagogy and the sista' professor: Teaching Black queer feminist studies through the self. In E. R. Meiners & T. Quinn (Eds.), *Sexualities in education: A reader* (pp. 33–40). New York, NY: Peter Lang.

Lewis, M. M. (2016). A genuine article: Intersectionality, Black lesbian gender expression, and the feminist pedagogical project. *Journal of Lesbian Studies, 21*(4), 420–431.

Lichtman, M. (2006). *Qualitative research in education: A user's guide*. Thousand Oaks, CA: Sage Publications.

Lingard, B., & Douglas, P. (1999). *Men engaging feminisms: Pro-feminism, backlashes and schooling*. Philadelphia, PA: Open University Press.

Lipman, P. (2004). *High stakes education: Inequality, globalization, and urban school reform*. New York, NY: RoutledgeFalmer.

Lipman, P. (2011). *The new political economy of urban education: Neoliberalism, race, and the right to the city*. New York, NY: Routledge.

Lobron, A. (2005, August 28). Subtraction problem. *Boston.com*. Retrieved from www.boston.com/news/globe/magazine/articles/2005/08/28/subtraction_problem/

Love, B. L. (2016). "She has a real connection with them": Reimagining and expanding our definitions of Black masculinity and mentoring in education through female masculinity. *Journal of Lesbian Studies, 21*(4), 443–452.

Lynn, M. (2002). Critical race theory and the perspectives of Black men teachers in the Los Angeles public schools. *Equity & Excellence in Education, 35*(2), 119–30.

Lynn, M. (2006a). Dancing between two worlds: A portrait of the life of a Black male teacher in South Central LA. *International Journal of Qualitative Studies in Education, 19*(2), 221–242.

Lynn, M. (2006b). Education for the community: Exploring the culturally relevant practices of Black male teachers. *Teachers College Record, 108*(12), 2497–2522.

Lynn, M., & Jennings, M. E. (2009). Power, politics, and critical race pedagogy: A critical race analysis of Black male teachers' pedagogy. *Race Ethnicity and Education, 12*(2), 173—196.

MacPherson, K. (2003, August 28). Study finds few male, minority teachers. *Pittsburgh PostGazette.* Retrieved February 5, 2017, from www.postgazette.com/news/nation/2003/08/28/Study-finds-few-male-minorityteachers/stories/200308280023

Madhubuti, H. R. (1990). *Black men: Obsolete, single, dangerous? The Afrikan American family in transition: Essays in discovery, solution, and hope* (1st ed.). Chicago, IL: Third World Press.

Madhubuti, H. R. (2002). *Tough notes: A healing call for creating exceptional Black men: Affirmations, meditations, readings and strategies.* Chicago, IL: Third World Press.

Majors, R. (1992). *Cool pose: The dilemmas of Black manhood in America.* New York, NY: Lexington Books.

Marcus, E. (2002). *Making gay history: The half-century fight for lesbian and gay equal rights* (1st ed.). New York, NY: Perennial.

Marsh, H. W., Martin, A. J., & Cheng, J. H. (2008). A multilevel perspective on gender in classroom motivation and climate: Potential benefits of male teachers for boys? *Journal of Educational Psychology; Washington, 100*(1), 78.

Martin, A., & Marsh, H. (2005). Motivating boys and motivating girls: Does teacher gender really make a difference? *Australian Journal of Education, 49*(3), 320–334.

Martino, W. J. (2008). Male teachers as role models: Addressing issues of masculinity, pedagogy and the re-masculinization of schooling. *Curriculum Inquiry, 38*(2), 189–223.

Martino, W. J., & Frank, B. (2006). The tyranny of surveillance: Male teachers and the policing of masculinities in a single sex school. *Gender and Education, 18*(1), 17–33.

Martino, W. J., & Rezai-Rashti, G. (2012). *Gender, race, and the politics of role modelling: The influence of male teachers.* New York, NY: Routledge.

Matus, R. (2005, June 3). Black male teachers needed. *Tampa Bay Times.* Retrieved May 29, 2016, from www.sptimes.com/2005/06/03/Tampabay/Black_male_teachers_n.shtml

Mawhinney, L. (2014). *We got next: Urban education and the next generation of Black teachers.* New York, NY: Peter Lang.

Maylor, U. (2009). "They do not relate to Black people like us": Black teachers as role models for Black pupils. *Journal of Education Policy, 24*(1), 1–21.

Mayo, J. B. (2008). Gay teachers' negotiated interactions with their students and (straight) colleagues. *The High School Journal, 92*(1), 1–10.

McClain, D. (2016, June 9). America needs more Black men leading its classrooms. *Slate.* Retrieved April 3, 2017, from www.slate.com/articles/life/tomorrows_test/2016/06/only_2_percent_of_teachers_a re_black_and_male_here_s_how_we_might_change.html

McCready, L. T. (2010). *Making space for diverse masculinities: Difference, intersectionality, and engagement in an urban high school.* New York, NY: Peter Lang.

McCready, L. T., & Mosely, M. (2014). Making space for Black queer teachers. In Y. Sealey- Ruiz, C. W. Lewis, & I. Toldson (Eds.), *Teacher education and Black communities: Implications for access, equity, and achievement* (pp. 43–58). Charlotte, NC: Information Age Publishing, Inc.

McCune, J. Q. J. (2014). *Sexual discretion: Black masculinity and the politics of passing.* Chicago, IL: The University of Chicago Press.

McLaren, P., & Kincheloe, J. L. (Eds.). (2007). *Critical pedagogy: Where are we now?* New York, NY: Peter Lang.

McWeeney, D. (2014, July 22). Male teachers needed in primary grades. *Hartford Courant.* Retrieved February 6, 2017, from www.courant.com/opinion/op-ed/hc-op-freshtalk-mcweeney-need-male-elementary-tea-20140722-story.html

Mehrotra, K. (2013, December 1). Black male teachers strive to be mentors and role models. *MYAJC.com.* Retrieved April 9, 2017, from www.myajc.com/news/black-maleteachers-strive-mentors-and-role-models/yYqWfLbq49Oz01RFtknlKP/

Meyer, E. J. (2010). *Gender and sexual diversity in schools: An introduction.* New York, NY: Springer.

Miller, S. S. (2016, June 17). What did my father mean to his Black male students? Everything. *Washington Post.* Retrieved April 8, 2017, from www.washingtonpost.com/posteverything/wp/2016/06/17/what-did-my-fathermean-to-his-black-male-students-everything/

Milloy, C. (2004, September 5). A Black man works magic in classroom. *Washington Post.* Retrieved from www.washingtonpost.com/wp-dyn/articles/A62637-2004Sep4.html

Milloy, M. (2003, October). The guy teacher. *NEA Today.* Retrieved from www.nea.org/neatoday/0310/cover.html

Mills, M. (2004). Male teachers, homophobia, misogyny and teacher education. *Teaching Education, 15*(1), 27–39.

Mills, M., Martino, W., & Lingard, B. (2004). Attracting, recruiting and retaining male teachers: Policy issues in the male teacher debate. *British Journal of Sociology of Education, 25*(3), 355–369.

Milner, H. R. (2006). The promise of Black teachers' success with Black students. *Educational Foundations, 20*(3–4), 89–104.

Milner, H. R. (2007). African American males in urban schools: No excuses— Teach and empower. *Theory Into Practice, 46*(3), 239–246.

Milner, H. R. (2011). Culturally relevant pedagogy in a diverse urban classroom. *The Urban Review, 43*(1), 66–89.

Milner, H. R. (2012). Challenging negative perceptions of Black teachers. *Educational Foundations, 26*(1/2), 27–46.

Milner, H. R. (2016). A Black male teacher's culturally responsive practices. *The Journal of Negro Education, 85*(4), 417–432.

Mitchell, C. (2016, February 16). Black male teachers a dwindling demographic. *Education Week.* Retrieved from www.edweek.org/ew/articles/2016/02/17/black-maleteachers-a-dwindling-demographic.html

Mitchell III, R. (2015, January 7). Holler if you hear me: Where are the Black male teachers? *Gigaré.* Retrieved January 4, 2016, from http://gigarelifestyle.com/education/holler-hearblack-male-teachers

Monroe, C. R. (2009). Teachers closing the discipline gap in an urban middle school. *Urban Education, 44*(3), 322–347.

Monroe, C. R., & Obidah, J. E. (2004). The influence of cultural synchronization on a teacher's perceptions of disruption: A case study of an African American middle-school classroom. *Journal of Teacher Education, 55*, 256–268.

Moore, D., & Moore, S. P. (2013). *Raise him up: A single mother's guide to raising a successful Black man.* Nashville, TN: Thomas Nelson.

Msibi, T. (2013). Denied love: Same-sex desire, agency and social oppression among African men who engage in same-sex relations. *Agenda: Empowering Women for Gender Equity, 27*(2), 105–116.

Mumford, K. J. (2016). *Not straight, not White: Black gay men from the March on Washington to the AIDS crisis.* Chapel Hill, NC: The University of North Carolina Press.

Munro, P. (1998). *Subject to fiction: Women teachers' life history narratives and the cultural politics of resistance.* Philadelphia, PA: Open University Press.

Mutua, A. D. (2006a). Introduction: Mapping the contours of profressive masculinities. In A. D. Mutua (Ed.), *Progressive Black masculinities* (pp. xi–xxviii). New York, NY: Routledge.

Mutua, A. D. (Ed.). (2006b). *Progressive Black masculinities.* New York, NY: Routledge.

Mutua, A. D. (2006c). Theorizing progressive Black masculinities. In A. D. Mutua (Ed.), *Progressive Black masculinities* (pp. 3–42). New York, NY: Routledge.

Myrie, M. (1992). *Boom bye bye [Recorded by Buju Banton]* [CD]. Queens, NY: VP Records.

National Education Association. (2004, April 28). *Are male teachers on the road to extinction?* Retrieved from www.nea.org/newsreleases/2004/nr040428.html

Nazaryan, A. (2015, March 25). Fighting to reclaim the future of Oakland's young Black men. *Newsweek.* Retrieved January 4, 2016, from www.newsweek.com/2015/04/03/oaktown-mans-316548.html

Neal, M. A. (2005). *New Black man.* New York, NY: Routledge.

Neal, M. A. (2006). Bringing up daddy: A progressive Black masculine fatherhood? In A. A. Mutua (Ed.), *Progressive Black masculinities.* New York, NY: Routledge.

Neal, M. A. (2013). *Looking for Leroy: Illegible Black masculinities.* New York, NY: New York University Press.

Neal, M. A. (n.d.). *Images of Black masculinity* [course synopsis]. Retrieved April 16, 2017, from https://aaas.duke.edu/courses/images-black-masculinity

Newell, J. (2013). They deserve it. In C. W. Lewis & I. A. Toldson (Eds.), *Black male teachers: Diversifying the United States' teacher workforce* (pp. 185–192). Bingley, UK: Emerald Publishing.

NewsOne Staff. (n.d.). Dr. Boyce: TD Jakes should stop defending Bishop Eddie Long. *News One.* Retrieved February 20, 2014, from http://newsone.com/1328755/td-jakesdefending-eddie-long/

Nichols, J. (2014, January 17). Kordale and Kaleb, gay Black fathers, respond to Twitter outrage over Instagram photos. *Huffington Post.* Retrieved February 20, 2014, from www.huffingtonpost.com/2014/01/17/gay-black-dads-twitter_n_4617226.html

Nicolas, D. G. (2014, February 26). Where are the Black male teachers? *Education Week.* Retrieved from www.edweek.org/ew/articles/2014/02/26/22nicolas_ep.h33.htmlNigel, D. (n.d.). Video: A wanna be gang member gets embarrassed on Facebook. *Uproxx.* Retrieved from http://realtalkny.uproxx.com/2011/01/topic/topic/videos/video-a-wannabe-gang-member-gets-embarrassed-on- facebook/

Noguera, P. (2008). *The trouble with Black boys: And other reflections on race, equity, and the future of public education* (1st ed.). San Francisco, CA: Jossey-Bass.

O'Connor, C., Lewis, A., & Mueller, J. (2007). Researching "Black" educational experiences and outcomes: Theoretical and methodological considerations. *Educational Researcher, 36*(9), 541–552.

Pabon, A. J-M. (2016). Waiting for Black superman: A look at a problematic assumption. *Urban Education, 51*(8), 915–939.

Pabon, A. J-M., Anderson, N. S., & Kharem, H. (2011). Minding the gap: Cultivating Black male teachers in a time of crisis in urban schools. *The Journal of Negro Education, 80*(3), 358–367.

Pascoe, C. J. (2007). *Dude, you're a fag: Masculinity and sexuality in high school.* Berkeley, CA: University of California Press.

Pascoe, C. J., & Bridges, T. (Eds.). (2016). *Exploring masculinities: Identity, inequality, continuity and change.* New York, NY: Oxford University Press.

Perlmann, J., & Margo, R. A. (2001). *Women's work? American schoolteachers, 1650–1920.* Chicago, IL: University of Chicago Press.

Perry, T., & Delpit, L. D. (Eds.). (1998). *The real Ebonics debate: Power, language, and the education of African-American children.* Boston, MA: Beacon Press.

Petchauer, E. (2016). Shall we overcome? Self-efficacy, teacher licensure exams, and African American preservice teachers. *The New Educator, 12*(2), 171–190.

Petok, M., & Greener, S. (Producers). (2001). *The Bernie Mac show* [Television series]. Los Angeles, CA: 20th Century Fox.

Pew Research Center. (2007, November 13). *Optimism about Black progress declines: Blacks see growing values gap between poor and middle class.* Retrieved from http://assets.pewresearch.org/wp-content/uploads/sites/3/2010/10/Race-2007.pdf

Piorkowski, J. (2015, October 27). Shaker Heights Schools looking at plan to attract Black male teachers. *Cleveland.com* Retrieved January 4, 2016, from www.cleveland.com/shakerheights/index.ssf/2015/10/shaker_heights_schools_1.html

Pitkin, R. (n.d.). A lack of Black male teachers in CMS inspired two local teachers to show kids it's possible. *Creative Loafing Charlotte.* Retrieved January 4, 2016, from http://clclt.com/charlotte/a-lack-of-black-male-teachers-in-cms-inspired-two-localteachers-to-show-kids-its-possible/Content?oid=3696599

Pleck, J. H. (1987). The theory of male sex-role identity: Its rise and fall, 1936 to the present. In H. Brod (Ed.), *The making of masculinities: The new men's studies* (pp. 21–38). Boston, MA: Allen & Unwin.

Poulson-Bryant, S. (2005). *Hung: A meditation on the measure of Black men in America.* New York, NY: Doubleday.

Prentice, A., & Theobald, M. R. (Eds.). (1991). *Women who taught: Perspectives on the history of women and teaching.* Toronto, ON: University of Toronto Press.

Punt, J. (2004). Biblical allusion in "The Matrix": Messiah and violence. *Journal of Theology for Southern Africa, 119*, 90–107.

Ramirez, S. (2017, May 31). Viral father-son selfie has heartfelt mission. *WHAS 11.com*. Retrieved June 1, 2017, from www.whas11.com/features/viral-father-son-selfiehas-heartfelt-mission/444495209

Reckdahl, K. (2015, December 15). Training more Black men to become teachers. *The Atlantic*. Retrieved from www.theatlantic.com/education/archive/2015/12/programs-teachers-africanamerican-men/420306/

Reeser, T. W. (2010). *Masculinities in theory: An introduction*. Malden, MA: Wiley-Blackwell.

Reid-Pharr, R. (2001). *Black gay man: Essays*. New York, NY: New York University Press.

Reinke, W. M., Herman, K. C., & Stormont, M. (2013). Classroom-level positive behavior supports in schools implementing SW-PBIS: Identifying areas for enhancement. *Journal of Positive Behavior Interventions, 15*, 39–50.

Reynolds, K. (1997). *187* [Motion picture]. Burbank, CA: Warner Bros.

Richard, A. (2005, October 12). Heeding the call. *Education Week*. Retrieved from www.edweek.org/ew/articles/2005/10/12/07mister.h25.html

Richardson, R. (2007). *Black masculinity and the U.S. South: From Uncle Tom to gangsta*. Athens: University of Georgia Press.

Riggs, M. T. (2006). *Tongues untied* [DVD]. Culver City, CA: Strand Releasing.

Roberts, N. (2016, April 20). Answering the call to train Black male teachers. *News One*. Retrieved April 4, 2017, from https://newsone.com/3414863/answering-the-call-to-trainblack-male-teachers/

Rodriguez, J. M. (2003). *Queer Latinidad: Identity practices, discursive spaces*. New York, NY: New York University Press.

Rofes, E. E. (2005). *A radical rethinking of sexuality and schooling: Status quo or status queer?* Lanham, MD: Rowman & Littlefield Publishers.

Romanski, A. (Producer), Gardner, D. (Producer), Kleiner, J. (Producer), & Jenkins, B. (Director). (2016). *Moonlight* [Motion picture]. New York, NY: A24 Films.

Ross, M. B. (2005). Beyond the closet as raceless paradigm. In E. P. Johnson & M. G. Henderson (Eds.), *Black queer studies: A critical anthology* (pp. 161–189). Durham, NC: Duke University Press.

Roulston, K., & Mills, M. (2000). Male teachers in feminised teaching areas: Marching to the beat of the men's movement drums? *Oxford Review of Education, 26*(2), 221–237.

Rowden-Racette, K. (2005, November 1). *Endangered species*. Retrieved February 5, 2017, from www.edweek.org/tm/articles/2005/11/01/03men.h17.html

Russell, V. T. (2010). Queer teachers' ethical dilemmas regarding queer youth. *Teaching Education, 21*(2), 143–156.

Sanlo, R. L. (1999). *Unheard voices: The effects of silence on lesbian and gay educators*. Westport, CT: Bergin & Garvey.

Sargent, P. (2001). *Real men or real teachers? Contradictions in the lives of men elementary school teachers*. Harriman, TN: Men's Studies Press.

Savage, C. (2001). "Because we did more with less": The agency of African American teachers in Franklin, Tennessee: 1860–1967. *Peabody Journal of Education, 76*(2), 170–203.

Savage, D., & Miller, T. (Eds.). (2011). *It gets better: Coming out, overcoming bullying, and creating a life worth living*. New York, NY: Dutton.

Sax, L. (2007). *Boys adrift: The five factors driving the growing epidemic of unmotivated boys and underachieving young men.* New York, NY: Basic Books.

Schniedewind, N., & Sapon-Shevin, M. (Eds.). (2012). *Educational courage: Resisting the ambush of public education.* Boston, MA: Beacon Press.

Schott Foundation for Public Education. (2012). *The urgency of now: The Schott 50 state report on public education and Black males—2012.* Retrieved from www.blackboysreport.org

Sealey-Ruiz, Y. (2011). The use of educational documentary in urban teacher education: A case study of Beyond the Bricks. *Journal of Negro Education, 80*(3), 310–324.

Sedgwick, E. K. (1990). *Epistemology of the closet.* Berkeley, CA: University of California Press.

Seidman, I. (1998). *Interviewing as qualitative research: A guide for researchers in education and the social sciences* (2nd ed). New York, NY: Teachers College Press.

Seidman, S. (2002). *Beyond the closet: The transformation of gay and lesbian life.* New York, NY: Routledge.

Server, A. (2012, August 10). *NOM thinks this Black preacher will convince you to oppose gay marriage.* Retrieved February 20, 2014, from www.motherjones. com/politics/2012/08/nom-newest-anti-gay-marriage-front-manwilliam-owens

Sexton, P. (1969). *The feminized male: Classrooms, White collars & the decline of manliness.* New York, NY: Random House.

Signorile, M. (1993). *Queer in America: Sex, the media, and the closets of power* (1st ed.). New York, NY: Random House.

Simmons, R. (1991). Some thoughts on the challenges facing Black gay intellectuals. In E. Hemphill (Ed.), *Brother to brother: New writings by Black gay men* (pp. 211–228). Boston, MA: Alyson Publications.

Simmons, R., Carpenter, R., Ricks, J., Walker, D., Parks, M., & Davis, M. (2013). African American male teachers and African American students: Working subversively through hip-hop in three urban schools. *International Journal of Critical Pedagogy, 4*(2), 69–86.

Simpson, K. (2011, February 7). *Increasingly, male teachers found at head of elementary class.* Retrieved from www.denverpost.com/2011/02/07/increasingly-male-teachersfound-at-head-of-elementary-class/

Singleton, J. (1991). *Boyz n the hood* [Motion picture]. Los Angeles, CA: Columbia Pictures.

Singleton, J. (2001). *Baby boy* [Motion picture]. Los Angeles, CA: Columbia Pictures.

Sirota, D. (2013, February 21). *Oscar loves a White savior.* Retrieved June 1, 2017, from www.salon.com/2013/02/21/oscar_loves_a_white_savior/

Skelton, C. (2001). *Schooling the boys: Masculinities and primary education.* Philadelphia, PA: Open University Press.

Skelton, C. (2009). Failing to get men into primary teaching: A feminist critique. *Journal of Education Policy, 24*(1), 39–54. Retrieved from https://doi.org/10.1080/02680930802412677

Skiba, R. J., Horner, R. H., Chung, C-G., Rausch, M. K., May, S. L., & Tobin, T. (2011). Race is not neutral: A national investigation of African American and Latino disproportionality in school discipline. *School Psychology Review, 40*(1), 85–107.

Slatton, B. C., & Spates, K. (Eds.). (2014). *Hyper sexual, hyper masculine? Gender, race and sexuality in the identities of contemporary Black men*. Burlington, VT: Ashgate.

Smiles, R. V. (2002). Calling all potential Misters. *Black Issues in Higher Education, 19*(17), 26, 28.

Smith, B. (Ed.). (1983). *Home girls: A Black feminist anthology* (1st ed.). New York, NY: Kitchen Table-Women of Color Press.

Snorton, C. R. (2014). *Nobody is supposed to know: Black sexuality on the down low*. Minneapolis, MN: University of Minnesota Press.

Snyder, T. (2008, April 28). *Male call: Recruiting more men to teach elementary school*. Retrieved February 6, 2017, from www.edutopia.org/male-teacher-shortage

Sokal, L., & Katz, H. (2008). Effects of technology and male teachers on boys' reading. *Australian Journal of Education, 52*(1), 81–94.

Sommers, C. H. (2000). *The war against boys: How misguided feminism is harming our young men*. New York, NY: Simon & Schuster.

Sonny, J. (2015, December 3). *This dad gets way too into his music while driving his son to school* (Video). Retrieved June 1, 2017, from http://elitedaily.com/social-news/crazydad-queenzflip-son-turn-up/1306202/

Souto-Manning, M., & Ray, N. (2007). Beyond survival in the ivory tower: Black and brown women's living narratives. *Equity & Excellence in Education, 40*(4), 280–290. Retrieved from https://doi.org/10.1080/10665680701588174

Spencer, M. B., Fegley, S. G., & Harpalani, V. (2003). A theoretical and empirical examination of identity as coping: Linking coping resources to the self processes of African American youth. *Applied Developmental Science, 7*(3), 181–188.

Sternod, B. M. (2011). Role models or normalizing agents? A genealogical analysis of popular written news media discourse regarding male teachers. *Curriculum Inquiry, 41*(2), 267–292. Retrieved from https://doi.org/10.1111/j.1467-873X.2011.00545.x

Stoudt, B. G. (2006). "You're either in or you're out": School violence, peer discipline, and the (re)production of hegemonic masculinity. *Men and Masculinities, 8*(3), 273–287. Retrieved from https://doi.org/10.1177/1097184X05282070

Strayhorn, T. L., & Jeffries, J. L. (2012). An introduction declaring . . . spectrum: A journal on Black men. *Spectrum: A Journal on Black Men, 1*(1), 1–4.

Strober, M. H., & Tyack, D. (1980). Why do women teach and men manage? A report on research on schools. *Signs, 5*(3), 494–503.

Tafari, D. N. H. (2013). "I can get at these kids": A narrative study exploring the reasons Black men teach. In C. W. Lewis & I. A. Toldson (Eds.), *Black male teachers: Diversifying the United States' teacher workforce* (pp. 93–106). Bingley, UK: Emerald Publishing.

Tarrant, A., Terry, G., Ward, M. R. M., Ruxton, S., Robb, M., & Featherstone, B. (2015). Are male role models really the solution? Interrogating the "War on Boys" through the lens of the "Male Role Model" discourse. *Boyhood Studies, 8*(1), 60–83. Retrieved from https://doi.org/10.3167/bhs.2015.080105

Tatum, A. W. (2005). *Teaching reading to Black adolescent males: Closing the achievement gap*. Portland, ME: Stenhouse Publishers.

Tavis Smiley Reports. (2011). *Too important to fail: Saving America's boys*. New York, NY: SmileyBooks.

Taylor, E. (2016, January 11). *Upon being called father*. Retrieved April 8, 2017, from http://youngteacherscollective.org/2016/01/11/upon-being-called-father/

Taylor, T. L., & Johnson, A. (2011). "Class, meet race": A critical re-scripting of the Black body through ghetto and bourgeois characters in American films. In R. L. Jackson & M. C. Hopson (Eds.), *Masculinity in the Black imagination: Politics of communicating race and manhood* (pp. 113–128). New York, NY: Peter Lang.

Thornton, M., & Bricheno, P. (2006). *Missing men in education*. Stoke on Trent, Staffordshire: Trentham Books.

Tillman, L. C. (2004). (Un)intended consequences? The impact of the Brown v. Board of education decision on the employment status of Black educators. *Education and Urban Society*, 36(3), 280–303.

Toldson, I. A. (2011). Diversifying the United States' teaching force: Where are we now? Where do we need to go? How do we get there? *Journal of Negro Education*, 80(3), 183–186.

Toldson, I. A. (2013a, April 23). Black male teachers: Becoming extinct? *The Root*. Retrieved January 4, 2016 from www.theroot.com/articles/culture/2013/04/ black_male_teacher_shortage_debunkin g_the_myth/

Toldson, I. A. (2013b). Race matters in the classroom. In C. W. Lewis & I. A. Toldson (Eds.), *Black male teachers: Diversifying the United States' teacher workforce* (pp. 15–21). Bingley, UK: Emerald Publishing.

Toldson, I. A., & Lewis, C. W. (2012). *Challenging the status quo: Academic success among school-age African American males*. Washington, DC: Congressional Black Caucus Foundation.

Torres, J. (2006, May 9). *Black male teachers rare in S.J.* Retrieved March 28, 2017, from www.recordnet.com/article/20060509/inschool/605090335

Twain, D. (Producer), & Avildsen, J. G. (Director). (1989). *Lean on me* [Motion picture]. Burbank, CA: Warner Bros.

Tyack, D. B., & Strober, M. H. (1981). Jobs and gender: A history of the structuring of educational employment by sex. In P. A. Schmuck, W. W. Charters, & R. O. Carlson (Eds.), *Educational policy and management: Sex differentials* (pp. 131–152). New York, NY: Academic Press.

Tyre, P. (2006, January 29). *Education: Boys falling behind girls in many areas*. Retrieved February 6, 2017, from www.newsweek.com/education-boys-falling-behind-girlsmany-areas-108593

Verdugo, R. R. (2002). Race-ethnicity, social class, and zero-tolerance policies: The cultural and structural wars. *Education and Urban Society*, 35, 50–75.

Vetter, A. (2013). "You Need Some Laugh Bones!": Leveraging AAL in a high school English classroom. *Journal of Literacy Research*, 45(2), 173–206. Retrieved from https://doi.org/10.1177/1086296X12474653

Videos of father and son goes [sic] viral for their incredible dancing. (2017, May 7). Retrieved June 1, 2017, from www.theblackloop.com/ adorable-father-son-go-viral-show-offdance-moves-video/

Villegas, A. M., & Lucas, T. (2002). Preparing culturally responsive teachers: Rethinking the curriculum. *Journal of Teacher Education*, 53(1), 20–32.

VIPMediaBlogs. (2017, January 25). *Dr. Boyce Watkins: Black men in America have become effeminate*. Retrieved April 21, 2017, from www.youtube.com/ watch?v=U0eGfdau-lI

Walker, L. (2016, January 27). *America's extreme need for more Black male educators*. Retrieved January 9, 2017, from www.ebony.com/news-views/ black-male-teachers

Walker, V. S. (1996). *Their highest potential: An African American school community in the segregated South.* Chapel Hill, NC: University of North Carolina Press.

Walker, V. S. (2001). African American teaching in the South: 1940–1960. *American Educational Research Journal, 38*(4), 751–779.

Walker, V. S. (2013). Tolerated Tokenism, or the injustice in justice: Black teacher associations and their forgotten struggle for educational justice, 1921–1954. *Equity & Excellence in Education, 46*(1), 64–80.

Wallace, M. O. (1979). *Black macho and the myth of the superwoman.* New York, NY: Dial Press.

Wallace, M. O. (2002). *Constructing the Black masculine: Identity and ideality in African American men's literature and culture, 1775–1995.* Durham, NC: Duke University Press.

Warren, C. A. (2016). Making relationships work: Elementary-age Black boys and the schools that serve them. In S. R. Harper & J. L. Wood (Eds.), *Advancing Black male student success from preschool through Ph.D.* (pp. 21–43). Sterling, VA: Stylus Publishing.

Watson, D. A. (2016, August 1). *Do we need more Black male teachers for young Black men?* Retrieved April 8, 2017, from www.theodysseyonline.com/do-we-needmore-black-male-teachers-for-young-black-men

Watson, D. A. (2017). "Male delivery": A critical investigation of what boys have to say about the influence of male teachers on literacy engagement and achievement. *Educational Review, 69*(1), 102–117.

Weaver-Hightower, M. B. (2011). Male preservice teachers and discouragement from teaching. *Journal of Men's Studies, 19*(2), 97–115. Retrieved from https://doi.org/10.3149/jms.1902.97

Webb, J. A. (n.d.). *U.S. secretary of education Duncan and film producer Spike Lee to call on morehouse students to pursue teaching careers.* Retrieved January 4, 2016, from www.ed.gov/news/media-advisories/us-secretary-education-duncan-and-filmproducer-spike-lee-call-morehouse-students-pursue-teaching-careers

Weedon, C. (1987). *Feminist practice and poststructuralist theory.* New York, NY: Basil Blackwell.

Weiler, K. (1989). Women's history and the history of women teachers. *Journal of Education, 171*(3), 9–30.

Weisenthal, J. (2013, January 18). *Newsweek likens Obama to Jesus—Calls second term "the second coming".* Retrieved June 5, 2017, from www.businessinsider.com/newsweek-on-obamas-second-coming-2013-1

West, M. G. (2013, November 23). New push to hire male teachers of color. *Wall Street Journal.* Retrieved from www.wsj.com/articles/new-push-to-hire-male-teachers-ofcolor-1448325157

Whitaker, M. C. (2005). *Race work: The rise of civil rights in the urban West.* Lincoln, NB: University of Nebraska Press.

White, A. M. (2008). *Ain't I a feminist? African American men speak out on fatherhood, friendship, forgiveness, and freedom.* Albany, NY: State University of New York Press.

White, D. G. (1993). The cost of club work, the price of Black feminism. In N. A. Hewitt & S. Lebsock (Eds.), *Visible women: New essays on American activism* (pp. 247–269). Urbana, IL: University of Illinois Press.

White, T. (2016). Teach for America's paradoxical diversity initiative: Race, policy, and Black teacher displacement in urban public schools. *Education Policy Analysis Archives, 24*(16), 1–37.

Williams, P., & Hugo, C. (1998). Caught out there [Recorded by Kelis]. On *Kaleidoscope* [CD]. London, UK: Virgin/EMI.

Williams, Z. (2005, February). *Moving beyond Black masculinity and towards a new theory of Black men's studies.* Presented at the Black Masculinities Conference, The CUNY Graduate Center, New York, NY.

Wolper, D. L. (Producer). (1977). *Roots* [Television series]. Burbank, CA: Warner Brothers Studios.

Woodson, A. N., & Pabon, A. (2016). "I'm none of the above": Exploring themes of heteropatriarchy in the life histories of Black male educators. *Equity & Excellence in Education, 49*(1), 57–71.

Worley, B. (2011, September 21). *Viral video of dad disciplining son leaves a mark.* Retrieved from http://thegrio.com/2011/09/21/dads-tough-love-caught-on-camera/

Yorkin, B., & Lear, N. (Producers). (1974). *Good times* [Television series]. Los Angeles, CA: CBS Television.

Young, V. A. (2007). *Your average nigga: Performing race, literacy, and masculinity.* Detroit, MI: Wayne State University Press.

Index

Page numbers in bold indicate tables. Notes are indicated by page numbers followed by n.